Instructor's Resource Manual

for

Dynamic Physical Education for Elementary School Children

Fifteenth Edition

Robert P. Pangrazi
Arizona State University

Carole M. Casten
California State University, Dominguez Hills

PEARSON

Benjamin
Cummings

San Francisco   Boston   New York
Cape Town   Hong Kong   London   Madrid   Mexico City
Montreal   Munich   Paris   Singapore   Sydney   Tokyo   Toronto

Development Manager: Claire Alexander
Senior Acquisitions Editor: Deirdre Espinoza
Project Editor: Marie Beaugureau
Supplements Project Editor: Sarah Kaminker
Managing Editor: Deborah Cogan
Production Supervisor: Mary O'Connell
Manufacturing Buyer: Stacy Wong
Senior Marketing Manager: Sandra Lindelof

ISBN 0-8053-7924-X

1 2 3 4 5 6 7 8 9 10 — OPM — 10 09 08 07 06
www.aw-bc.com

Table of Contents

Preface

The 15th edition of the **Instructor's Resource Manual** is specifically designed to complement the 15th edition of the textbook **Dynamic Physical Education for Elementary School Children**. This edition of the **Instructor's Resource Manual** contains a new format, expanded content, Internet links, and a Cooperative Learning Task Sheet for each chapter. These materials offer you an expanded learning experience never before available. The icon is placed in the Instructional Resource Manual wherever an Internet link has been identified.

> In addition to the resources and websites listed here, the Companion Website for this book will provide you and your students with materials to supplement the textbook:
> www.aw-bc.com/pangrazi

The purpose of this guide is to provide you with material to supplement and expand the information offered in the textbook. This Instructor's Resource Manual approaches each chapter with the following organizational format:

Summary: Provides a brief synopsis of the chapter content.

Student Outcomes: Lists the basic objectives that should result from reading the chapter.

Main Concepts: This section summarizes important concepts from the chapter. In this section, you will find Internet links, when appropriate, to sites you may visit for expanded reading material and ideas.

Discussion Topics: Offers suggestions for in-class discussions.

Sample Written Assignments: Contains examples of written assignments that could be completed outside the classroom setting.

Cooperative Learning Task Sheet: The Task Sheet provided with each chapter offers topics that can be completed by the student during the class period for review of the topics presented in each chapter. Additionally, there are topics for additional research and Internet links to assist research. The Cooperative Learning method of teaching grew out of the realization that in most learning situations students compete against each other for a grade or success. In competitive situations, students perceive they can only reach their goal if other students in the class fail. In traditional learning situations, students often learn to distrust each other, yet people need to work together in society to accomplish common goals. Cooperative learning allows the student to work in groups to reach common goals. In the cooperative learning setting, the student seeks outcomes that are beneficial to oneself and to the group. An emphasis is placed on joint rather than individual outcomes and peers are given the opportunity to work with each other. Students are expected to assist the success of their peers rather than hoping they will fail. This teaching method has the potential to enhance the social and psychological growth of students.

Acknowledgments

I would like to thank my husband, Richard, for his computer assistance "extraordinaire" in the preparation of this guide. My friend and colleague, Robert P. Pangrazi, is gratefully thanked for giving me the opportunity to write this Instructor's Resource Manual and for his continued support.

Sarah Kaminker is thanked for her support and thoughtfulness in the production of this guide. The production staff at Benjamin Cummings is also appreciated for their assistance and support.

CHAPTER 1

Elementary School Physical Education

SUMMARY

This chapter addresses physical education as the phase of the general educational program that contributes to the total growth and development of each child, primarily through movement experiences. Program objectives provide the framework and direction for the physical education curriculum. Systematic and properly taught physical education can help achieve the major content standards, including movement competence, maintaining physical fitness, learning personal health and wellness skills, applying movement concepts and skill mechanics, developing lifetime activity skills, and demonstrating positive social skills. Modern programs of physical education have been influenced by cultural and educational factors related to games, sports, fitness, educational movement, perceptual-motor competency, federal mandates, value and attitude development, the Surgeon General's report, and the nationwide emphasis on physical activity.

STUDENT OUTCOMES

Upon completion of the reading of this chapter, the student will:

- Justify the need for a quality physical education program in the elementary school setting based on the health benefits it can offer children.

- Cite the NASPE national standards for physical education.

- List program objectives and recognize the distinctive contributions of physical education.

- Describe the educational reasons for including physical education as part of the elementary school experience.

- Define physical education and its role in the elementary school experience.

- Articulate how various pedagogical influences changed the course of elementary school physical education programs.

- Identify essential components of a quality physical education program.

- Verbally portray how a variety of societal influences and federal mandates impacted elementary school physical education.

MAIN CONCEPTS

Physical education means many things to many people. Physical education professionals often describe it as essential subject matter dedicated to learning in the psychomotor domain and committed to developing lifetime physical activity patterns. Some individuals mistakenly consider physical education to be the same as athletics or competitive sports. Some perceive physical education to be recess or free-time play. In general, some view it as a meaningful subject matter area, while others report having less than satisfactory physical education experiences, if they had physical education at all.

So, what is physical education? It is part of the total educational program that contributes, primarily through movement experiences, to the total growth and development of all children. *Physical education* is defined as education through movement. It is an instructional program that gives attention to all learning domains: psychomotor, cognitive, and affective. No other area of the curriculum is designed to help children learn motor and lifetime activity skills. This makes physical education a necessary component of the total school curriculum. It is not enough to educate children academically; they must also be educated physically. Too often, physical educators try to do all things for their students including improving their academic skills. Certainly, whenever possible, it is important to do so. However, physical education programs should always place the majority of emphasis on learning physical skills. If students, particularly the unskilled, don't receive quality instruction in physical education, there is little opportunity for them to learn skills as adults. Unskilled youngsters often have little opportunity to learn new skills as compared to those who are skilled. For example, there are all types of opportunities for skilled youngsters to participate in little league, gymnastics clubs, and sport clubs. However, for the unskilled youngster, physical education may be the only place that offers an option to learn new skills. Therefore, a strong physical education program places emphasis on helping all youngsters succeed regardless of ability or skill level.

THE EVOLUTION OF ELEMENTARY SCHOOL PHYSICAL EDUCATION

A number of concerns, historical events, and pedagogical influences have significantly impacted elementary school physical education programs. Often these programs are created as responses to events that are publicized by the press and other interested parties. The many changes that have occurred in elementary school physical education programming clearly point out how the public's needs and concerns shape the direction of U.S. education.

Elementary physical education has evolved due to the influence of a number of historical factors.

- The public's needs and concerns shaping the direction of American education

- The German and Swedish influence

- The emphasis on games and sports

- National concern about physical fitness

- Physical fitness testing and the President's Council

Recently, the Council has begun to focus on increasing the activity of youngsters rather than just promoting fitness. This emphasis is manifested in a forthcoming award program for individuals who participate in regular physical activity and show the ability to maintain a physical activity regimen over an extended period of time.

Information about the President's Council on Physical Fitness and Sport can be read at
🏃 http://www.fitness.gov

The President's Challenge and guidelines are listed at

🏃 http://www.presidentschallenge.org

Pedagogical influences are described in the chapter as:

- Movement education programs.

- Perceptual-motor programs.

For more information related to perceptual-motor learning, go to
http://www.frontrowexperience.com/Page07.html

Conceptual learning is described in the chapter content.

Value and attitude development (Affective Domain Learning) is explained in the chapter.

This site provides you with an outline of the Affective Learning:
http://chiron.valdosta.edu/whuitt/col/affsys/affdom.html

Federal mandates including the following in this chapter:

- Title IX: Equal opportunity for the sexes

  To read about Title IX go to http://www.dol.gov/oasam/regs/statutes/titleix.htm

  This site offers you commentary on Title IX: http://www.ed.gov/pubs/TitleIX/part3.html

- Background information on PL 94-142 can be obtained at
  http://www.scn.org/~bk269/94-142.html

Additional information can be found at http://asclepius.com/angel/special.html

Child Nutrition and WIC Reauthorization Act of 2004

Nationally, there is widespread concern about the health status of Americans, particularly related to physical activity and nutrition. The number of overweight Americans has increased rapidly during the past 15 years. Statistics show that over 60% of Americans are overweight. (National Center for Health Statistics, 2004). Much of this increase has been attributed to a decrease in physical activity patterns and an increase in the amount of calories consumed.

Physical education programs must place their focus on improving the health status of students, particularly with respect to eating habits and physical activity. In the Child Nutrition and WIC Reauthorization Act of 2004, the U.S. Congress established a new requirement that all school districts with a federally funded school meals program develop and implement wellness policies that address nutrition and physical activity by the start of the 2006-2007 school year. This act offers an excellent opportunity for physical educators to implement physical activity and eating behavior programs in their classes. Changing activity and eating behaviors takes the efforts of an entire community. Physical educators can make this an opportunity to change the environment of the school rather than focus on a minor curriculum change. Making changes in the school environment will require the efforts of parents, classroom teachers, administrators, and students. If implemented correctly, there is a strong possibility that this mandate can lead physical education programs to a prominent role in the total school curriculum.

A nationwide concern for health and wellness exists.

This site connects you to numerous health and fitness links: http://www.health-fitness-tips.com

This site has even more information: http://about.com/health

A demand for "Back-to-Basics" schools exists and is explained.

A national focus on physical activity has taken place and examples are written in the chapter.

A variety of professional organizations have had a strong effect on physical education over the past two decades. The organizations are: American Alliance for Health, Physical Education, Recreation and Dance (AAHPERD), NASPE, Council on Physical Education for Children (COPEC), and the American Academy of Pediatrics (AAP).

Recreation societies are available at 🏃 http://www.lib.uwaterloo.ca/society/recreation_soc.html

Additional information on youth and fitness is available at the American Heart Association site: 🏃 http://www.justmove.org

THE CURRENT STATUS OF PHYSICAL EDUCATION IN THE UNITED STATES

The differences in perceptions of physical education are a result of the wide variety of experiences offered under the physical education umbrella.

The School Health Policies and Programs Study (SHPPS) 2000 report shows that when physical education requirements by grade are analyzed, each grade shows a decline from about 50 percent in grades 1–5 to about 5 percent in grade 12 (Burgeson et al., 2001). Many states and schools allow exemptions from physical education classes so that the actual percentage of kids receiving instruction is even less. Few children in America receive daily physical education instruction. Only about 8 percent of elementary schools provide daily physical education for their students. When physical education is taught in these grade levels, a "specialist" often teaches it, though many people having this designation do not hold valid credentials. In fact, only 17 percent of states require elementary level physical education teachers to be certified in physical education (U.S. Department of Health and Human Services, 1994). Classroom teachers often teach physical education and because these teachers have wide ranges of interests and qualifications, instruction often varies dramatically among schools.

A common picture of elementary school physical education might look something like this. Youngsters go to school and receive about 25 hours of overall instruction weekly. Out of the 25 hours, physical education may be scheduled for 30 to 60 minutes a week in a school that cares about physical education. This amounts to 2 to 4 percent of the total instructional time devoted to the health and wellness of students. Instruction may be carried out by a physical education specialist, classroom teacher, or paraprofessional. Often, up to 4 classes are sent to physical education at once so that the student to teacher ratio is 120 to 1 with one or two paraprofessionals sent to help. Small wonder that obesity and hypokinetic disease has become rampant throughout the United States. Many of America's schools do not value physical education and do little to ensure that all children receive daily physical education instruction as a minimum.

THE NEED FOR PHYSICAL EDUCATION PROGRAMS

During the past decade, the interest in the benefits derived from an active lifestyle has spawned a wide assortment of health clubs, a vast array of books and magazines concerning exercise and fitness, a weekly smorgasbord of distance runs and triathlons, streamlined exercise equipment, and apparel for virtually any type of physical activity. Unfortunately, most of this interest and lifestyle change has occurred among middle- and upper-class Americans. Little change in activity patterns has occurred in lower-middle and lower-class families.

The nation's enthusiasm for physical activity has not trickled down to elementary school youngsters. A statement issued by the American Academy of Pediatrics (1991) reported that children from the ages of 2 to 12 watch about 25 hours of television per week. Another study, (Anderson, et al., 1998) showed that children who watched 4 or more hours of television per day had significantly greater BMI compared to children watching fewer than 2 hours per day. Health goals for the nation for the year 2010 (U.S. Department of Health and Human Services [USDHHS], 2000) are based on increasing daily levels of physical activity. Many of the goals directly target schools, or programs that can take place within the school setting. These goals place emphasis on reducing inactivity and increasing light-to-moderate physical activity. The need is clear: implement physical education programs to teach youngsters how to live an active and healthy lifestyle. What evidence is available that shows the benefits of a quality physical education program?

1. The percentage of youth who are overweight has more than tripled in the past 30 years (USDHHS, 2002). The prevalence of being overweight is more strongly related to decreases in energy expenditure than to increases in energy intake (Jebb & Moore, 1999). The school environment discourages physical activity. A 30-minute physical education class can offer 1200 to 2000 steps of moderate to vigorous physical activity to counteract the effects of an inactive day (Beighle & Pangrazi, 2000; Morgan, Pangrazi, & Beighle, 2003). This can be a substantial contribution to the daily energy expenditure of students, particularly those students who are inactive. For example, for a student who is averaging 8,000 steps a day, a quality physical education class could increase the number of steps by 20%. This would increase the number of steps to 10,000, which is a substantial increase in physical activity.

2. A positive experience in physical education classes will encourage youngsters to be active as adults. In a survey sponsored by the Sporting Goods Manufacturers Association (2000), 60 percent of respondents ages 18–34 reported that a positive experience in physical education classes encouraged them to be active in later life. On the other hand, of those respondents who said they were sedentary, only 10 percent said their physical education classes encouraged them to be active.

3. Overweight children grow into overweight adults. Studies (Guo et al., 1994; Must et al., 1992) show that adolescent weight is a good predictor of adult obesity. A study by Whitiker, et al., (1997) showed that the risk of being overweight in adulthood is much higher among overweight adolescents than younger children. The chance for childhood obesity persisting into adulthood increases from 20% at 4 years of age to 80% by adolescence (Guo & Chumlea, 1999). This supports the case for dealing with overweight children in elementary school before the problem becomes much more difficult to rectify. Since a quality program encourages active behavior, it makes sense that a program be in place to help youngsters understand the importance of proper weight management and an active lifestyle.

4. A quality physical education program educates youngsters physically but does not detract from the academic performance of the school.

5. Physical education gives students the skills they need to be active as adults. One commodity that youngsters have in contrast to adults is the time to practice and learn new skills.

6. Physical activity (which most often occurs in physical education classes) provides immediate and short-term health benefits for children (Bar-Or, 1995). For overweight children, increased physical activity results in a reduction of the percentage of body fat. Additionally, increased activity reduces blood pressure and improves the blood lipid profile for high health-risk children. Finally, there is evidence to show that weight-bearing activities performed during the school years offer bone mineral density benefits that carry over into adulthood (Bailey et al., 1996).

7. Active children become active adults. This clearly delineates the legacy given to youth when we place them in an inactive school environment.

The NASPE website listed here gives you more important information on the subject:
http://www.aahperd.org/NASPE/pdf_files/pos_papers/pe_critical.PDF

Outcomes for all developmental levels of students are described in detail in the remainder of this chapter.

INSTRUCTIONAL FORMATS

The material in this chapter can be presented using the lecture style plus the Power Point materials and overhead transparencies providing students an overview of the chapter. The introduction may be followed by cooperative learning assignments that provide active learning and critical thinking activities for the student. In the cooperative learning groups, the students will discuss the materials listed on the Task Sheet and/or other topics you may assign. Each group can become a "content expert" for sections of the Task Sheet. Oral summary reports of the group may be presented to the entire class covering all or part of the discussion items.

KEY TERMS

physical education	social skills	body management skills
physical education specialist	hidden curriculum	IEP
personal wellness	movement competence	specialized motor skills
psychomotor domain	self-concept	human wellness
process of activity	movement concepts	manipulative skills
cognitive domain	movement education	health-related fitness
experiential physical fitness	fundamental skills	rhythmic movement skills
affective domain	perceptual motor programs	Healthy People 2010
movement principles	locomotor skills	gymnastics skills
pedagogical influences	Title IX	games skills
determinants of active living	nonlocomotor skills	Child Nutrition and WIC
principles of wellness	PL 94-142	Reauthorization Act

REFLECTION AND REVIEW QUESTIONS

How and Why

1. How have your perceptions of physical education changed based on your understanding of its evolution?

2. How does physical education fit into a school's curriculum?

3. How can the nationwide focus on health, wellness, and physical activity influence the lives of children?

4. How do the NASPE national standards help teachers?

5. Why is it important to understand the essential components of physical education?

Content Review

1. Are physical education programs and physical education teachers necessary? Defend your answer.

2. Why is physical education a unique component of the total school curriculum?

3. Discuss the evolution of physical education.

4. What contributions have different pedagogical approaches made to the evolution of physical education?

5. How have federal mandates influenced physical education?

6. Discuss the content standards and explain the role they play in physical education.

7. State the essential components of a quality physical education program and discuss the significance of each.

DISCUSSION TOPICS

1. Who teaches elementary physical education in your area?

2. Observe an elementary physical education class in your area. Discuss the physical environment in which the instruction took place as well as the quantity of equipment provided. If equipment was used, were there enough for each student to have a piece of equipment to practice individual skills? Was the environment conducive to teaching?

3. How much time is allocated per week to physical education instruction in the schools in your area?

4. What is the state requirement for minutes per week allocated to elementary physical education? Are schools really adhering to the state requirement?

SAMPLE WRITTEN ASSIGNMENTS

1. Interview a principal in your area and ask his/her views on elementary physical education. Write a one to two page report describing the views of the principal you interviewed. Compare and contrast your views with those of the principal in the paper.

2. Write a speech that you could use at a school board meeting to defend the importance of having elementary physical education specialists teaching children versus the classroom teacher. Check Internet sites for possible speeches/defenses that are available online.

3. Interview a school board member in your area. Ask this person their perception of a good physical education instructional program. Write a one-page report describing what you learned.

4. Interview a school board member and discuss the funding of Elementary Physical Education Specialists in the district. Do they fund such positions? If so, are the classes the same size as what the multiple subjects' faculty member works with in the classroom? If not, why? If the district does not fund Physical Education Specialists, why don't they? Has it ever been considered? Have they considered cutting some other fringe areas to support the hiring of specialists?

5. Interview an elementary physical education specialist to find out about their job duties, support from their administration, support from parents and other teachers, and attitude toward their job assignment. Write a report explaining what you learned.

ACTIVITY SESSION EXPERIENCE

Lead the students through the following activity:

1. Teach a model lesson using the 4-part Dynamic Elementary Physical Education model demonstrating how you will expect students to peer teach.

COOPERATIVE LEARNING TASK SHEET

Chapter 1: Elementary School Physical Education

Directions: Your cooperative learning group will become the content experts by finding the answers to the items listed below. Discuss the following items with your group and be ready to report on one or all of them at the end of the class period.

1. What is physical education?

2. Why do children need physical education?

3. Describe the contribution physical education makes to the general education program of each child.

4. Briefly cite the NASPE content standards of elementary physical education for each developmental level.

5. Define the term Physical Education Specialist.

6. Describe Title IX and its implications at the elementary school level.

7. What is PL 94-142?

8. State the statistics describing the time most first through sixth grade children receive physical education instruction per week. How much physical education instruction should they receive?

9. What are your state guidelines on how much physical education should be taught daily? Is that being met in most schools in your area? You may need to discuss this with your instructor, call schools, or conduct an online search for the answers.

10. List the learning domains physical education covers.

11. How can content standards help teachers?

12. Define the following terms: motor skills, movement competence, movement concepts skills, fundamental motor skills, locomotor skills, nonlocomotor skills, body management skills, specialized motor skills, manipulative skills, rhythmic movement skills, gymnastics skills, game and sport skills.

13. Describe how the physical education program contributes to personal wellness.

14. Describe how students learn to maintain a personalized active lifestyle.

15. Discuss the contribution elementary physical education plays towards lifetime participation in activity.

16. Describe how elementary physical education contributes to the development of social skills.

17. Summarize the historical evolution of elementary physical education.

18. State the essential components of a quality physical education program and discuss the significance of each.

19. Are physical education programs and physical education teachers necessary? Defend your answers based on material in this chapter.

20. What is the current status of physical education in the United States?

21. Describe the Child Nutrition and WIC Reauthorization Act of 2004.

CHAPTER 2

Teaching Children in the Physical Education Environment

SUMMARY

This chapter describes the ways in which physical activity impacts the growth and development of children. Research supports the value of an active lifestyle for optimum growth and development. There is a positive correlation between the incidence of certain health disorders and a sedentary lifestyle. Lifetime involvement in physical activity often depends on early participation and gratification gained from such participation. Developing motor skills at an early age provides the tools needed to be physically active throughout life. Guidelines for safe participation in physical activity, including weight lifting, running, exercising in heat, and fitness testing, are delineated.

STUDENT OUTCOMES

Upon completion of the reading of this chapter, the student will:

- Describe the need for physical activities.

- Cite stages of the growing child.

- Understand the relationship between physical activity and the development of muscular strength and endurance and skeletal growth.

- Define aerobic capacity and discuss its relationship to health and physical activity.

- Understand how body composition impacts the health and well-being of an individual.

- Discuss the role organized youth sports should play in the proper growth and development of children.

- Identify guidelines to follow for exercising children safely.

- Describe the proper approach to distance running and weight training for preadolescent children.

MAIN CONCEPTS

The Growing Child and Growth Patterns

Growth patterns are generally controlled by genetic makeup at birth. An unhealthy environment can have a negative impact on proper growth and development.

Maturation patterns that are common to the majority of youngsters are examined in this chapter.

Children go through a rapid period of growth from birth to age 5. From age 6 to the onset of adolescence, growth slows to a steady but increasing pattern. A general rule of thumb in regard to motor learning is that when growth is rapid, the ability to learn new skills decreases. Because the rate of growth slows during the elementary school years, this is an excellent window for learning motor skills.

During the elementary school years, boys are generally taller and heavier. Girls reach the adolescent growth spurt first, and grow taller and heavier during the sixth- and seventh-grade years. Boys quickly catch up and grow larger and stronger.

Young children have relatively short legs for their overall height. The trunk is longer in relation to the legs during early childhood. The ratio of leg length (standing height) to trunk length (sitting height) is similar for boys and girls through age 11. The head makes up one-fourth of the child's total length at birth and about one-sixth at age 6. K-2 students appear to be "top heavy" due to their proportions and fall more easily than adults.

Skeletal Maturity

Physical maturity has a strong impact on the performance of children in physical education. Maturity is usually measured by comparing chronological age with skeletal age. Children whose chronological age is beyond skeletal age are said to be late (or slow) maturers. If skeletal age is ahead of chronological age, children are labeled early (fast) maturers. Studies examining skeletal age (Gruelich & Pyle, 1959; Krahenbuhl & Pangrazi, 1983) consistently show that a five- to six-year variation in skeletal maturity exists in a typical classroom of youngsters. This means that some youngsters are actually 5-year-olds skeletally and are trying to compete with others who are as mature as 11-year-olds.

Body Physique

A child's physique (somatotype) affects the quality of his or her motor performance. There are three major physiques: endomorph, mesomorph, and ectomorph. The mesomorph is characterized as having a predominance of muscle and bone and is often labeled "muscled." The ectomorph is identified as being extremely thin, with a minimum of muscle development, and is characterized as "skinny." These children may be less able in activities requiring strength and power, but able to perform well in aerobic endurance activities such as jogging, cross-country running, and track and field. The third classification is the endomorph, characterized as soft and round, with an excessively protruding abdomen.

Go to this website to read an article about somatotypes and personality traits: http://www.rider.edu/~suler/somato.html

Skeletal maturity is described. Physical maturity has a strong impact on the performance of children in physical education. Maturity is usually measured by comparing chronological age with skeletal age. Effective programs must offer activities that are developmentally appropriate and suited to their level of maturity.

Muscular Development and Strength

Muscular strength increases linearly with chronological age. When differences in strength between the sexes are adjusted for height, there is no difference in lower body strength from age 7-17. Boys do have more upper extremity and trunk strength. Boys and girls can participate on somewhat even terms in activities requiring leg strength if their size and mass are similar. Boys have the advantage in activities demanding arm or trunk strength.

Muscle Fiber Type and Performance

Muscle fibers include fast twitch and slow twitch and are defined and related to motor performance. Elementary-aged children who do best in activities requiring fast twitch fibers also do best in distance running. Muscle fiber metabolic specialization does not occur until adolescence; this fact is a strong argument of keeping all youngsters involved in varied physical activity throughout the elementary years.

Relative Strength and Motor Performance

Relative strength (strength in relation to body size) has been identified as the most important factor contributing to motor performance of children. Overweight children are less proficient at performing motor skills. Deadweight has a negative impact on motor performance because it reduces relative strength when strength is adjusted for body weight.

Aerobic Capacity: Children Are Not Little Adults

Maximal aerobic power is an individual's maximum ability to use oxygen in the body for metabolic purposes. Aerobic capacity in relation to performance is explained. Oxygen uptake is the major determinant of endurance-oriented performance. Studies indicate that training caused little, if any, increase in aerobic power in prepubescent children.

Children exercising at a certain workload perceive the activity to be easier than do adults working at a similar level. Youngsters demonstrate a rapid recovery rate after strenuous exercise. This implies that teachers should not judge workloads for children based on how they perceive the difficulty of an activity. Interval training is an effective method to use with children because it allows them to exercise aerobically and recover while stretching or performing nonlocomotor movements.

Overweight Children and Physical Performance

Overweight children are restricted in motor performance because the excess weight reduces their relative strength. As weight increases, the impulse for physical exertion decreases. Diets of overweight and normal children showed no substantial differences in caloric consumption. Overweight children tend to be less active than normal weight children. Overweight children seldom perform physical activities on a par with leaner children.

Exercise programs for overweight children should be designed to increase caloric expenditure rather than improve cardiovascular fitness.

Additional reading is available on the subject by going to this website:
http://www.familyhaven.com/health/fitkids.html

Go to this site for an article on nutrition for children:
http://www.nutritionforkids.com

TEACHING SPECIALIZED MOTOR SKILLS

Allow youngsters to play all positions when teaching sport skills. If the best athletes are always assigned to skilled positions, it becomes a situation of the rich getting richer and the poor getting poorer. Because all children deserve equal opportunity to learn sport skills, it should be a mandate to teachers that all children play all positions and receive similar amounts of practice time.

Understand that maturity plays an important role in dictating how youngsters learn motor skills. One of the reasons for helping children learn all skills and play all positions is that it will give them the opportunity to be successful when they reach maturity.

Ensure Success for All Students

The willingness to try new experiences and participate in activities is driven by how people feel about their ability level—their perceived competence. Perceived competence becomes more specific as students mature. Young students think they are good and competent at everything. As they become older (third or fourth grade), they start to realize that other students are better in some areas. If these students are not given the chance to succeed in class, low perceived competence about their ability to perform physical skills is the result. This "learned helplessness" (Harter, 1978) eventually results in the students' disliking and dropping out of physical education.

Assume All Youngsters Have the Ability to Achieve

Avoid identifying athletes at a young age. Predictions based on elementary school performance were correct only 25% of the time. All children should be treated as if they have the potential to become successful. It is not the purpose of a physical education program to develop athletes, but rather to help all students develop physical skills within the limits of their potential. Perceived competence can influence attitudes toward pursuing an active lifestyle.

Physical education should help all students develop physical skills within the limits of their potential.

> A related article is available at this site:
>  http://kidshealth.org/parent/nutrition_fit/index.html

Understand that Starting Young Doesn't Ensure Excellence

There is no evidence to support the idea that starting a child at a young age assures the child will become an outstanding athlete.

Children who have been in organized sports programs for many years may burn out at an early age. Extrinsic versus intrinsic motivation is discussed in this chapter. Evidence shows that extrinsic motivation may ultimately decrease intrinsic motivation, particularly in children age 7 years and older.

> To read additional articles related to the pressure children feel when competing, go to these two sites:
>  http://kidshealth.org/kid/stay_healthy/fit/pressure.html
>  http://www.cnn.com/2005/US/06/20/youth.sports

GUIDELINES FOR EXERCISING CHILDREN SAFELY

Moderation is a way to ensure that children are safe and grow up enjoying physical activity. Moderate exercise, coupled with opportunities to participate in recreational activity, helps develop a lasting desire to move. Children can withstand a gradual increase in workload and are capable of workloads comparable to those of adults when the load is adjusted for height and size. Fatigue causes healthy children to stop exercising long before any danger to health occurs (Shephard, 1984a).

Exercising in the Heat

Caution must be exerted when exercising children in hot weather to avoid heat-related illness.

Children are not little adults and do not adapt to extremes of temperature as effectively as adults do for the following physiological reasons (Bar-Or, 1983; American Academy of Pediatrics, 2000):

1. Children have higher surface area/mass ratios than those of adults. This allows a greater amount of heat
    to transfer between the environment and the body.

2. When walking or running, children produce more metabolic heat per unit mass than adults produce. Youngsters are not as efficient in executing movement patterns, so they generate more metabolic heat than do adults performing a similar task.

3. Sweating capacity is not as great in children as in adults, resulting in a lowered ability to cool the body.

4. The ability to convey heat by blood from the body core to the skin is reduced in children due to a lower cardiac output at a given oxygen uptake.

The American Academy of Pediatrics (2000) offers the following guidelines for exercising children during hot days:

1. The intensity of activities that last 15 minutes or more should be reduced whenever relative humidity and air temperature are above critical levels. Table 2.1 in the textbook shows the relationship between humidity and air temperature and when activity should be moderated.

2. At the beginning of a strenuous exercise program or after traveling to a warmer climate, the intensity and duration of exercise should be restrained initially and then increased gradually over a period of 10 to 14 days to acclimatize to the effects of heat. When such a period is not available, the length of time for participation should be curtailed.

3. Children should be hydrated 20 to 30 minutes before strenuous activity (Figure 2.9 in the textbook). During the activity, periodic drinking (e.g., 150 ml of cold tap water every 20 minutes for a child weighing 40 kg) should be enforced.

4. Clothing should be lightweight and limited to one layer of absorbent material to facilitate evaporation of sweat and to expose as much skin as possible. Sweat-saturated garments should be replaced by dry ones. Rubberized sweat suits should never be used to produce weight loss.

The committee identifies children with the following conditions as being at a potentially high risk for heat stress: Overweight, febrile (feverish) state, cystic fibrosis, gastrointestinal infection, diabetes insipidus, diabetes mellitus, chronic heart failure, caloric malnutrition, anorexia nervosa, sweating insufficiency syndrome, and mental retardation.

Distance Running

An often-asked question is how much and how far children should be allowed to run, particularly in a competitive or training setting. The American Academy of Pediatrics Executive Committee (1991) identifies some of the concerns.

Psychological and social problems for the child runner can result from spending long hours in training and setting unrealistic goals. A prepubertal child should be allowed to participate for the enjoyment of running without fear of parental or peer rejection or pressure.

Due to the potential for injuries, the International Athletics Association Federation (IAAF) Medical Committee does not encourage training and competition for long-distance track and road-running events. Up to the age of 12, it is suggested that not more than 800 m (one-half mile) should be run in competition. An increase in this distance should be introduced gradually—with, for example, a maximum of 3,000 m (nearly 2 miles) in competition for 14-year-olds.

Fitness Testing Considerations

The practice of testing children at the start of the school year in a one-mile run/walk or other high-effort aerobic tests should be discouraged, since many children may not have ample conditioning to participate safely in the activity. A recommendation is to test only at the end of the school year after youngsters have had the opportunity to be conditioned. If this is not possible, at least allow youngsters 4 to 6 weeks to condition themselves.

The PACER aerobic fitness test should be used in place of the mile run for fitness evaluation. The PACER can be administered indoors and does not require running to exhaustion. As a cardiovascular fitness measure, the PACER is as accurate as the mile run and produces much less emotional stress for participants.

> This website connects you to the Cooper Institute with information on the Fitnessgram test:
> http://www.cooperinst.org/ftgmain.asp

> This website connects you to the President's Challenge test:
> http://www.presidentschallenge.org

Resistance Training

Resistance training for preadolescent children has generated concern among educators. Many worry about safety and stress-related injuries, while others question whether such training produces significant strength gains.

Accepted thinking for years was that prepubescent youngsters are incapable of making significant strength gains because they lack adequate levels of circulating androgens. Evidence is continuing to build that contradicts this point of view (Faigenbaum, 2003). A study by Cahill (1986) demonstrated significant increases in strength among 18 prepubescent boys. A study by Servedio et al. (1985) showed significant strength gains in shoulder flexion. Weltman et al. (1986) conducted a 14-week, three-times-a-week program using hydraulic resistance training (circuit training using 10 different stations) in 6- to 11-year-old boys. Results showed an 18 to 37 percent gain in all major muscle groups. Strength can be increased through weight training in prepubescent youngsters; however, the way prepubescent children gain strength differs from adolescents and adults (Tanner, 1993). In preadolescent children, it appears that strength gains occur from motor learning rather than muscle hypertrophy.

The term resistance training is in this textbook to denote the use of barbells, dumbbells, rubber bands, or machines as resistance. This is in sharp contrast to weight lifting or power lifting, which is a competitive sport for the purpose of determining maximum lifting ability. There is agreement among experts that weight training is acceptable for children, but weight lifting is highly undesirable and may be harmful.

When a variety of physical activities are experienced in elementary school physical education, there is little need for weight training within the school curriculum. There are many ways to enhance strength in children besides using weights, which may offer a safety issue. For a number of alternative ways to develop strength, see the text by Roberts and Pillarella (1996). However, weight training is acceptable on an individual basis with parental approval in a club setting.

> Go to this site to read a related article on strength training and children:
> http://kidshealth.org/parent/nutrition_fit/fitness/strength_training.html

> Go to this site to read another related article:
> http://kidshealth.org/parent/nutrition_fit/index.html

> This website connects you to the American College of Sports Medicine Youth Strength Training site:
> http://www.acsm.org/pdf/YSTRNGTH.pdf

INSTRUCTIONAL FORMATS

The material in this chapter can be presented using the lecture style plus the Power Point materials and overhead transparencies providing students an overview of the chapter. The introduction may be followed by cooperative learning assignments that provide active learning and critical thinking activities for the student. In the cooperative learning groups, the students will discuss the materials listed on the Task Sheet and/or other topics you may assign. Each group can become a "content expert" for sections of the Task Sheet. Oral summary reports of the group may be presented to the entire class covering all or part of the discussion items.

KEY TERMS

somatotype	fast twitch fibers	deadweight
endomorph	slow twitch fibers	endurance training
perceived competence	PACER	aerobic capacity
ectomorph	resistance training	perceived competence
extrinsic rewards	relative strength	
mesomorph	strength training	
intrinsic motivation	overweight	

REFLECTION AND REVIEW QUESTIONS

How and Why

1. How have your views of what is appropriate for children changed as a result of reading this chapter?

2. Why is it important for physical education teachers to understand "The Growing Child?"

3. How might physical education be different for an overweight child as compared to a leaner peer?

4. Should children under 9 years old be permitted to play youth sports?

5. Is fitness testing in elementary physical education an appropriate practice? Defend your answer.

DISCUSSION TOPICS

1. What impact do growth patterns, body physique, and skeletal maturity have on skill acquisition and performance?

2. Explain the importance of physical activity for children.

3. Discuss the influence of muscular development and strength on physical activity for children.

4. Is training designed to improve aerobic capacity appropriate for children? Explain.

5. What can be done to maximize the youth sport experience for all children?

6. Describe the relationship between physical activity and intelligence.

7. Role-play the following situation: You are the physical education specialist at an elementary school. The principal wants to hold a mile race for the kindergarten children. Discuss the pros and cons of this situation with the principal. Can you offer any alternative activities for the children?

SAMPLE WRITTEN ASSIGNMENTS

1. Write a paper describing how adults and children differ with respect to exercising in the heat. Be sure to include the guidelines described in the chapter for exercising students in heat.

2. Write an editorial to a local newspaper describing the difference between physical education at your school and organized youth sports participation.

3. Write an article for the PTA/PTSO newsletter describing the importance of physical education in your curriculum.

4. Write an article for parents regarding the pressures students feel when involved in competition.

5. Go to this site for additional information:
    http://kidshealth.org/parent/nutrition_fit/index.html

6. Write a newsletter to parents about your physical education program. Conduct an Internet search to assist you in newsletter ideas.

    Go to this site to view some examples:
    http://primusweb.com/fitnesspartner/library/libindex.htm

    If you go to this site, you will see an article you could use as a model:
    http://www.usaweekend.com/98_issues/981108/981108education.html

7. Create a variety of safe and interesting running activities for a class.

ACTIVITY SESSION EXPERIENCE

Lead the students through the following activity:

1. Have the students perform a given aerobic activity. Then, have them wear a scuba weight belt or attach 10-pound weights to their clothes, and have them try to perform the same aerobic activities at the same pace. In this activity, students will see how much more difficult it is to perform when overweight. The exercise will give the student more appreciation for the efforts the overweight student gives in class.

COOPERATIVE LEARNING TASK SHEET

Chapter 2: Teaching Children in the Physical Education Environment

Directions: Your cooperative learning group will become the content experts by finding the answers to the items listed below. Discuss the following items with your group and be ready to report on one or all of them at the end of the class period.

1. Describe the need for physical activities for the growing child.

2. Discuss the trends of today regarding fitness versus physical activity development.

3. Describe the relationship between physical activity and the development of muscular strength, endurance, and skeletal growth.

4. State the characteristics of each somatotype and their effects on motor performance.

5. Define aerobic capacity and discuss its relationship to the health and physical activity levels of normal and overweight children.

6. Describe the elements of body composition and their relationship to the health and well-being of a child.

7. Discuss the role organized youth sports play in the growth and development of children. Conduct an Internet search to assist your discussion on the role youth sports play in the growth and development of children.

8. How might physical education be taught differently for an overweight child as compared to a leaner child?

9. Write guidelines to follow for exercising children safely under a variety of weather conditions.

10. Describe safe approaches to distance running for preadolescent children.

11. Describe appropriate practices for weight lifting for preadolescent children.

12. Is fitness testing in elementary physical education an appropriate practice? Defend your answer.

13. Describe the relationship between physical activity and intelligence.

14. Discuss how adults and children differ with respect to exercising in the heat. Discuss guidelines for exercising students in the heat.

CHAPTER 3

Preparing a Quality Lesson

SUMMARY

Effective teachers are able to use more than one style of teaching and may, in fact, use several styles during a particular lesson. In this chapter, planning strategies associated with effective and quality instruction are described. Pre-instructional decisions such as selection of the teaching style, use of time, use of space and equipment, and student instructional formations are explained. Skill progression guidelines are presented. Objective writing and its purpose are covered along with lesson plan writing. Sample Task Sheets for your use are also presented in this chapter.

STUDENT OUTCOMES

Upon completion of the reading of this chapter, the student will:

- Describe various teaching styles and the best time to use each style to increase student learning.

- Describe the role of planning in preparing for quality instruction.

- Understand the relationships between instruction and the developmental and experiential level of students.

- List pre-instructional decisions that must be made before the actual delivery of the lesson.

- Know the basic mechanical principles required for efficient performance of motor skills.

- Cite effective ways to use equipment, time, space, and formations in the instructional setting.

- Understand how to optimize skill learning. Include discussions of developmental patterns, arousal, feedback, practice sessions, and skill progression.

- Understand the rationale for the four components of a lesson and describe characteristics of each.

- Know how to improve the quality of instructional presentations through reflection and critique.

MAIN CONCEPTS

Teachers must plan for effective and quality instruction. Pre-instructional decisions include: selection of teaching style, time allotment, teaching space, equipment use, and instructional and student formations.

CHOOSE FROM A VARIETY OF TEACHING STYLES

Teachers make numerous decisions while teaching each class. One of the first steps to take when planning is to decide on the teaching style to use for each lesson. There are a variety of styles to choose from and there is no one "best" or universal teaching style. Good planning aids the teacher in making the best decision. Using different teaching styles can improve the environment for students and teachers and increases the effectiveness of the program. The styles presented in this chapter include: Direct, Task (Station), Mastery Learning (Outcomes-Based), Individualized Style, Cooperative Learning (Reciprocal), Inquiry, Guided Discovery (Convergent), Problem Solving (Divergent), and Free Exploration.

OPTIMIZE SKILL LEARNING

Be cognizant of developmental growing patterns in reference to learning. Three development patterns typify the growth of the primary-grade children:

- Development proceeds from head to foot (cephalocaudal).

- Development occurs from inside to outside (proximodistal).

- Development proceeds from general to specific.

Know the Effect of Arousal

Arousal is the level of excitement stress produces. Arousal levels can have a positive or negative impact on motor performance. A good teacher will attempt to find the amount that is "just right" to maximize learning.

Competition affects the arousal level of children. When competition is introduced in the early stages of skill learning, stress and anxiety reduce a child's ability to learn. If competition is used after a skill has been overlearned, it can improve the level of performance.

Offer Meaningful Skill Feedback

Feedback must be offered to students to enhance learning. Feedback is important in teaching because it impacts what is to be learned, what should be avoided, and how the performance can be modified. A variety of feedback styles are presented including intrinsic feedback and extrinsic feedback.

Knowledge of Results

Knowledge of results is extrinsic feedback given after a skill has been performed. Knowledge of results is a requisite for learning new motor skills. Knowledge of results assures students they are performing and practicing a skill correctly though guided practice. Knowledge of results focuses on the outcome of a skill; knowledge of performance relates to the process of the skill performance. Knowledge of performance can increase a youngster's level of motivation because it provides feedback about improvement. Knowledge of performance is a strong reinforcer when an instructor mentions something performed correctly. If choosing between knowledge of results and knowledge of performance, focus on knowledge of performance. Knowledge of results relies on the performance outcome and doesn't consider whether the skill was performed correctly.

Design Effective Practice Sessions

Practice is a key part of learning motor skills. Practice must focus on quality of movement.

Focus skill practice sessions on process.

Use mental practice techniques.

Decide on whole vs. part practice.

Determine the length and distribution of practice sessions. Short practice sessions usually produce more efficient learning than longer sessions.

Blocked practice is where all the trials of one task are completed before moving on to the next task. This is effective during the first stages of skill practice.

Random practice is where the order of multiple task presentations is mixed and no task is practiced twice in succession. Random practice has been proven to be the most effective approach to use when learning skills. Block practice gave the best results during the acquisition phase of skill learning. However, students who learned a skill using random practice demonstrated higher levels of retention.

Developmental Levels and Progression

Teach skills in a progressive, developmentally appropriate order. Children learn skills in a natural progression, but not at the same rate. Encourage youngsters to progress at a rate that is best suited for them. This usually means that all children will be learning a similar class of skills (throwing or striking, for instance), but will progress at different rates and practice different skills within the category.

Developmental Level I activities (used most often with kindergarten through second-grade children) are the least difficult and form the foundation for more complex skills.

In Developmental Level II (usually grades 3–4), the tasks become more difficult and many are performed individually or within small groups. Environmental factors such as different speeds of objects, different sizes of objects, and games requiring locomotor movements and specialized skills (throwing, catching, and so on) are introduced at this level.

In Developmental Level III (grades 5–6), students use skills in a number of sport and game situations. Simple skills previously learned are sequenced into more complex motor patterns. Cognitive decisions about when to use a skill and how to incorporate strategy into the game are integrated into the learning experiences at this level.

INTEGRATE MECHANICAL PRINCIPLES INTO INSTRUCTION

Mechanical principles need to be considered as an integral part of skill performance.

- Stability: Reflects balance and equilibrium. A stable base is necessary when one applies force to a projectile or absorbs force.

- Force: A measure of the push or pull that one object or body applies to another. Force is necessary to move objects of various types and sizes. The larger the object to be moved, the greater the amount of force required to cause the movement.

- Leverage and Motion: Body levers amplify force into motion. Levers offer a mechanical advantage so that less effort is needed to accomplish tasks. Motion occurs after force has been applied or when force is absorbed. The types of levers are described in this chapter.

- Motion and Direction: The majority of skills in physical activities are associated with propelling an object. Trajectory, rebound angles, and release points are discussed in this chapter.

CONSIDER THE LEARNING ENVIRONMENT

The teaching environment can have an impact on the effectiveness of instruction and learning.

Predetermine Your Space Needs

Plan the best method of using equipment and space. Delineate the practice area so that it is appropriate to the tasks being taught. An easy way to do that is to set up cones around the perimeter of the area. Available space can be divided into smaller areas to maximize student participation.

Use Equipment Efficiently

Ideally, a teacher will have one necessary apparatus per student. If there are fewer items, instruction should be planned to still maximize participation of all students. Using Task Style or Station Style can enhance the learning environment with limited equipment.

Effective distribution of individual equipment is important. Place the equipment around the perimeter of the teaching area before beginning the lesson.

Ensure a Safe Environment

Set up the teaching environment with safety in mind. Have a written curriculum that guides instructional presentations in proper progression.

Conduct safety inspections of your teaching environment daily.

CHOOSE AN INSTRUCTIONAL FORMATION

Select appropriate formations for teaching to assure maximum activity, facilitate learning, and ensure safety for all students. The formations described in the chapter include: Mass/Scattered Formation; Squad Formation; Partner Formation; Lane/File; Line and Leader; Double Line; Regular Shuttle Formation; Shuttle Turn-Back Formation; and Simultaneous Class Movement.

DESIGN A LESSON PLAN FORMAT

Written lesson plans ensure that thought has been given to the lesson before children enter the activity area. Lesson plans give focus and direction to instruction. Standardized lesson plans allow teachers and substitute teachers to interchange plans within a school/district. Include the following in your lesson plan:

- Objectives: Objectives are written for the purpose of accomplishing content standards.

- Equipment required: Identify the amounts of materials/supplies required for the lesson and the format for distribution.

- Instructional activities: List the movements and skill experiences to be taught. The planned learning experience should be based on the developmental level of children.

- Teaching hints: Include organizational tips and teaching-learning cues.

A common format is the four-part lesson plan described in this chapter and in the accompanying lesson plan book.

The Four-Part Lesson Components

The four-part Dynamic Physical Education Model consists of: Introductory Activity, Fitness Activity, Lesson Focus, and Closing Activity.

Introductory (Warm-Up) Activity: lasts 2–3 minutes and sets the tone for the rest of the lesson.

Purposes of the Introductory Activities:

- Students receive immediate activity when they enter the activity area.

- They serve as a physiological warm-up, preparing students for physical activity.

- Can be used to review skills or for an anticipatory set.

Fitness Activity: lasts 7–10 minutes. This portion of the lesson is designed to enhance health-related fitness and promote lifetime physical activity.

Lesson Focus: is designed to teach physical skills. This portion of the lesson lasts 15–25 minutes.

Closing Activity: The closing activity may be a game that uses skills developed in the lesson focus or simply a low-organized game/activity. Bring closure to the end of each lesson to increase retention and allow students to review what they have learned.

REFLECTIVE TEACHING

Caring, hard working, effective teachers reflect on their teaching and evaluate themselves to improve instruction in future lessons. Instruction improves when teachers reflect on why some things worked and others didn't.

Questions to Aid the Reflection Process

Planning

- Did I prepare ahead of time? Mental preparation prior to a lesson assures flow and continuity occurs in a lesson.

- Did I understand the "whys" of my lesson? Knowing why you are teaching something will give you greater strength and conviction in your presentation.

- Did I state my instructional goals for the lesson? Students are more focused if they know what they are supposed to learn.

- Did I plan the lesson so students can participate safely such as areas for running, no slippery spots, broken glass, objects to run into, adequate room for striking activities, etc.?

Equipment

- Was my equipment arranged prior to class? Proper equipment placement reduces management time and allows more time for instruction and practice.

- Did I use enough equipment to keep all students involved and assured of maximum practice opportunities?

- Did I notify the principal about equipment that needs to be repaired or replaced? On a regular basis, do I record areas where equipment is lacking or insufficient in quantity? Do I inform the principal of these shortcomings?

- Did I select equipment that is appropriate for the developmental level of the students, i.e., proper size and types of balls, basketball hoop height, hand implements?

Methodology

- Did I constantly move and reposition myself during the lesson? Moving allows you to be close to more students so you can reinforce and help them. It usually reduces behavior problems.

- Did I teach with enthusiasm and energy? My energy and zest rubs off on my students.

- Did I try to show just as much energy for the last class of the day as I did for the first class of the day? Do I work just as hard on Friday as I did at the start of the week?

- Did I keep students moving during lesson transitions? Did I plan my transitions carefully so little time was needed to proceed to the next part of the lesson?

Instruction

- Was I alert for children who were having trouble performing the activities and needed some personal help? Youngsters want to receive relevant but subtle help.

- Did I praise youngsters who made an effort or improved? Saying something positive to children increases their desire to perform at a higher level.

- Did I give sufficient attention to the personalization and creativity of each student? Everybody feels unique and different and wants to deal with learning tasks in a personal manner.

- Did I teach for quality of movement or just offer a large quantity of activities in an attempt to keep students on task? Repetition is a necessary part of learning new skills.

Discipline/Management

- Did I teach students to be responsible for their leaning and personal behavior? Students need to learn responsibility and self-direction skills.

- Did I evaluate how I handled discipline and management problems? Did I preserve the self-esteem of my students during behavior correction episodes? What are some ways I could have handled situations better?

- Did I make positive calls home to reinforce students who are really trying and working hard?

Assessment

- Did I bring closure to my lesson? This gives me feedback about the effectiveness of my instruction. It also allows students a chance to reflect on what they have learned. Did I ask for answers in a way that allows me to quickly check that all students understand?

- Did I evaluate the usefulness of activities I presented? Did I make changes as quickly as possible to ensure my lessons were improving and better meeting the needs of my students?

- Did I communicate with teachers and the principal about things that need to be improved or better understood? For example, did I say something about classes arriving late, teachers arriving late to pick up their class, schedule problems that cause excessive work, etc.?

INSTRUCTIONAL FORMATS

The material in this chapter may be presented using the lecture style and the Power Point and overhead transparencies to provide students an overview of the chapter. The instructor may also use the Guided Discovery method of teaching to introduce and review the materials read by the students. In this style, the instructor asks questions guiding the students toward one answer. The instructor rephrases the questions until the students discover the answer to the question. The introduction/ review of the chapter may be followed by cooperative learning assignments that provide active learning and critical thinking activities for the student. In the cooperative learning groups, the students will discuss the materials listed on the Cooperative Learning Task Sheet and/or other topics you may assign. Each group can become a "content expert" for sections of the Task Sheet. Oral summary reports of the group may be presented to the entire class covering all or part of the discussion items.

The four-part lesson can be demonstrated to the class with the use of the prepared videotapes, which accompany the adoption of this textbook. Additionally, an activity session can be taught to demonstrate the four-part lesson.

KEY TERMS

mastery learning	intrinsic feedback	blocked practice
part method	knowledge of results	problem-solving style
individualized style	knowledge of performance	random practice
objectives	mental practice	free-exploration style
guided discovery	direct style	skill progression
arousal	whole method	instructional progression
extrinsic feedback	cooperative learning	

REFLECTION AND REVIEW QUESTIONS

How and Why

1. Why is it important for teachers to understand and use a variety of teaching styles?

2. How can knowledge of motor learning help teachers maximize learning in physical education?

3. Why are mechanical principles taught in elementary physical education? How might these principles help teachers and students?

4. How does the college learning environment differ from an appropriate learning environment for elementary physical education?

5. How did your elementary physical education learning environment differ from that advocated in the chapter?

Content Review

1. What variables must be considered when choosing a teaching style?

2. Describe the teaching styles used in physical education. Include comments on the effective use of the different styles.

3. Discuss the basic tenets of motor learning required to "optimize skill learning."

4. Explain several mechanical principles and how they are used in elementary physical education.

5. Describe four instructional formations. How can these formations be used?

6. What are the four parts of a lesson? Discuss the characteristics of each part and its significance.

7. State several issues that physical education teachers must address when preparing to teach.

DISCUSSION TOPICS

1. Why do instructors need to write lesson plans when they know the material well and can teach without writing things down each day?

2. Explain self-evaluation/reflection of teaching and how it can improve the quality of each lesson.

3. Who are instructional objectives written for: the student or the teacher?

4. How does instructional planning relate to accountability?

SAMPLE WRITTEN ASSIGNMENTS

1. Write two instructional objectives for a physical education lesson making them as complete as possible.

2. List the content of a selected activity unit. *Lesson Plans for Dynamic Physical Education for Elementary School Children, 15th edition* may be used as a resource guide for this assignment.

3. Interview a school administrator about the importance of planning and lesson plan writing in the educational process. Write a summary of the interview.

ACTIVITY SESSION EXPERIENCES

Lead the students through the following activities:

1. A mini lesson using the Direct Style of teaching.

2. A mini lesson using the Task Style of teaching.

3. A mini lesson using the Reciprocal Style of teaching.

4. A mini lesson using the Guided Discovery Style of teaching.

5. A mini lesson using the Problem-Solving Style of teaching.

COOPERATIVE LEARNING TASK SHEET

Chapter 3: Preparing a Quality Lesson

Directions: Your cooperative learning group will become the content experts by finding the answers to the items listed below. Discuss the following items with your group and be ready to report on one or all of them at the end of the class period.

1. Describe the role and importance of planning in preparing for quality instruction.

2. Discuss the interaction between instruction and the developmental and experiential level of students.

3. State the essential elements of instruction and discuss the manner in which each relates to the learning environment.

4. List pre-instructional decisions that must occur before the actual delivery of the lesson.

5. Cite effective ways to use equipment, time, space, and formations in the instructional setting.

6. Discuss developmental patterns, arousal, feedback, practice sessions, and skill progression in the learning environment.

7. State what the relationship is between instruction and the developmental and experiential levels of students.

8. Describe the four components of a Dynamic Physical Education lesson and the characteristics of each component.

9. Define each teaching style and the best use of each to increase student learning. This question may be divided among several people with each person selecting a particular teaching style to discuss.

10. Describe strategies and techniques that can be used to give students meaningful feedback regarding their performance of a skill.

11. Identify methods for evaluating your lessons following a teaching session.

12. Discuss how your elementary physical education learning experience differed from what is advocated in this chapter.

CHAPTER 4

Curriculum Development

SUMMARY

This chapter offers a systematic approach for developing a curriculum and suggested formats for organization and evaluation. A written curriculum gives direction to the instructional program. A sequence of steps is presented for planning, designing, and implementing a comprehensive curriculum. The concepts of scope, sequence, and balance help assure the curriculum will meet the needs of all students.

STUDENT OUTCOMES

Upon completion of the reading of this chapter, the student will:

- Define scope, sequence, and balance as each relates to curriculum development.

- List elements common to quality curriculum.

- Delineate your philosophy of physical education for children.

- List environmental factors that impact curriculum development.

- Specify the six-step approach in developing a quality curriculum.

- Specify the needs, characteristics, and interests of children and be able to explain how these age and maturity factors influence program development.

- Describe the difference between content standards and student-centered objectives.

- Cite the three learning domains and discuss characteristics of each.

MAIN CONCEPTS

Curriculum is a framework for instructional activities that focuses on subject matter, student development, social-cultural goals or some combination of all three areas. Curriculum gives sequence and direction to the learning experiences of students. Value orientation is a set of personal and professional beliefs that provides a basis for determining curricular decisions.

> If you would like to read the curriculum guide for schools in a section of Canada go to this website: http://www.sasked.gov.sk.ca/docs/physed/physed1-5/index.html

When developing or revising an existing curriculum, the value orientation of the physical education staff toward the existing curriculum and proposed changes is a necessary consideration. Determining the value orientation of the curriculum involves consideration of three major components: subject matter; the students for whom the curriculum is being developed; and the social-cultural goals that have been established in the school/district.

Priorities in curriculum vary depending on the value orientations of the physical educators involved in the planning. A professional learns to teach activities that will enrich the needs of all students even if they are uncomfortable with the subject matter.

Instructors who favor a student-centered approach select activities that develop the individual student. In contrast, physical educators who place the highest priority on subject matter mastery include an emphasis on sports, dance, outdoor adventure activities, physical fitness activities, and aquatic activities. Still other faculties see student autonomy and self-direction as the most important goals. These faculty members focus curricula on lifetime sport skills and non-traditional activities such as cooperative games and group activities, in an attempt to foster problem-solving and interpersonal skills.

Before accepting a teaching position, ask questions about the existing curriculum and program philosophies to see if your values and beliefs match the position being offered. Make an informed decision and be aware of the situation when deciding if the position will afford you an enjoyable, rewarding teaching experience.

Ask the following questions of administrators before you accept a job in the district:

- Will the curriculum express a point of view about subject matter that is consistent with mine?

- Does the curriculum express a point of view about student learning that I believe?

- Does the curriculum express a point of view about the school's role in accomplishing social-cultural goals that is similar to my beliefs?

- Can I implement instructional strategies I value within this model?

DESIGNING A QUALITY CURRICULUM

Curriculum design involves following a sequential approach for constructing a meaningful, well-planned curriculum. These steps are: Developing a Guiding Philosophy; Defining a Conceptual Framework for the Curriculum; Environmental Factors; Determining Content Standards and Student Objectives; Selecting Child-Centered Activities; Organizing Selected Activities into Instructional Units; and Evaluating and Modifying the Curriculum. Other factors that need to be taken into consideration in curriculum planning, development, and implementation are: the administration; the community; facilities and equipment; state and federal laws and requirements; school scheduling; and budget.

Step One: Develop a Guiding Philosophy

The initial step in curriculum design is to define a philosophy of physical education that reflects the educator' beliefs. A philosophical statement defines how physical education fits into the total school curriculum and what it will accomplish for each student.

When developing a philosophy, remember the three major and unique contributions of physical education to the total school curriculum:

1. To develop personal activity and fitness habits.

2. To develop and enhance movement competency and motor skills.

3. To gain a conceptual understanding of movement principles.

Class sizes should be similar to other teachers in the school, and an assigned teaching area appropriate for physical education instruction should be provided. The school should provide one piece of individual equipment for each youngster and ample apparatus to assure small learning groups. This will afford maximum opportunity for learning and retention.

Activities in the curriculum need to be presented in an educationally sound sequence.

Go to these websites to see curriculum plans from a variety of states:

http://www.pecentral.com

http://pelinks4u.org

The curriculum includes an appropriate means of assessing student progress on a consistent and regular basis.

Physical education is that portion of the child's overall education that is accomplished through movement.

For effective learning, activities and skills must be presented in a developmentally appropriate form, one that assures success.

Successful physical education programs educate all students and employ educationally sound teaching strategies.

Movement is the basis of physical education. Children do not profit from standing in line, waiting for equipment to be arranged, listening to lengthy teacher explanations, or participating in an activity dominated by a few students.

The curriculum offers students skills to maintain an active lifestyle with a variety of activity choices.

Children should be taught movement based on their individual motor development level, not just their grade level.

Step Two: Define a Conceptual Framework for the Curriculum

A conceptual framework is a series of statements that characterize the desired curriculum. The following are conceptual statements that define a child-centered, developmental curriculum:

- Curriculum goals and objectives are appropriate for all youngsters.

- Activities in the curriculum are selected based on their potential to help students reach content standards.

- The curriculum helps youngsters develop lifelong physical activity habits and understand basic fitness concepts.

- The curriculum includes activities that enhance cognitive and affective learning.

- The curriculum provides experiences that allow all children to succeed and feel satisfaction.

- The curriculum is planned and based on an educational environment that is consistent with other academic areas in the school.

- Activities in the curriculum are presented in an educationally sound sequence.

- The curriculum includes an appropriate means of assessing student progress.

Assessment and evaluation schedules and suggested techniques for modifying the curriculum are an integral part of the curricular structure, evaluation, and regeneration.

Step Three: Consider Environmental Factors

Environmental factors are all those conditions within the community and school district that limit or extend the scope of the curriculum. Restrictive factors are conditions within the community or school district that limit the scope of the curriculum development. Examples of environmental factors are the amount and type of equipment, budget size, school administrators, and the cultural makeup of the community.

School Administrators

The support of school administrators has a significant impact on the curriculum. It is important to communicate program goals to administrators. Many administrators have misconceptions about physical education and its contribution to the overall education of students.

> Going to this site will allow you to read about a particular school district's physical education program including philosophy, curriculum, and testing procedures:
> http://www.geocities.com/Athens/Forum/8208/pe.html

The Community: People and Climate

Occupations, religions, educational levels, cultural values, and physical activity habits within the community are factors that might affect curriculum development.

Facilities and Equipment

Available teaching facilities and equipment determine which activities can be offered. One piece of equipment per child is necessary if students are to learn at an optimum rate.

Laws and Requirements

Laws, regulations, and requirements at the national, state, and local levels may restrict or direct a curriculum. Examples of two national laws affecting physical education programs are Title IX and PL 94-142.

Scheduling

Scheduling should be done to maximize the educational experience for students. The most common length of period is 30 minutes. Some teachers like 40 minutes for upper-grade youngsters. Some schools try to compress periods for primary-grade children to 20 minutes. This is too short a period to present a balanced and complete lesson and places undue stress on the physical educator.

Physical education teachers should have the same workload as other teachers in their school and district.

Classes should be scheduled by developmental levels. Because physical education is equipment-intensive, scheduling by developmental level reduces equipment and teaching preparations

Budget and Funding

Physical educators deserve parity in funding with other school program areas.

Step Four: Determine Content Standards and Student Objectives

Content standards determine the direction of the program as dictated and desired by the state, district, or individual school. They determine what students should know and be able to do when they complete their schooling. Student progress is dictated by how students compare to the fixed standards rather than how they compare with other students. Content standards determine what criteria will be used to select instructional activities for the curriculum.

Content standards determine what criteria will be used to select instructional activities for the curriculum. The National Association for Sport and Physical Education (NASPE) has identified six national standards that are used to guide content in this textbook. See Chapter 1 for an in-depth discussion of each standard.

1. Demonstrates competency in motor skills and movement patterns needed to perform a variety of physical activities.

2. Demonstrates understanding of movement concepts, principles, and tactics as they apply to the learning and performance of physical activities.

3. Participates regularly in physical activity

4. Achieves and maintains a health-enhancing level of physical fitness.

5. Exhibits responsible personal and social behavior that respects self and others in physical activity.

6. Values physical activity for health, enjoyment, challenge, self-expression, and/or social interaction.

The major criterion to follow when selecting activities for the curriculum is: Do the activities contribute to institutional and student objectives? This approach contrasts with selecting activities because they are fun or because you enjoy them.

Write Student-Centered Instructional Objectives

After defining content standards, student-centered objectives are written. They dictate the specific activities students will need to learn throughout the school year. Student-centered objectives are written in behavioral terms. Behavioral objectives contain three key characteristics: (a) a desired behavior that is observable; (b) a behavior that is measurable; and (c) a criterion for success that can be measured. They are written for all three of the learning domains: cognitive, affective, and psychomotor.

Step Five: Select Child-Centered Activities

When selecting activities for a child-centered curriculum, a clear understanding of children is requisite. A program should be designed that flows with children and supports their urges, characteristics, and interests.

Know the Basic Urges of Children

All children have similar basic urges closely linked to societal and familial influences. Instruction should provide for the development of these urges. The urges represent broad traits that are typical of children regardless of age, sex, or race. The urges are:

- The Urge for Movement

- The Urge for Success and Approval

- The Urge for Peer Acceptance and Social Competence

- The Urge to Cooperate and Compete

- The Urge for Physical Fitness and Attractiveness

- The Urge for Adventure

- The Urge for Creative Satisfaction

- The Urge for Rhythmic Expression

- The Urge to Know

- The Urge to Understand the Characteristics and Interests of Children

Understand the Characteristics and Interests of Children

The urges of children represent broad traits that are typical of children regardless of age, sex, or race. In contrast to the urges, children have age and maturity specific attributes and characteristics that influence learning objectives. Children have interests grouped under each learning domain: psychomotor, cognitive, and affective. The chapter provides a chart (Table 4.1) that will aid in the selection of appropriate selection and sequencing of curriculum activities based on developmental levels and the domains discussed.

Step Six: Organize Selected Activities into Instructional Units

The textbook is divided into descriptions of movements appropriate to Levels I, II, or III. Generally, students placed in Developmental Level I are K–2; Level II includes grades 3–4; and Level III includes grades 5–6.

Level I: Focus activities on those that are individual in nature and center on learning movement concepts through theme development. Children learn about movement principles, body identification, and body management skills.

Level II: Activities focus on refinement of fundamental skills and the ability to perform specialized skills begins to surface.

Level III: Activities focus on specialized skills and sports skills while participating in cooperative sport lead-up games.

Activities in the lesson focus section of the lesson plans begin with skills all students can perform and progress to a point where further instruction and skill practice is necessary because students are challenged. Starting each lesson with basic activities ensures all students begin with success. This is critical for developing positive attitudes toward new activities. If the first thing youngsters experience is failure, the rest of the unit is a tough sell. Build instructional sequences for each day based on the preceding lesson. Keep the length of units of instruction to one or two weeks, so students do not become bored or discouraged. Long units force children who are unskilled or who dislike the activity to have to live with failure for long periods of time. If more time is needed for a specific unit, add another week or two later in the year. Use a game activity to provide a change of pace when the motivational level of the class (and, in turn, the teacher) appears to be waning.

Check the Scope, Sequence, and Balance of the Curriculum

An important step in creating a quality program is to review and monitor the scope, sequence, and balance of the curriculum. The curriculum should be broad in scope, sequence, and balance and offer as much variety and depth as possible.

Scope is the yearly content of the curriculum; also known as the horizontal articulation of the curriculum.

Sequence defines the skills and activities to be covered on a year-to-year basis. It is known as a vertical articulation of the curriculum.

Balance ensures that all objectives in the program receive adequate coverage. To assure balance, major areas of emphasis are determined based on program objectives. Balance ensures children do not have to stay with one type of activity too long.

If you would like to read about the curriculum developed in three different school districts, go to this website:
 http://www.republic.k12.mo.us

Step Seven: Evaluate and Modify the Curriculum

Evaluation schedules and suggested techniques for modifying the curriculum are an integral part of the curricular structure. Following an evaluation process, educators must analyze the data and make changes to improve their curriculum based on the data.

INSTRUCTIONAL FORMATS

The material in this chapter may be presented using the lecture style and the Power Point/overhead transparencies providing students an overview of the chapter. The instructor may also use the Guided Discovery method of teaching to introduce and review the materials read by the students. In this style, the instructor asks questions guiding the students toward one answer. The instructor rephrases the questions until the students discover the answer to the question. The introduction/review of the chapter may be followed by cooperative learning assignments that provide active learning and critical thinking activities for the student. In the cooperative learning groups, the students will discuss the materials listed on the Cooperative Learning Task Sheet and/or other topics you may assign. Each group can become a "content expert" for sections of the Task Sheet. Oral summary reports of the group may be presented to the entire class covering all or part of the discussion items.

KEY TERMS

value orientation
conceptual framework
scope
Developmental Levels I-III

horizontal articulation
basic urges
sequence
psychomotor domain

vertical articulation
cognitive domain
affective domain

DISCUSSION TOPICS

1. Discuss cultural/religious restrictions that may limit curriculum development. Brainstorm ways to meet the needs of children, yet not offend particular groups in the community.

2. Share with your students specific state/federal laws that must be adhered to in your area. Open up discussion regarding how this enhances the educational experience for students or challenges the teacher attempting to offer a broad-based curriculum.

3. Evaluate a videotape of a physical education class. Ask the students to identify the urges displayed by the children in the class.

SAMPLE WRITTEN ASSIGNMENTS

Write a philosophy of teaching physical education at the elementary school level.

1. Describe in writing specific activities that you will teach in your elementary physical education class that support the cognitive and affective domains.

2. If you go to this site, you can read research related to physical education and the affective domain: http://coe.sdsu.edu/eet/Articles/BloomsLD/index.htm

3. Write a one-day, four-part lesson plan at an assigned developmental level including objectives for the lesson.

4. Develop the outline of a yearlong sequence of learning experiences for a particular developmental level.

ACTIVITY SESSION EXPERIENCES

Lead the students through the following activities:

- Teach a Dynamic Physical Education lesson demonstrating each of the four parts of the lesson. Any lesson from the Lesson Plan book would work for this demonstration.

- Demonstrate a motor skill appropriate for Level 1 and demonstrate the progression of the same or similar activity appropriate for a Level 2 lesson.

COOPERATIVE LEARNING TASK SHEET

Chapter 4: Curriculum Development

Directions: Your cooperative learning group will become the content experts by finding the answers to the items listed below. Discuss the following items with your group and be ready to report on one or all of them at the end of the class period.

1. List and discuss the six steps for designing a quality physical education curriculum.

2. Define scope, sequence, and balance as each relates to curriculum development. Give examples of each.

3. List guidelines for well-balanced curriculum planning. Give examples.

4. What environmental factors can impact a curriculum? Discuss your answers.

5. Explain the conceptual framework underlying the elementary physical education curriculum.

6. Specify the needs, characteristics, and interests of children and discuss how age and maturity factors influence program development.

7. Cite the three learning domains and discuss characteristics of each. Apply each to a specific topic in a selected physical education class.

8. If you go to this website, you can read more about Bloom's taxonomy of learning domains: http://coe.sdsu.edu/eet/Articles/BloomsLD/index.htm

9. Characterize a program that would satisfy the needs and interests of elementary-age children. Contrast that approach with a teacher-centered approach.

10. Describe student-centered objectives for physical education and categorize each by learning domain.

11. What components are common to quality physical education curricula?

CHAPTER 5

Improving Instructional Effectiveness

SUMMARY

Quality instruction cuts across all teaching presentations regardless of the students' ages, grade levels, or lesson content. Diversity and gender are two areas that need attention in instruction in physical education. Strategies for enhancing diversity and reducing gender stereotyping are outlined in this chapter. Instructional effectiveness can be improved by effective use of instructional cues, demonstration, modeling, and feedback. Offering one or two key points while simultaneously demonstrating the desired behavior increases the effectiveness of instructional cues. Listening skills are just as important as speaking skills when working with students. A productive class environment demands consistent monitoring of student performance, an emphasis on safety, and keeping students on-task. Feedback can be positive, negative, or corrective. Over time, positive feedback is the most effective for developing positive attitudes toward activity. Instruction is best when it is personalized and offers something of value to each individual.

STUDENT OUTCOMES

Upon completion of the reading of this chapter, the student will:

- Know how to teach for the promotion of diversity in physical education classes.

- Understand how gender stereotypes can be minimized.

- Identify various ways to effectively communicate with youngsters in a physical education learning environment.

- Understand the procedures needed to develop effective instructional cues.

- Cite various ways to enhance the clarity of communication between the teacher and the learner.

- Identify essential elements of instruction and discuss the manner in which each relates to the learning environment.

- Describe the value of nonverbal behavior in the physical education setting.

- Describe various demonstration and modeling skills that facilitate an environment conducive to learning.

- Understand how instructional cues can be used to increase student performance.

- Articulate techniques that supply youngsters with meaningful feedback regarding performance.

- Describe ways to personalize instruction within the physical education setting.

MAIN CONCEPTS

Quality instructors create a positive atmosphere for learning. They may not know more about skills and activities than less capable teachers, but they are able to apply a set of effective instructional skills and lessons for children. This chapter deals with instructional techniques all teachers can master to become an effective teacher. Communicating effectively with the learner is critical.

CHARACTERISTICS OF A QUALITY LESSON

Regardless of the teaching style utilized, an effective learning environment can be identified by a set of instructional behaviors that occur regularly.

1. Students are engaged in appropriate activities for a large percentage of class time.

2. The learning atmosphere is success oriented, demonstrating a positive, caring climate.

3. Students are given clear objectives and receive high rates of information feedback from the teacher and the environment.

4. Student progress is monitored regularly, and students are held accountable for learning in physical education.

5. Low rates of management time and smooth transitions from one activity to another characterize the learning environment.

6. Students spend a limited amount of time waiting in line or in other unproductive activities.

7. Teachers are organized with high but realistic expectations for student achievement.

8. Teachers are enthusiastic about what they are doing and are actively involved in the instructional process.

INCORPORATE ESSENTIAL ELEMENTS OF INSTRUCTION

Learning occurs when a well-planned curriculum is presented in a sound instructional manner. Education is effective when both a quality curriculum and able instruction are smoothly meshed. The curriculum is a critical component of the educational process; however, when the curriculum is poorly taught, student progress is limited.

Design measurable student outcomes/objectives. They can be written for the three learning domains included in physical education: psychomotor, affective, and cognitive.

Determine the instructional entry-level. Instruction in a new activity should always begin with a successful experience to provide a positive experience.

Use the anticipatory set at the beginning of each class.

Deliver meaningful, sequential delivery of skill instruction.

1. Limit instruction on one or two key points.

2. Refrain from lengthy skill descriptions. Keep instructional episodes to 30 seconds ideally, and no more than 60 seconds. Speak to your class in an exciting and dynamic manner.

3. Present information in its most basic, easy-to-understand form. Continually check for understanding and re-phrase your instruction as necessary.

4. Separate management and instructional episodes.

Monitor student performance. Move your instructional position around the room. Deliver instruction from the perimeter of the area and vary that location regularly during the class period. Make sure you have teacher movement during the period to enhance observational effectiveness, feedback, and instruction.

The Use of Appropriate Instructional Cues:

- Develop precise, short, descriptive phrases for cues.

- Use short, action-oriented cues.

- Use voice inflections, body language, and action words to motivate movement.

- Integrate cues so the student can focus on the skill as a whole.

Use appropriate demonstration of skills during instruction. Teachers cannot be expected to demonstrate all physical activities well. Media, students, and pictures can be used effectively to enhance demonstrations.

For additional information go to this website:
www.pecentral.org/climate/monicaparsonarticle.html

Check for Understanding through Written and Skill Monitoring:

- Use hand signals to indicate understanding.

- Ask questions that can be answered in choral response.

- Direct a forthcoming check to the entire class rather than to a specified student.

- Use peer-checking methods.

- Use tests and written feedback to monitor cognitive concepts.

Offer guided practice. This helps ensure that students are performing a skill correctly. Offer practice sessions quickly after instructions so students remember the activity.

Bring closure. Lesson closure and review increases retention because students review what they have learned. Leave the class spaced out as you ask review and evaluation questions. Bringing them into a line may cause disruptive behavior.

PROVIDE INSTRUCTIONAL FEEDBACK

Feedback when properly delivered enhances a student's self-concept, improves the focus of performance, increases the rate of on-task behavior, and improves student understanding. Meaningful feedback helps students learn when skills are performed correctly or need refinement. Corrective to negative feedback should be at a 4:1 ratio. Feedback should be evenly distributed to all students by systematically moving from student to student during the class period. Offer feedback as soon as possible after a correct performance.

Types of Feedback:

- Specific or value feedback improves desired student behavior.

- General/group-oriented feedback is not as valuable to student learning as specific feedback.

- Use first names in feedback.

- Negative/corrective feedback needs to be delivered privately.

- When using nonverbal feedback, know the cultural implications of hand signals before using one you feel should be well understood. In fact, it might be misunderstood if a youngster is from a select culture.

CONSIDER THE PERSONAL NEEDS OF STUDENTS

Teach for Diversity

Multicultural education allows students to reach their potential regardless of the diversity among learners. It creates an educational environment where students from a variety of backgrounds and experiences come together to participate in educational equality. Four variables influence how teachers and students think and learn: race/ethnicity, gender, social class, and ability. Multicultural education creates an environment in which students from a variety of backgrounds come together to experience educational equality (Manning & Baruth, 2004). Good teaching requires the ability to communicate across cultures, with an awareness of gender differences, similarities, stereotyping, social class, and diverse abilities of students. It is the teacher's responsibility to teach children to live comfortably and to prosper in this diverse and changing world. The chapter lists a number of things teachers can do to teach students to value diversity.

It is important that students celebrate their own culture while learning to integrate into the diversity of the world.

Teachers should instill respect for all people regardless of race/ethnicity, gender, social class, and ability.

> Promising programs and practices in multicultural education are available by going to this site:
> http://www.ncrel.org/sdrs/areas/issues/educatrs/leadrshp/le4pppme.htm

One of the best ways to facilitate student diversity in group instruction is to vary teaching presentations. Some students learn easily via auditory methods while others learn better using visual means. Combining instructional methods by explaining and then demonstrating gives students the opportunity to learn through different modes.

Showing students that you care is important to the learning success of all youth.

> If you go to this site, you can read an article on caring teachers:
> http://www.ncrel.org/sdrs/areas/issues/students/atrisk/at6lk10.htm

> If you go to this site, you can read an article that offers tips on how to stay out of gangs and gang activity.
> http://www.nagia.org/Gang%20Articles/Kids%20and%20Gangs.htm

> A teacher needs to treat all students with respect and can expect students to treat each other with dignity.

Teachers need to know and educate themselves so they better understand the needs of all youth.

In working with diverse youth, ask the following questions:

1. What is their history?

2. What are their important cultural values?

3. Who are influential individuals in their group?

4. What are their major religious beliefs?

5. What are their important political beliefs?

6. What political, religious, and social days do they celebrate?

Gender Differences

Teachers play a large role in how children learn to behave.

Research shows that teachers don't treat boys and girls alike.

Teachers give more praise for achievement to boys and call on girls less than boys.

Aggression is tolerated more in boys than girls.

Disruptive talking is tolerated more in girls than boys. Boys are reprimanded more than girls and teachers use more "intense" means of disciplining boys.

Expectations for boys and girls strongly impact how they interact in different ways. Teachers expect boys to be more active and more precocious than girls and not to be as good academically. Girls are expected to be more reserved and to do well academically, so they tend to be overlooked when they are doing "what they are supposed to do." Some teachers believe that girls aren't able to perform at a level similar to boys even though research shows otherwise.

Written communications, evaluations, and grades must be written in gender-neutral or gender-inclusive terms.

Information on gender equity in schools is available at this site:
http://www.academic.org

Here are some guidelines to minimize stereotyping by gender:

- Reinforce the performances of all students regardless of gender.

- Provide activities that are developmentally appropriate and allow all students to find success.

- Design programs that assure success in coeducational experiences. Boys and girls can challenge each other to higher levels if the atmosphere is positive.

- Don't use and don't accept student stereotypical comments such as "You throw like a girl."

- Include activities in the curriculum that cut across typical gender stereotypes, such as "rhythms are for girls," "football is for boys."

- Arrange activities so the more aggressive and skilled students do not dominate. Little is learned if students are taught to be submissive or play down their ability.

- Arrange practice sessions so all students receive equal amounts of practice and/or opportunity to participate. Practice sessions should not give more practice opportunities to the skilled while the unskilled stand aside and observe.

- Expect all boys and girls to perform equally well. Teacher expectations communicate much about a student's ability level. Students view themselves through the eyes of their teacher.

Encourage Creative Responses

Offering students an opportunity to create and modify new experiences is an important part of the total learning environment. Encouraging creativity in the classroom helps students develop habits of discovery and reflective thinking. Self-discovered concepts are often better retained and retrieved for future use.

Allow Students to Make Educational Decisions

Decision-making is a large part of behaving in a responsible manner, but responsibility is a learned skill that takes practice. Below are strategies than can be used to help youngsters learn to make decisions in a safe environment.

- Limit the number of choices presented to students.

- Allow student modifications of activities in which they engage as needed.

- Offer open-ended tasks using the problem-solving technique.

Develop Positive Affective Skills

Physical education offers the opportunity for affective domain development. Occasions are available to learn to share, express feelings, set personal goals, and function as a team or independently. Effective instruction includes teaching the whole person rather than just physical skills.

Personalize Instruction

Be aware that the ability levels of students in one class vary widely. Modify tasks so all students can find success. Guidelines for personalizing instruction to accommodate developmental differences among youngsters are:

- Modify the conditions, tasks, and activities to help all children experience success.

- Use self-competition and encourage students to set personal goals for themselves.

- Offer different task challenges to accommodate the varying skill levels in class.

For more information on lesson presentation elements, go to this website:
www.humboldt.edu/~tha1/hunter-eei.html

EMPLOY EFFECTIVE COMMUNICATION SKILLS

Communicating with a learner is critical and communication skills can always be improved. Quality instructors are able to create a positive atmosphere for learning. They may not know more about skills and activities than less able teachers, but they often know how to communicate effectively. Meaningful feedback helps students learn when skills are performed correctly or need refinement.

When talking with students, assume a physical pose that expresses interest and attention.

The following are suggestions to help establish a positive bond with students and create a learning environment enjoyed by everyone:

- Speak about behavior rather than about their personal character.

- Try to understand the child's point of view.

- Identify your feelings about the learner.

- Accentuate the positive when communicating with a student.

- Accent positive performance points rather than stating what not to do.

- Speak precisely.

- Optimize speech patterns. Focus on correct performance of an activity. Silence can be effective.

- Conduct lengthy discussions in a classroom setting.

- Respect student opinions. Avoid humiliating a child who gives a wrong answer.

Be a Good Listener:

- Be an active listener.

     This site gives you tips and insight into being an active listener:
     http://crs.uvm.edu/gopher/nerl/personal/comm/e.html

- Listen to the hidden message of the speaker/student.

- Paraphrase what the student said.

- Let students know you value listening.

For more information on enhancing teacher effectiveness, see this website:
www.hcc.hawaii.edu/intranet/committees/FacDevCom/guidebk/teachtip/enhance.htm

INSTRUCTIONAL FORMATS

The material in this chapter may be presented using the lecture style incorporating the Power Point presentation and/or overhead transparencies providing students an overview of the chapter. The introduction may be followed by cooperative learning assignments, which provide active learning and critical thinking activities for the student. In the cooperative learning groups, the students will discuss the materials listed on the Task Sheet and/or other topics you may assign. Each group can become a "content expert" for sections of the Task Sheet. Oral summary reports of the group may be presented to the entire class covering all or part of the discussion items.

KEY TERMS

anticipatory set	nonverbal behavior	teacher movement
multicultural education	instructional cues	corrective feedback
active listener	negative feedback	student diversity

REFLECTION AND REVIEW QUESTIONS

How and Why

1. Were the characteristics of a quality lesson present for all students in your elementary physical education classes as a child?

2. Using teacher talk, state 5 meaningful feedback statements. Use statements other than those presented in the chapter and discus why your statements are meaningful.

3. How can you promote diversity in your classes? Why is this important?

4. What are your strengths and weaknesses with respect to communicating?

Content Review

1. What are the characteristics of a quality elementary physical education lesson? Explain each.

2. Explain the importance of several essential elements of instruction.

3. What are the key components of instructional feedback? Discuss each.

4. What methods can be used to make instruction personal and meaningful for students?

5. Discuss several important communication skills for teachers.

DISCUSSION TOPICS

1. Discuss methods that can be used to communicate with students who do not speak English or a language that you speak.

2. Identify an appropriate multicultural movement-oriented activity that would be appropriate to a grade level you may teach. Conduct an Internet search for ideas.

3. Demonstrate acceptable nonverbal cues, feedback, and behavior. Identify methods that can be used to make hand signals acceptable for all populations enrolled in a class.

4. Role-play acceptable methods for stating corrective feedback.

5. Role-play situations modeling active listening techniques.

6. Role-play inappropriate body language that sometimes is observed in teaching.

SAMPLE WRITTEN ASSIGNMENTS

1. Write an observation report of a physical education class taught by a physical education specialist or multiple subjects' instructor at the elementary level and tally the types of feedback the teacher offers during the class.

2. Interview an elementary physical education specialist to assess the types of conferences the teacher has engaged in with students. Replicate the topic with a classmate practicing active learning techniques. Analyze your success as an active listener by discussing the experience with your classmate. You may invite an observer to participate and compare your analysis with that of the observer. Write the results into a report.

3. Write a list of ten phrases using constructive/corrective feedback stated in a positive, meaningful manner.

4. Conduct an Internet search on gender equity issues. Report the findings to your class. Listed below is a site to begin the search:

> Information on gender equity in schools is available at this site:
> http://www.academic.org

ACTIVITY SESSION EXPERIENCES

Lead the students through the following activities:

1. Teach and explain a dance from one of the cultures represented in the class.

2. Teach and explain a game from one of the cultures represented in the class.

COOPERATIVE LEARNING TASK SHEET

Chapter 5: Improving Instructional Effectiveness

Directions: Your cooperative learning group will become the content experts by finding the answers to the items listed below. Discuss the following items with your group and be ready to report on one or all of them at the end of the class period.

1. Discuss and identify a variety of ways to effectively communicate with youngsters in a physical education learning environment. Conduct an Internet search on effective forms of communication to assist your discussion.

2. Develop a list of effective and ineffective instructional cues and statements.

    Go to this Internet site for teaching cue examples:
    http://www.pecentral.org/climate/monicaparsonarticle.html

3. Cite the ways described in the chapter to enhance the clarity of communication between the teacher and the learner. Role-play a situation.

    Go to this Internet site for effective communication examples:
    http://web.cba.neu.edu/~ewertheim/interper/commun.htm

    Describe the value of nonverbal behavior in the physical education setting. Demonstrate acceptable and unacceptable nonverbal signals to your cooperative learning group. Identify methods that can be used to ensure that nonverbal signals will not be misinterpreted.

    Go to this Internet site for further information on nonverbal communication.
    http://nonverbal.ucsc.edu

4. State demonstration and modeling skills that facilitate an environment conducive to learning. Discuss the purpose and value of demonstrations. Describe methods that can be used to provide demonstrations when the instructor cannot demonstrate the movement.

5. Describe how verbal cues can be used to increase student performance. Create a list of 10 effective verbal cues.

6. Discuss and then demonstrate appropriate and inappropriate body language sometimes observed by teachers during a lesson.

7. Describe the many methods listed in the chapter to personalize instruction within the physical education setting.

8. Use the Internet to conduct research and then develop a meaningful multicultural lesson for physical education. For this assignment you are to develop a lesson that requires (a) students to use some form of technology to help them learn about a "traditional" content area (i.e., dance, sport, games), (b) the student will need to access technology in the development of the unit and lesson, or (c) both. You may select any content area. You can also assume that your classroom has the necessary technology to engage in the lesson. Please note that this assignment is not about teaching students how to use technology. Rather, it is about using technology to help students improve their knowledge and understanding of the multicultural topic you have selected.

   The assignment consists of two parts:

   The first part is a description about why or how technology can be used to support the learning goals identified in the lesson.

   The second part of the assignment should provide a detailed rationale about why this lesson is important and how it fits into the overall multicultural curriculum you work with for this grade.

9. Discuss how you can promote diversity in your classes. Why is this important?

CHAPTER 6

Management and Discipline

SUMMARY

Management and discipline are a requisite part of effective instruction. Management requires designing and implementing a preventive approach to discipline. Dealing with behavior involves two major parts: the first part requires modifying and maintaining acceptable behavior. The second phase is an approach to decrease unacceptable behavior. Procedures such as time-out, reprimands, and removal of privileges are described. Minimizing the use of criticism and punishment is reviewed and specific recommendations listed.

Successful teachers effectively manage student behavior. Management skills characterize quality teaching. Effective teachers make three assumptions: teaching is a profession, students are in school to learn, and the teacher's challenge is to promote learning. The majority of children in a class are relatively easy to teach, but making appreciable gains among low-aptitude and indifferent students is the result of effective instruction.

STUDENT OUTCOMES

Upon completion of the reading of this chapter, the student will:

- Describe the role of the teacher as it pertains to managing children in a physical education setting.

- Implement management and discipline skills that result in a positive and constructive learning environment.

- Identify techniques used to start and stop the class, organize the class into groups and formations, employ squads, and prepare youngsters for activity.

- Cite acceptable and recommended procedures for dealing with inappropriate behavior.

- Describe techniques to increase or decrease specific behaviors.

- Explain the role of teacher reaction in shaping and controlling student behavior.

- Design or modify games that are effective in changing the behavior of children.

- Know the shortcomings of criticism and punishment when used to change and improve student behavior.

- Understand the legal ramifications associated with expelling a student from school.

MAIN CONCEPTS

Successful teachers effectively manage student behavior. Management skills characterize quality teaching.

Effective teachers make three assumptions: teaching is a profession; students are in school to learn, and the teacher's challenge is to promote learning.

Classroom management ideas are available at this site:

    http://www.honorlevel.com/techniques.xml

Successful teachers realize that making appreciable learning gains among low-aptitude and indifferent students is the result of effective instruction.

EFFECTIVE MANAGEMENT AND DISCIPLINE: A COORDINATED APPROACH

Managing student behavior is a learned skill. A class of children is really a group of individuals, each of whom must be uniquely treated and understood. Effective management and discipline is basic to allow children to learn effectively without encroaching on the rights of others. U.S. society is based on freedom partnered with self-discipline. Americans have much personal freedom as long as they do not encroach on the rights of others. In similar fashion, children can enjoy freedom as long as their behavior is consistent with educational objectives and does not prevent other students from learning.

Most children choose to cooperate and participate in the educational setting. No one can be taught who chooses not to cooperate. Effective management of behavior means maintaining an environment in which all children have the opportunity to learn. Students who choose to be disruptive and off-task infringe on the rights of students who choose to cooperate.

A smoothly functioning class is a well-managed class. Teachers behave in ways that promote positive student behavior and, in turn, students perform in a positive manner. Management and discipline techniques are interrelated and one impacts the other. **Management** is defined as organizing and controlling the affairs of a class. It refers to how students are organized, started and stopped, grouped, and arranged during class. Effective management means students are moved quickly, called by their names, moved into instructional formations, and taught in an efficient manner, etc. **Discipline** is defined as changing student behavior when it is unacceptable. When things don't go so smoothly, and some students decide not to follow the management requests of the teacher, discipline techniques are required to create a constructive teaching environment. In a nutshell, effective management implies students follow class procedures and when such class procedures are not followed, discipline techniques must be used.

For further reading on classroom management, go to:

    http://www.pecentral.org/climate/disciplinelinks.html

    http://www.honorlevel.com/techniques.html

    http://www.glencoe.com/sec/teachingtoday/tiparchive.phtml/4

In working with children there is bound to be some type of discipline problem. There are a number of steps that lead to a well-managed and disciplined class.

Steps that should be followed:

1. Develop an assertive approach to discipline.

2. Use effective management skills.

3. Teach acceptable student behavior.

4. Incorporate positive discipline techniques.

5. Use effective discipline techniques when positive discipline techniques fail.

USE PROPER TEACHING BEHAVIORS

In a well-managed class, teacher and students assume dual responsibility for learning. Presentations and instructional strategies used are appropriate for the capabilities of students and the nature of activity sequences. How teachers teach determines what students learn. Effective class management and organizational skills create an environment that gives students freedom of choice in harmony with class order. When an instructor prevents problems before they occur, less time is spent dealing with deviant behavior.

Be aware of the impact your behavior has on students. What students learn reflects your personality, outlook, ideals, and background. A basic requisite is the ability to model behavior you desire from students. This means hustling if you demand that students hustle. Modeling acceptable behavior has a strong impact on students. The phrase, "Your actions speak louder than your words," has significant implications.

Develop an Assertive Communication Style

- **Passive communicator.** A passive teacher "hopes" to make all children happy in order to avoid being upset. Passive means trying to avoid all conflict and trying to please others.

- **Aggressive communicator**. An aggressive responder wants to overpower others by coming on strong. Aggressive people feel it is a competition and they must win at all costs whenever communication occurs. A common trait with aggressive communicators is that they use the word "You" all the time. A number of statements keep students feeling defensive and attacked.

- **Assertive communicator.** An assertive responder does not beg, plead, or threaten. Rather, he or she uses a straightforward approach to express feelings and expectations. Assertive people are not afraid to say what they want and do not worry about what others will think of them.

Create a Personal Behavior Plan

One of the key elements of a management approach is to understand and plan for how you will behave when disciplining students. Serious misbehavior can cause some teachers to become angry, others to feel threatened, and others to behave in a tyrannical manner. Part of your behavior plan will be to remind yourself how you should act when misbehavior occurs. Personal behavior plans usually include the following points:

1. Maintain composure.

2. Acknowledge your feelings when student misbehavior occurs.

3. Design a plan for yourself when such feelings occur.

4. Know the options you have for dealing with the deviant behavior.

Be a Leader, Not a Friend

Students want a teacher who is knowledgeable, personable, and a leader.

Students are not looking for a friend in a teacher. They often feel uncomfortable if you try to be "one of them."

Communicate High Standards

Students respond to your expectations. If you expect students to perform at high levels, the majority of them will strive to do so.

Understand Why Students Misbehave

A number of situations cause students to misbehave. There are times when students misbehave because they didn't understand the instructions. Give instructions and then proceed with the activity.

Discipline Individually and Avoid Group Negative Feedback

When negative feedback is delivered, it should be done privately and personally to individual students. Few people want to have negative comments delivered globally for others to hear.

Avoid Feedback That Offers the Possibility for Backlash

Some verbal types of interactions may work in the short term but cause long-term negative consequences. The following types of feedback often work immediately but cause greater problems over the long haul:

- Preaching or moralizing

- Threatening

- Ordering and commanding

- Interrogating

- Refusing to listen

- Labeling

Give Positive Group Feedback

Positive feedback delivered to a class develops group morale.

Maintain and Increase Desirable Behavior

Managing student behavior is a difficult task. Teachers often question themselves in terms of their ability to control and manage a classroom.

DEFINE CLASS PROCEDURES, RULES, AND CONSEQUENCES

Effectively managing a class depends on letting students know what you expect of them.

Step 1. Determine Routines for Students

- Be assertive.
- Students feel best when they know expectations.
- Students expect to follow established routines.
- Explain your routines so students understand why the chosen procedures are used.

Examples of routines that teachers often use are:

1. How students are supposed to enter the teaching area.
2. How the teaching area is defined.
3. Where and how they should meet—in sitting squads, moving and freezing on a spot, in a semicircle, etc.
4. What students should do if equipment is located in the area.
5. What signal is used to freeze a class.
6. How students procure and put away equipment.
7. How students will be grouped for instruction.

Step 2. Determine Rules and Procedures for the School Year

Rules are an expected part of the school environment. Typical rules for the class are:

- *Stop, look, and listen.* This implies freezing on signal, looking at the instructor, and listening for instructions.
- *Take care of equipment.* This includes caring for equipment, distributing, gathering, and using it properly.
- *Respect the rights of others.*

Make rules reasonable for the age level of students. Meaningful rules cut across all ages and can be used throughout the elementary school years.

Limit the number of rules (three to five).

State rules briefly, positively, and broadly.

Step 3. Determine Consequences When Rules Are Not Followed

Make a sign that lists the consequences for breaking rules and post it in a prominent place in the teaching area.

Step 4. Share your Rules with Parents, Teachers, and Administrators

A newsletter to parents at the start of the year explaining your program and your approach to class management will set the tone for students immediately.

Step 5. Have the Class Practice Rules Systematically

Rules stipulate expected class behavior. If a rule is in place for proper care of equipment, students need the opportunity to practice how the teacher wants equipment handled.

INCORPORATE EFFICIENT MANAGEMENT SKILLS

Class management skills are prerequisites to effective instruction.

Deliver Instruction Efficiently

Instructions should be specific and seldom last longer than 20 to 30 seconds. An effective approach is to alternate short instructional episodes with periods of activity.

When giving instructions, tell students "**when before what.**"

Stop and Start a Class Consistently

Pick a consistent signal you want to use to stop a class.

Move Students into Groups and Formations Quickly

Place some spots in the center of the area and call it the "friendship spot." Students who don't have a partner nearby, run to the friendship spot, raise their hands, and look for a partner.

Finding Partners

Use the activity *Toe-to-Toe, Back-to-Back, Elbow-to-Elbow,* to teach children to find partners quickly.

Dividing a Class in Half

Have students get toe-to-toe with a partner. For Developmental Level I students, have one partner sit down while the other remains standing. Ask those standing to go to one area, after which those sitting are then moved to the acceptable space. With Developmental Level II and III students, one partner can raise a hand. Move the students with their hands up to one side of the area and the other student to the other side of the area.

Creating Small Groups

Use *Whistle Mixer*

Creating Circles or Single-File Lines

Have students run randomly throughout the area until a signal is given. On the signal to "fall in," students continue jogging, move toward the perimeter of the area, and fall in line behind someone until a circle is formed.

Use Squads to Expedite Class Organization

Some teachers find that placing students into squads helps them manage a class effectively. An effective was to use squads is "Home Base."

Know Students' Names

Effective class management requires learning the names of students and using them in feedback.

Establish Pre- and Post-Teaching Routines

Effective teaching demands that a number of procedures be routinely handled.

Nonparticipation

Entering the Teaching Area

Starting the Lesson

Closing the Lesson

Equipment Procedures

Dealing with Student Behavior Problems

Use Equipment Effectively

Distribute equipment to students as rapidly as possible.

TEACH ACCEPTABLE STUDENT BEHAVIOR AND RESPONSIBILITY THROUGH PHYSICAL ACTIVITY

Strategies for Increasing Responsible Behavior

- Model acceptable behavior

- Use reinforcement

- Offer time for responsibility and reflection

- Allow student sharing

- Encourage goal setting

- Offer opportunities for responsibility

- Allow student choice

Teacher-Directed Conflict Resolution

Conflict between students often results in aggression and violence.

Effective Conflict Resolution Steps:

- Stop the aggressive behavior immediately.

- Gather data about what happened and define the problem.

- Brainstorm possible solutions.

- Test the solutions generated through brainstorming.

- Help implement the plan.

- Evaluate the approach.

Peer Mediation

Peer mediation is similar to conflict resolution except that it is student-directed. Disputes and conflicts are resolved between students with a neutral peer acting as a moderator in the process.

USE BEHAVIOR MANAGEMENT TO INCREASE ACCEPTABLE BEHAVIOR

Positive discipline focuses on reinforcing acceptable behavior. Increasing positive behavior may help reduce negative behavior because the student will receive increased feedback and attention. Lavay, et al., (2006) provide an excellent resource for taking a systematic approach to positive behavior management.

Increase Acceptable Behavior

"Catch them doing what you want them to do" is the secret to increasing acceptable behavior. Behavior that is followed by appropriate positive reinforcement occurs more often in the future.

Social Reinforcers

Teachers most often use this class of reinforcers. Your positive behavior is the reinforcement given when students perform desired behavior.

The following are examples of reinforcers that can be used with students in a physical education setting:

Words of Praise

Great job	Nice going
Exactly right	I really like that job
Perfect arm placement	That's the best one yet
Way to go	Nice hustle

Physical Expressions

Smiling	Winking
Nodding	Clenched fist overhead
Thumbs up	Clapping

Physical Contact

Handshake   High five

Activity Reinforcers

Various types of activities that children enjoy can be used as reinforcement.

Token Reinforcers

Many teachers feel a need to offer some type of token as a reinforcer. It may be points, gold stars, certificates, or trophies. Physical education is closely related to athletic competition, where awards are often given to winners. This causes some teachers to believe that tokens should be used to motivate children in physical education.

Selecting Reinforcers

A common question among teachers is, "How do I know what will be reinforcing to my students?" It is impossible to know what will reinforce a student until it is administered. Fortunately, there are a lot of things to which most children will respond, such as praise, attention, smiles, games, free time, and privileges.

Using Social Reinforcers

Effective use of social reinforcers requires praise and makes positive statements. You may feel uncomfortable when learning to administer positive reinforcement to youngsters because such behavior feels inauthentic.

The Premack Principle

The Premack principle (Premack, 1965) is often used unknowingly to motivate students. This principle states that a highly desirable activity can be used to motivate students to learn an activity they enjoy to a lesser degree. In practice, this principle allows students to participate in a favorite activity if they perform a less enjoyable one.

Prompt Acceptable Behavior

Prompts are used to remind students to perform desired behavior.

There are a number of ways to prompt children in the physical education setting. The most common are the following:

1. Modeling

2. Verbal cues

3. Nonverbal cues

Shape Acceptable Behavior

Shaping techniques can be used to build new and desired behavior. When desired behavior does not exist, shaping—using extinction and reinforcement—is used to create new behavior. Shaping is slow and inefficient, so it is used only if prompting is not possible. Two principles are followed when shaping behavior.

Differential reinforcement is used to increase the incidence of desired behavior.

The criterion that must be reached for reinforcement to occur is increased. In this step, you gradually shift the criterion standard toward the desired goal.

DECREASE UNACCEPTABLE BEHAVIOR WITH DISCIPLINE

Most effective techniques for improving class behavior are designed to guide the student away from behavior that is disrupting the class. Corrective feedback and the use of consequences can be an effective means for decreasing undesirable behavior.

Use Corrective Feedback

As a first step, try using positive reinforcement to increase desired behavior with the hope that it will replace undesirable behavior.

The following steps will prevent teacher-student conflicts from occurring in front of other students. Whether delivering corrective feedback or consequences, use these steps to avoid embarrassing students and yourself.

1. Do not address the student publicly.

2. Isolate the student and yourself.

3. Deal with one student at a time.

4. State your position once; repeat it once if you believe the student didn't understand. Don't argue or try to prove your point. Take no more than 10–15 seconds to tell the student the unacceptable behavior and what acceptable behavior you would like to see.

5. Deliver and move away. Avoid eyeballing the behavior to completion; walk away after you have delivered the behavior you desire.

6. Don't threaten or bully the student. It builds resentment in students and may cause greater problems at a later time.

7. Avoid touching the student when correcting behavior.

8. Don't curse or raise your voice excessively.

Use Consequences to Decrease Unacceptable Behavior

When corrective feedback fails to cause the desired change in behavior, consequences must be used. Students need to understand that undesirable behavior will bring consequences.

Reprimands

This is a common approach used to decrease undesirable behavior. If done in a caring and constructive manner, reprimands can serve as effective reminders to behave.

Identify the unacceptable behavior, state briefly why it is unacceptable, and communicate to students what behavior is desired.

Don't reprimand in front of other students. Not only does it embarrass students, it also can diminish their self-esteem.

Reprimands should speak about behavior, not the person.

After reprimanding and asking for acceptable behavior, reinforce it when it occurs.

Removal of Positive Consequences

This is a common approach used by parents, so many students are familiar with it. The basic approach is to remove something positive from the student when misbehavior occurs.

For removal of positive consequences to be effective, make sure students really want to be a part of the removal activity. A few key principles should be followed when removing positive consequences using this technique:

- Assure that the magnitude of the removal fits the crime.

- Be consistent in removal, treating all students and occurrences the same.

- Make sure students understand the consequences of their misbehavior before the penalties are implemented.

- It is helpful to chart a student's misbehavior to see if the frequency is decreasing.

Time-Out

The time-out procedure is an equitable technique for dealing with youngsters in a manner that is consistent with society. Rules are clearly posted and consequences are clear and easy to comprehend. Time out is an effective approach for dealing with unacceptable behavior that occurs randomly on an individual basis. Time-out means time out from reinforcement.

First misbehavior: warn student that the unacceptable behavior must stop.

Second misbehavior: student goes to a time-out area and stays until ready to return and behave in an acceptable manner.

Third misbehavior: student stays in time-out area until the end of the class period.

Implement Behavior Contracts with Older Students

A behavior contract is a written statement specifying certain student behaviors that must occur to earn certain rewards or privileges. The contract is drawn up after a private conference to decide on the appropriate behaviors and rewards.

Incorporate Behavior Games for Overall Class Behavior

Behavior games are an effective strategy for changing class behavior in the areas of management, motivation, and discipline.

USE CRITICISM SPARINGLY

Use criticism and punishment with caution and good judgment. Criticism and punishment lend a negative air to the instructional environment and have a negative impact on both the student and the teacher.

Criticism does not offer a solution to problems.

MAKE PUNISHMENT A LAST RESORT

Punishment should always fit the crime. Punish youngsters softly, calmly, and privately. Offer warnings; do not threaten students; the punishment should follow the misbehavior as soon as possible; punish softly and calmly in private.

EXPULSION: LEGAL CONSIDERATIONS

Many times deviant behavior is part of a larger, more severe problem that is troubling a child. Work with the classroom teacher and principal on the problems you notice. Legal concerns involving the student's rights in disciplinary areas are an essential consideration.

INSTRUCTIONAL FORMATS

The material in this chapter may be presented using the lecture style and the Power Point/overhead transparencies available to provide students an overview of the chapter. The instructor may also use the Guided Discovery method of teaching to introduce and review the materials read by the students. In this style, the instructor asks questions guiding the students toward one answer. The instructor rephrases the questions until the students discover the answer to the question. The introduction/review of the chapter may be followed by cooperative learning assignments, which provide active learning and critical thinking activities for the student. In the cooperative learning groups, the students will discuss the materials listed on the Cooperative Learning Task Sheet. Oral summary reports of the group may be presented to the entire class covering all or part of the discussion items.

KEY TERMS

token reinforcers	shaping technique	behavior contract
self-control	conflict resolution	social reinforcers
extrinsic rewards	extinction	behavior games
self-responsibility	reprimand	activity reinforcers
Premack principle	nonparticipation	expulsion
reinforcement	time-out	

REFLECTION AND REVIEW QUESTIONS

How and Why

1. How would you respond to a child that consistently misbehaves?

2. How does it make you feel when a professor knows your name?

3. How might pre- and post-teaching routines change depending on the school?

4. Why is it important for teachers to know their own trigger points? What are your trigger points?

5. What rules would you have in your classes?

6. What types of emotions might you feel when placing a child in time-out?

7. As an adult, how does criticism make you feel?

Content Review

1. What class management skills are necessary to be an effective teacher?

2. Discuss the importance of using efficient instruction, a consistent stop signal, and moving students into formation quickly in an effective lesson.

3. How can knowing the names of the students help teachers?

4. Discuss the effective use of equipment.

DISCUSSION TOPICS

1. Discuss the variety of formations used to enhance class management. Practice several of the formations using management skills to quickly demonstrate how to move into each formation quickly and efficiently.

2. Demonstrate assertive discipline techniques. Role-play a variety of situations applying assertive discipline. Following the role-playing, discuss each situation and the appropriateness of the behavior management technique applied.

3. Discuss traits/reactions teachers might exhibit in response to student misbehavior.

4. Discuss behavior games and contracts to manage behavior. Create a behavior management contract model with the students.

5. Discuss social and activity reinforcers that work well with children in the physical education setting.

6. State and discuss the two techniques that work when "shaping" desired behavior.

SAMPLE WRITTEN ASSIGNMENTS

1. Interview students and teachers to develop a profile of descriptive characteristics of a teacher who effectively manages children. Cite specific personality characteristics and actions that assist the teacher in being effective. Type the report for a letter grade evaluation.

2. Write a list of common actions of children who misbehave in class. Write solutions to effectively manage each of the situations.

3. Create a Behavior Rules Chart for your future class. Discuss the categories of expected behavior among your peers and/or current teachers and the consequences for inappropriate behavior before you make the chart.

4. Conduct an Internet search on teaching responsible behavior to children. Write a one- to two-page report on your findings.

    If you go to this site, you will find a summary of a reference book on the subject:
    http://www.onlinesports.com/pages/I,HK-BHEL0654.html

5. Develop a written behavior contract specifying certain student behaviors that must occur to earn certain rewards or privileges. Build into the contract a place where both the student and the teacher can sign the contract.

ACTIVITY SESSION EXPERIENCES

Lead the students through the following activities:

1. During an activity session, demonstrate handling misbehaving children using a First, Second, and Third warning.

2. Demonstrate management games to create groups including:

    *   Toe-to-toe

    *   Back-to-back

    *   Whistle Mixer

    *   Home Base

    *   "Fall-In" to create a circle formation

COOPERATIVE LEARNING TASK SHEET

Chapter 6: Management and Discipline

Directions: Your cooperative learning group will become the content experts by finding the answers to the items listed below. Discuss the following items with your group and be ready to report on one or all of them at the end of the class period.

1. State at least three management and discipline skills that result in a positive and constructive learning environment. Practice each one in your group. Be prepared to lead your classmates through one of the techniques you have practiced and discussed.

2. Identify techniques used to start and stop the class, organize the class into groups and formations, employ squads, and prepare youngsters for activity. Select people within the group to identify certain techniques and then share them with your group. Be prepared to lead the class through an exercise exemplifying each technique.

3. Select two management games cited in this chapter. Play the games with your group. Let two people practice playing the management games.

4. Discuss the numerous ways and values to using squads to organize class activities. Describe two ways to create squads.

5. List a variety of organizational techniques to distribute equipment efficiently and effectively as described in this chapter. Discuss the effective use of equipment as described in the chapter.

6. Cite recommended procedures for dealing with inappropriate behavior. Role-play a situation demonstrating inappropriate behavior and how the teacher should best handle the student(s).

7. Describe techniques to increase or decrease specific behaviors as described in this chapter.

8. Describe appropriate activities in which to engage students who are unable to participate in class.

9. Explain the role of teacher reaction in shaping and controlling student behavior. Role-play examples within your group.

10. How would you respond to a child that consistently misbehaves?

11. Discuss the five levels of responsible behavior described in this chapter. Describe three activities/opportunities for responsibility available to students in the classes you will be teaching.

    If you go to this site, you can read further about teaching responsible behavior:
    http://www.sasked.gov.sk.ca/docs/physed/physed1-5/ep_perspective3.html

12. Describe five techniques described in this chapter to manage conflict resolution. Brainstorm a problem and resolve it using one of the techniques you have just identified as a way to resolve conflicts.

13. State the games that are effective in changing the behavior of children. Practice two of the games and be prepared to lead the class through the games.

14. Develop a personal behavior management plan for your future life as a teacher. Cite examples from the chapter.

15. Identify the shortcomings of criticism and punishment when used to change and improve student behavior. Role-play a situation whereby a teacher uses criticism. Identify an alternative technique to change the behavior of the student(s).

16. Explain the legal ramifications associated with expelling a student from school. State situations when expulsion is generally considered acceptable.

CHAPTER 7

Children with Disabilities

SUMMARY

Every state is required by federal law to develop a plan for identifying, locating, and evaluating all children with disabilities. Due process for students and parents is an important requisite when conducting formal assessment procedures. Mainstreaming involves the practice of placing children with disabilities into classes with able youngsters. Moving a child to a less restrictive learning environment is based on achievement of specified competencies that are required for moving into the new environment. The most common types of disabilities and ways to modify activities for successful participation are discussed in this chapter. Programs for children with weight problems, motor deficiencies, and postural problems are detailed in a step-by-step manner.

STUDENT OUTCOMES

Upon completion of the reading of this chapter, the student will:

- Understand the implications of PL 94-142 and the IDEA as it applies to the physical education teaching environment.

- Explain due-process guidelines associated with assessment procedures.

- Develop a plan for identifying, locating, and evaluating all children with disabilities.

- Cite standards associated with assessment procedures for special children.

- Identify essential elements of an individualized educational program and list the stages of development.

- List guidelines for successful inclusion of students and ways of modifying activities for inclusion.

- Describe characteristics of specific impairments and ways to modify learning experiences in physical education to accommodate children with disabilities.

- Locate nationally validated programs to assist in the screening, assessment, and curriculum development for children with special needs.

- Indicate a step-by-step approach used to develop a success profile for obese youngsters in the elementary school.

- Describe the attributes of good posture and explain its importance in successful physical performance.

MAIN CONCEPTS

Providing a quality educational experience for all students is the responsibility of the educational system. It should be the goal of all professionals to view this responsibility as an ethical and professional duty. It is the appropriate thing to do for all children–and all children come to school with varying ability levels, disabled or not. Dr. Claudine Sherrill in her text (2004) states that, "in a sense, all good physical education is adapted physical education."

The Education for All Handicapped Children Act (Public Law 94-142) was passed by Congress in 1975. This legislation introduced new requirements, vocabulary, and concepts into physical education programs across the United States. These concepts include individual education programs (IEP), mainstreaming, least restrictive environments, zero reject, and progressive inclusion. The purpose of the law is clear and concise:

It is the purpose of this act to assure that all handicapped children have available to them ... a free appropriate public education which emphasizes special education and related services designed to meet their unique needs, to assure that the rights of handicapped children and their parents or guardians are protected, to assist states and localities to provide for the education of all handicapped children, and to assess and assure the effectiveness of efforts to educate handicapped children.

In short, the law requires that all youth with disabilities, ages 3 to 21, receive a free and appropriate education in the least restrictive environment. The law indicates that the term special education "means specially designed instruction, instruction in physical education, home instruction, and instruction in hospitals and institutions." A 1997 amendment, Public Law 105-17 (also known as IDEA—Individuals with Disabilities Education Act), continues with the objective of providing handicapped individuals with the least restrictive environment in the school setting. The Individuals with Disabilities Education Act states, *"Physical education services, specially designed if necessary, must be made available to every child with a disability receiving a free appropriate public education."* Autism and traumatic brain injury have been added to the list of handicapping conditions that should receive the least restrictive environment. IDEA provides that an individual transition plan be developed no later than age 16 as a component of the IEP process. Rehabilitation and social work services are included as related services.

To comply with PL 94-142, secondary schools must locate, identify, and evaluate all students who might have a disability. A screening process must be followed by a formal assessment procedure. An assessment must be made and an IEP developed for each student before placement into a special program can be made. The law states who will be responsible for developing the IEP and what the contents of the IEP will include.

The passage of PL 94-142 shows that a strong commitment has been made to equality and education for all Americans. Prior to 1970, these students had limited access to schools. They certainly did not have an equal opportunity to participate in school programs. The government also assured that funding would be made available to assure quality instruction. The law authorizes a payment to each state of 40 percent of the average per-pupil expenditure in U.S. elementary and secondary schools, multiplied by the number of youngsters with disabilities who are receiving special education and related services.

For additional reading on this subject, go to this site:
http://asclepius.com/angel/special.html

Additional reading about IDEA is available by going to this site:
http://www.ed.gov/offices/OSERS/Policy/IDEA/the_law.html

LEAST RESTRICTIVE ENVIRONMENT

PL 105-17 uses the term *least restrictive environment* to help determine the best placement of students with disabilities. This concept refers to the idea that not all individuals can do all of the same activities in the same environment. However, the concept of *zero reject* entitles everyone of school age to some aspect of the school program. No one can be totally rejected because of a disability. The focus should be on placing students into settings that offer the best opportunity for educational advancement and success. It would be debilitating to put a student in a setting that is more restrictive than necessary.

The least restrictive environment also varies depending on the unit of instruction and the teaching style. For example, for a student in a wheelchair, a soccer activity might be very restrictive, whereas in a basketball or Frisbee activities, the environment would less restrictive. For a student with emotional disabilities, the direct style of instruction might be the least restrictive environment, while a problem-solving method with group cooperation may be too difficult and would end up being more restrictive. Consistent and regular judgments need to be made since curriculum content and teaching styles change the type of environment the student enters. Evaluation and modification of environments need to be ongoing. The concept of *progressive inclusion* focuses on the idea that students make progress as a result of educational experiences. Thus, students with disabilities should have the opportunity to progress to the least restrictive environments and experience more and more of the mainstream of our schools and their programs.

Additional material related to this can be found at:

 www.pelinks4u.org/sections/adapted/adapted.htm

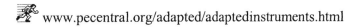 www.pecentral.org/adapted/adaptedinstruments.html

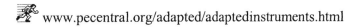 www.twu.edu/inspire

Mainstreaming

Physical educators usually speak in terms of mainstreaming rather than least restrictive environments. Mainstreaming means that students with disabilities have opportunities to integrate with other students in public schools. Prudent placement in a least restricted educational environment means that the setting must be as normal as possible (normalization), while ensuring that the student can fit in and achieve success in that placement. There are several categories of placement relative to physical education classes.

- *Full mainstreaming.* Students with disabilities function as full-time members of a regular school routine. They go to all classes with able students. Within the limitations of their disability, they participate in physical education with able peers.

- *Mainstreaming for physical education only.* Students with disabilities can participate in physical education with able peers. This setting may include students with emotional disabilities who are grouped in the classroom and are separated into regular physical education classes.

- *Partial mainstreaming.* Students participate in selected physical education experiences but do not attend on a full-time basis because they can be successful in only a few of the offerings. Their developmental needs are usually met in special classes.

- *Special developmental classes.* Students with disabilities are in segregated special education classes.

- *Reverse mainstreaming.* Able students are brought into a special physical education class to promote intergroup peer relationships.

Segregation can be maintained only when it is in the best interests of the student. The purpose of segregated programs is to establish a level of skill and social proficiency that will eventually enable the special student to be transferred to a less-restricted learning environment. The goal of the process is to place students in the least restrictive environment, where they can benefit most.

Students with disabilities need contact with support personnel during mainstreaming. Even though the physical education teacher is responsible for the mainstreamed students during class time, these students may still require access to special education teachers, school psychologists, and speech therapists. Support personnel may view physical education as a time to get rid of their students; however, they are a source of information and support for the physical education teacher in charge.

To read more on inclusion programs and examples, go to:

🏃 www.ed.gov/pubs/EPTW/eptw12/index.html

🏃 www.palaestra.com/Inclusion.html

🏃 http://clerccenter2.gallaudet.edu/KidsWorldDeafNet/e-docs/IDEA/section-1.html#historyofidea

SCREENING AND ASSESSMENT

Screening is a process that involves all students in a school setting and is part of the "child find" process. The physical educator usually conducts screening tests, which may include commonly used test batteries.

Assessment is conducted after screening evaluations have been made. Assessment is performed by a team of experts that may include the physical educator.

For further information on assessment, go to:

🏃 www.pecentral.org/adapted/adaptedinstruments.html

Due Process Guidelines

Written Permission: A written notice must be sent to parents stating that their child has been referred for assessment. The notice must explain that the district requests permission to conduct an evaluation to determine if special education services are required for their child.

Interpretation of the Assessment: The results of the assessment must be interpreted in a meeting with parents (Interpretation of the Assessment).

External Evaluation: If parents are not satisfied with the results of the assessment, they may request an evaluation outside the school setting (External Evaluation).

Negotiation and Hearings: If parents and the school district disagree on the results of the assessment, the district is required to try to negotiate the differences (Negotiation and Hearings).

Confidentiality: Only parents of the child or authorized school personnel can review the student's records.

Procedures for Ensuring Assessment Standards

PL 94-142 requires that assessment is held to certain standards to ensure fair and objective results.

Selection of Test Instruments

Test instruments used must be valid examinations that measure what they purport to measure.

Administration Procedures

Many disabilities, cultural backgrounds of students, native language, and socio-economic background of students can interfere with standardized tests. Administrators must be sensitive to these situations.

Team Evaluation

A number of experts should be used for assessment to ensure that all facets of the child will be properly reviewed and evaluated.

To find out more about legal issues on the subject, go to:

www.asclepius.com/angel/special.html

www.ed.gov/offices/OSERS/Policy/IDEA/the_law.html

DEVELOPING AN INDIVIDUALIZED EDUCATION PROGRAM

PL 94-142 requires that an IEP be developed for each child with a disability receiving special education and related services. A committee stipulated by the law must develop the IEP. The committee consists of a member of the local education association, the child's parents, the teachers who have direct responsibility for implementing the IEP, and when appropriate, the student. Specific elements of the IEP are explained in-depth in this section of the chapter.

A SYSTEMATIC APPROACH TO SUCCESSFUL MAINSTREAMING

Mainstreaming is a moral issue. Educators have the responsibility to see that all students have the opportunity to experience activity and related social experiences. All parents desire the best experiences for their youngsters, and the goal of teachers is to help facilitate this need. Attitudinal change is important since the teacher must accept the student as a full-fledged participant and assume the responsibilities that go along with special education. Mainstreaming increases the difficulty of teaching to all students; however, teachers who support it show their concern for the human spirit regardless of condition.

1. Determine How to Teach

The success or failure of the mainstreaming process depends largely on the interaction between the teacher and the student with a disability. Purposes and derived goals are perhaps more important to students with disabilities than to so-called normal peers. It is important to accept responsibility for meeting the needs of students, including those with disabilities that permit some degree of mainstreaming. Physical education teachers must be able to: (1) analyze and diagnose motor behavior of students with disabilities; (2) provide appropriate experiences for remediation of motor conditions needing attention; and (3) register data as needed on the student's personal record. Record keeping is important. When time between classes is short, the teacher can use a portable tape recorder to record evaluative comments during or after class time.

To work successfully with students with disabilities, teachers have to understand specific impairments and how they affect learning. Also, it is necessary to know how to assess motor and fitness needs and how to structure remediation to meet those needs. Avoid placing students with disabilities in situations where they could easily fail.

2. Determine What to Teach

This step involves reviewing the existing physical education curriculum and determining how it will impact students who have differing needs. One important consideration is whether certain activities completely exclude certain students. Many students with disabilities have severe developmental lags that work against successful integration if the curriculum is not modified. It should be the responsibility of the teacher to try to individualize activities as much as possible so youngsters with disabilities are smoothly integrated.

3. Find Ways to Modify Instruction and Activities for Student Success

Students may need additional consideration when participating in group activities, particularly when the activity is competitive. Much depends on the physical condition of the student and the type of disability. Students like to win in a competitive situation, and resentment can be created if a team loss is attributed to the presence of a student with a disability. Rules can be changed for everyone so that the student with a disability has a chance to contribute to group success. On the other hand, all students need to recognize that everyone has a right to play.

Be aware of situations that devalue the student socially. Avoid using the degrading method of having captains choose teams from a group of waiting students. Elimination games should be changed so that points are scored instead of players being eliminated.

Students with disabilities have to build confidence in their skills before they will want to participate with others. Individual activities give them a greater amount of practice time without the pressure of failing in front of peers. The aim is to make students with disabilities less visible and not set apart from able classmates. Using students with disabilities as umpires or scorekeepers is a last resort.

There are many instructional modifications that can be made that will not be obvious to other students but will improve the opportunity for students to succeed. For example, factors such as teaching styles, verbal instructions, demonstrations, and the elimination of distractions might easily be manipulated in a manner that improves the lesson for all.

A Reflection Check

When making modifications to the lesson, it impacts many people. It impacts the youngsters with differing needs, the other students in the class, and the teacher. It is relatively easy to modify activities, but it can be quite difficult to make modifications that add to the total environment rather than create unsafe conditions or reduce the educational value of the experience. The following questions should be considered as you formulate modifications.

1. Do the changes allow the student with differing needs to participate successfully yet still be challenged?

2. Does the modification make the setting unsafe for the student with differing needs as well as for those students without disabilities?

3. Does the change negatively impact the quality of the educational experience? Is learning seriously hampered because of the changes made?

4. Does the change cause an undue burden on the teacher? This is important because many teachers come to resent students with differing needs because they feel the burden is too great.

5. Activities need to be modified because all students have differing needs. Effective teachers always examine an activity and know that it is their responsibility to make the environment better for all students. The idea of "doing the most good for the most students" is a good adage to follow. The following are ways to modify activities that may help all students.

Modifications for Students Lacking Strength and Endurance

1. Lower or enlarge the size of the goal. In basketball, the goal can be lowered; in soccer the goal might be enlarged.

2. Modify the tempo of the game. For example, games might be performed using a brisk walk rather than running. Another way to modify tempo is to stop the game regularly for substitution.

3. Reduce the weight and/or modify the size of the projectile. A lighter object will move more slowly and inflict less damage upon impact. A larger object will move more slowly and be easier for students to track visually and catch.

4. Reduce the distance that a ball must be thrown or served. Options are to reduce the dimensions of the playing area or add more players to the game.

5. In games that are played to a certain number of points, reduce the number required for a win. For example, volleyball games could be played to 7 or 11, depending on the skill and intensity of the players.

6. Modify striking implements by shortening and reducing their weight. Racquets are much easier to control when they are shortened. Softball bats are easier to control when the player "chokes up" and selects a lighter bat.

7. Slow the ball by letting out some air. This will reduce the speed of rebound and make the ball easier to control in a restricted area. It will also keep the ball from rolling away from players when it is not under control.

8. Play the games in a different position. Some games may be played in a sitting or lying position, which is easier and less demanding than standing or running.

9. Provide matching or substitution. Match another student on borrowed crutches with a student on braces. Two players can be combined to play one position. A student in a desk chair with wheels can be matched against a wheelchair student. Permit substitute courtesy runners.

10. Allow students to substitute skills. For example, a student may be able to strike an object but may lack the mobility to run. Another student can be selected to run.

Modifications for Students Lacking Coordination

1. Increase the size of the goal or target. Another alternative might be to offer points for hitting the backboard near a goal.

2. Offer protection when appropriate. The lack of coordination will make the student more susceptible to injury from a projectile. Use various types of protectors (such as glasses, chest protectors, or face masks).

3. When teaching throwing, allow students the opportunity to throw at maximum velocity without concern for accuracy. Use small balls that can be grasped easily. Fleece balls and beanbags are easy to hold and release.

4. Use a stationary object when teaching striking or hitting. The use of a batting tee or tennis ball fastened to a string can offer the student an opportunity for success. In addition, a larger racquet or bat and "choking up" on the grip can be used.

5. Make projectiles easily retrievable. Place them near a backstop or use a goal that rebounds the projectile to the shooter.

6. When teaching catching, use a soft, lightweight, and slow-moving object. Beach balls and balloons are excellent for beginning catching skills since they allow the student to track their movement visually. In addition, foam rubber balls eliminate the fear of being hurt by a thrown or batted projectile.

Modifications for Students Lacking Balance and Agility

1. Increase the width of rails, lines, and beams when practicing balance. Carrying a long pole will help minimize rapid shifts of balance and is a useful lead-up activity.

2. Increase the width of the base of support. Students should be taught to keep the feet spread at least to shoulder width.

3. Emphasize use of many body parts when teaching balance. The more body parts in contact with the floor, the easier it is to balance the body. Beginning balance practice should emphasize controlled movement using as many body parts as possible.

4. Increase the surface area of the body parts in contact with the floor or beam. For example, walking flat-footed is easier than walking on tiptoes.

5. Lower the center of gravity. This offers more stability and greater balance to the youngster. Place emphasis on bending the knees and slightly leaning forward.

6. Make sure that surfaces offer good friction. Floors and shoes should not be slick or students will fall. Carpets or tumbling mats will increase traction.

7. Provide balance assistance. A barre, cane, or chair can be used to keep the student from falling.

8. Teach students how to fall. Students with balance problems will inevitably fall. Practice in learning how
to fall should be offered so that they gradually learn how to absorb the force.

4. Determine What Support and Aid Are Necessary

When a student is deemed ready for placement, consultation between the physical education teacher and the special education supervisor is of prime importance. In a setting where emotions and feelings run high, it is important to ensure that communication and planning occur on a regular basis. Special and physical education professionals must discuss the needs of the student and the needs of the physical education teacher on a regular basis, and develop realistic expectations. It is quite possible that the special education teacher may have to participate in the physical education class to ensure a smooth transition.

Full information about the needs of the student is due the physical education teacher before the student participates. Physical education teachers must feel able to tell the support personnel what kind of help they need. Negative feelings toward students with differing needs will occur if the physical educator feels students are dropped into their class without asking what kind of help they need. This procedure should also be implemented when the student moves from one mainstreaming situation to another. Both able students and students with disabilities need opportunities to make appropriate progress.

5. Teach Tolerance to All Students

An important part of the physical education experience is to help all students understand the problems related to being disabled. Students need to learn to understand, accept, and live comfortably with persons with disabilities. They should recognize that students with disabilities are functional and worthwhile individuals who have innate abilities and can make significant contributions to society. The concept of understanding and appreciating individual differences is one that merits positive development and should concentrate on three aspects:

a. Recognizing the similarities among all people: their hopes, rights, aspirations, and goals.

b. Understanding human differences and focusing on the concept that all people are disabled. For some, disabilities are of such nature and severity that they interfere with normal living.

c. Exploring ways to deal with those who differ without overhelping, and stressing the acceptance of all students as worthwhile individuals. People with disabilities deserve consideration and understanding, based on empathy, not sympathy.

6. Integrate Students with Differing Needs into the Class Setting

Once the mainstreamed student, able students, and teacher have undergone preliminary preparation, consideration can be given to integrating the disabled youngster into the learning environment. Guidelines for successful integration of students with disabilities into physical education are:

1. Students with disabilities must be able to meet target goals specified in the IEP in addition to participating in the regular program of activities.

2. Build ego strength; stress abilities. Eliminate established practices that unwittingly contribute to embarrassment and failure.

3. Foster peer acceptance, which begins when the teacher accepts each student as a functioning, participating member of the class.

4. Concentrate on the student's physical education needs and not on the disability. Give strong attention to fundamental skills and physical fitness qualities.

5. Provide continual monitoring and assess periodically the student's target goals. Anecdotal and periodic record keeping are implicit in this guideline.

6. Be constantly aware of students' feelings and anxiety concerning their progress and integration. Provide positive feedback as a basic practice.

POSTURE

The physical education program should include vigorous physical activities that lead to fitness and strengthening of the muscle groups that maintain proper body alignment. Strengthening the abdominal wall and the musculature of the upper back and neck helps maintain proper body alignment. Flexibility is also necessary so that children can move their body with ease and proper postural alignment.

Posture refers to the habitual or assumed alignment and balance of the body segments while the body is standing, walking, sitting, or lying. Appropriate posture radiates a positive self-image; improper posture may reflect fatigue or a lack of confidence.

Elementary school teachers and/or school nurses are responsible for detecting and reporting physical problems of children; some programs of posture evaluation can help identify posture problems. Evaluation procedures are described in this chapter.

What Is Correct Posture?

Posture varies with the individual's age, gender, and body type. Very young children often toe out while standing and walking to provide a wider, more stable base. Standing position exhibits an exaggerated lumbar curve and rounded shoulders, which are normal at this developmental stage. By age 6 or 7, however, the lumbar curve lessens and the prominent abdominal protrusion begins to disappear. At this stage, the feet and toes generally point ahead. The educational process should assist the child in making the transition from the normal exaggerated curves of young children to proper adult posture in adolescence.

Evaluating Posture

A program of posture evaluation by the teacher and or school nurse can help identify posture problems. Evaluation can be done through observation, both formal and informal, and with measurement devices. A referral system should be established for individuals who exhibit marked posture deviations.

REFLECTION AND REVIEW QUESTIONS

How and Why

1. How do you feel about teaching individuals with disabilities?

2. Why is it important for children with disabilities to participate in physical education?

3. Do all children have disabilities? Explain your answer.

4. How can teachers generate parent and social support for children with disabilities?

5. How does our society look at obese children? Are the assumptions accurate?

Content Review

1. What implications do PL 94-142 and IDEA have for the physical education teacher?

2. Discuss the screening and assessment procedures for evaluating students.

3. How are individual educational programs developed? Include comments on who is involved and what the IEP contains.

4. What are inclusion and mainstreaming? Discuss guidelines for successful inclusion.

5. Identify methods of modifying activities for inclusion.

6. Identify several disabilities and techniques for modifying activities to accommodate these disabilities.

7. Explain the process of designing programs for obese children with motor deficiencies.

8. Why is posture an important topic for physical education teachers?

INSTRUCTIONAL FORMATS

The material in this chapter can be presented using the lecture style plus the overhead transparencies and Power Point slides available from the publisher to provide students an overview of the chapter. The introduction may be followed by cooperative learning assignments that provide active learning and critical thinking activities for the student. Videotape recordings may be used to demonstrate the types of disabilities described in the chapter. Videotapes of good teaching techniques demonstrating mainstreaming could also be used to illustrate the topics presented. In the cooperative learning groups, the students will discuss the materials listed on the Task Sheet and/or other topics you may assign. Each group can become a "content expert" for sections of the Task Sheet. Oral summary reports of the cooperative learning group may be presented to the entire class covering all or part of the discussion items.

KEY TERMS

mainstreaming	due process guidelines	scoliosis
zero reject	least restrictive environment	assessment
IDEA	partial mainstreaming	progressive inclusion
PL 94-142	posture	PL 105-17
screening	reverse mainstreaming	

DISCUSSION TOPICS

1. Invite a special education teacher or an adapted physical education teacher to your class to discuss mainstreaming and reverse mainstreaming. Suggested focus areas: "Modifying Activities in Physical Education to Enhance the Inclusion Experience" and "Mainstreaming in Physical Education." Have the specialist share actual experiences with the students.

2. Invite a Resource Specialist, appropriate district evaluator, or an attorney to speak to your class to explain the legal implications of providing due process for all individuals with disabilities.

3. Invite a school counselor to class to walk the class through the development of an IEP.

SAMPLE WRITTEN ASSIGNMENTS

1. Write an outline of an IEP created for a student with a given disability.

2. Write a sample letter to parents identifying the need for testing their child for special education.

3. List methods for modifying teaching to meet the needs of specific disabilities.

4. List a variety of activities most suitable for inclusion activities. Demonstrate a lesson focus idea explaining the inclusion activities you have created.

5. Conduct an Internet search and write a report on a topic such as obesity and its implications for students in physical education and for a lifetime. Other topics covered in this chapter for consideration should be discussed with the instructor. The paper should be typed, two pages long, and reference the sites you have used.

ACTIVITY SESSION EXPERIENCES

Lead the students through the following activities:

1. Demonstrate a lesson and assign selected students to represent an individual with a particular disability or learning challenge.

2. Demonstrate methods of adjusting your instruction to adapt to the needs of the special student(s) and modify activities such that they will be rewarding for all students. Discuss the experience with the entire class.

COOPERATIVE LEARNING TASK SHEET

Chapter 7: Children with Disabilities

Directions: Your cooperative learning group will become the content experts by finding the answers to the items listed below. Discuss the following items with your group and be ready to report on one or all of them at the end of the class period.

1. Within your group, identify two students to demonstrate posture aberrations. Conduct an informal posture screening for your group. Discuss the implications of poor posture on performance and conversely, the importance of good posture in successful physical performance.

2. Explain the purpose and applications of PL 94-142 and IDEA as applied to the physical education environment.

3. Discuss and explain the due process guidelines associated with assessment procedures.

4. Develop a plan for identifying, locating, and evaluating all children with disabilities.

5. Cite standards associated with assessment procedures for special children.

   The National Standards for an Adapted Physical Education teacher are listed at this site:
   http://www.pecentral.org/adapted/adaptedapens.html

6. Identify essential elements of an individualized educational program and list the stages of development.

7. Discuss the guidelines for successful mainstreaming experiences.

   This site provides you with mainstreaming ideas:
   http://www.pelinks4u.org/sections/adapted/adapted.htm

8. Describe the characteristics of specific impairments and ways to modify learning experiences in physical education to accommodate children with disabilities. Set up a peer teaching assignment within your group to demonstrate appropriate adaptations for specific disabilities.

9. Identify methods of modifying activities for inclusion.

10. Describe and discuss the nationally validated programs listed in the chapter available in assisting the screening, assessment, and curriculum development for children with special needs.

11. Describe a systematic approach to treating underachievers in physical fitness, children with weight problems, and youngsters with motor deficiencies. An Internet search might provide you with additional facts and material to bring to your discussion.

12. Discuss a step-by-step approach that could be used to develop a success profile for obese youngsters in the elementary school. Practice administration of the skin fold test using calipers on several of your classmates within this cooperative learning group. Evaluate each other's techniques.

CHAPTER 8

Evaluation

SUMMARY

The purpose of student, teacher, and program evaluation is to determine whether progress is being made toward objectives. Evaluation is done to increase student learning and improve instruction. There are many ways to evaluate student learning including the use of checklists, logs, tests, and scoring rubrics. A grading system that communicates student progress to parents is difficult to design. There are many good reasons for giving grades and just as many reasons for avoiding grading in elementary schools. A student progress report can be a useful approach for helping parents understand their child's progress in physical education. Growth in instructional effectiveness occurs when teachers choose to self-evaluate their instruction. A program checklist can be used to score the total physical education setting.

STUDENT OUTCOMES

Upon completion of the reading of this chapter, the student will:

- Differentiate between formal and informal evaluation.

- Explain the differences between process and product evaluation.

- Cite a number of ways to assess student learning.

- Know the advantages of a progress report for parents.

- Develop arguments for and against grading in physical education.

- Identify methods of instructional analysis of teacher behavior.

- Identify ways to self-evaluate instructional behavior.

- Recognize the key elements of an effective physical education evaluation form.

MAIN CONCEPTS

The purpose of evaluation is to determine whether progress is being made toward objectives. Evaluation should review all phases of education, including pupil progress, teacher performance, and program effectiveness.

ASSESSMENT OF STUDENT PERFORMANCE

Assessment is defined as the collection of information about student performance. Traditionally, assessment in physical education has been directed at functions of participation, attendance, and effort, but not on components that reflect student learning (Lund, 1993). Even when performance is considered, it is done in ways that are suspect in recording true learning. Matanin and Tannehill (1994) suggest the use of ongoing, daily assessments to obtain measures that reliably reflect student learning. The purpose of assessment in this chapter will be to obtain knowledge about student performance that can be used for grading and student accountability.

Within the field of physical education, assessment is a difficult issue. Classes are often larger than traditional classroom settings, the area covered is more expansive, and there is often no permanent record (like a written example of work for an English class) of work completed for teachers to take home and thoroughly inspect. Obstacles are stacked against physical education teachers to produce a quality assessment routine for students. The assessment process is crucial in providing feedback to students, teachers, and parents.

Many components are evaluated in physical education. A major part of assessment is examining the skill learning and development that occurs through the instructional process. Even though skill development is a primary focus of physical education, it is not enough; students need to learn about strategy, skill performance techniques, and positive attitudes towards physical activity. Written exams can evaluate whether students have requisite knowledge for successful participation. Finally, the area of attitudes and values is important to the program. Students will choose not to participate if their attitudes and values have not developed concurrently with skills and knowledge.

Using assessment instruments serves a number of purposes (Strand and Wilson, 1993). Some of the more common reasons for assessment include the following:

- Grading.

- Motivation.

- Diagnosis.

- Placement and equalization.

- Program assessment.

- Program support. Results of regular assessment can be used to validate and support the program. The data gained through assessment is objective and can reveal what students are expected to learn and how effectively they are learning. Accountability is a buzzword among educators as schools try to document what students are learning in order to gain public support. When administrators need to make cutbacks in programs, they usually ask faculty members to justify continuation of their program. Data gained through consistent assessment of students is a strong and effective way to defend the program.

Assessment: Process of Learning or Product Outcomes?

Physical education is different than academic areas because it demands physical performance. In physical education, skills are learned only to be lost if not practiced. It is never possible to say in physical education that a skill or fitness level will be maintained at a high level if it isn't used. Therefore, it becomes important to look at physical education in a slightly different perspective.

Two types of outcomes pertain to students: process of learning and product. The process of learning outcomes relate to the performance of general movement and skills with emphasis on correct technique. The form used to execute the movement is the point of assessment rather than the outcome of the skill performed. Product outcomes focus on performance in terms of measurable increments of what learners accomplish.

Develop Athletes or Teach All Students?

Should elementary school physical education focus on product outcomes or should it emphasize the process of learning skills correctly? Should physical education experiences be designed to develop high-quality performances or should it focus on teaching all students the proper way to perform skills?

The role of physical education in the curriculum is unique. Nowhere else can students receive skill instruction and physical activity.

Is Perfection Possible in Physical Education?

Perfection of a skill usually does not occur in physical education or sport. This contrasts with other academic areas that demand accuracy and correctness. In physical education, correct performance is impossible to predict and errors are expected. Even the best of athletes miss half of the baskets they shoot or make an error in baseball about 70% of the time.

Skill Refinement or Skill Performance?

Skill refinement is not synonymous with performance improvement. Teachers can teach youngsters how to perform skills properly, but can't guarantee that all students will be high-level performers.

Winning or Feeling Good?

The ultimate goal of physical education is to graduate students who feel competent and willing to perform skills throughout a lifetime of activity. Leaving students a legacy of knowing how to live an active lifestyle is more important than their knowing that they could make 10 out of 15 free throws or hit 20 successful tennis serves.

Students should be taught that the process of doing one's best is the important issue in physical education.

A reminder is in order here: Physical education teachers are not coaches (who focus on winning) in the physical education setting. They are coaches when they work in the athletic arena. Quality teachers and coaches are able to separate the two domains to assure that proper outcomes are reached in both arenas.

ASSESSING STUDENT OUTCOMES

Assessing student performance can be accomplished in a variety of ways. They include: informal assessment on the spot when a teacher corrects or reinforces a student's performance; checklist rubrics; observation checklists; skill checklists; anecdotal record sheets; student self-assessments; student logs; and written tests. Assessment covers all three major learning domains: psychomotor, cognitive, and affective.

Checklist Rubrics

A checklist rubric is a rating scale that lists multiple criteria related to a task or motor skill performance. The criteria are performance levels students are expected to achieve.

Observation Checklists

Observation checklists are another means of process evaluation. Criteria governing proper technique for the movement pattern are listed, and the child's performance is checked against these points.

Rating Scales

Rating scales have long been used as a system for reporting progress to students and parents. Rating scales are usually most effective when skills are listed in the sequence in which they should be learned. In this way, instruction is designed to achieve diagnosed needs.

Anecdotal Record Sheets

A record sheet that contains student names and has room for comments about student behavior can be used to assess student progress. Anecdotal records of student progress can be reinforcing to both student and teacher, as it is often difficult to remember how much progress has been made over time.

Student Self-Assessments

Intermediate grade students are capable of performing self-evaluations making judgments about their achievement. Self-evaluation reduces the amount of teacher evaluation time and allows the teacher more time for instruction.

Student Logs

Intermediate-grade youngsters are capable of maintaining a log that indicates progress toward a goal over time. The log should include goals the students have set, decisions and choices made, time spent on working toward the goal behaviors, and a reflection area to record their perceptions of the experience.

Written Tests

Written tests are administered to check the cognitive learning that has accompanied physical skill learning.

GRADING

There is wide variation in physical education grading policies in elementary schools, ranging from no grading to grading with letter grades similar to high school classes. Arguments can be made on each side of the issue, to grade or not to grade, and there is no clear-cut answer. If a decision is made to grade, a more difficult question arises: What type of grading approach should be used? School report cards should contain a section devoted to a physical education grade.

Points against Using a Grading System

- Grades are difficult to interpret between teachers and schools.

- Physical education does not place emphasis on content and product. Physical education judges success by improvement on skills. Academic subjects reflect achievement and accomplishment in contrast to improvement.

- Often, physical education classes in elementary schools only meet once or twice a week. Conducting testing for grade requirements is time-consuming and takes away from learning opportunities. Physical educators in this setting are trying to squeeze as much learning as possible into a minimal amount of time, and grading reduces their instructional time.

- Since physical education instruction covers all learning domains, it is difficult to decide which domain to overlook when grading. Grading all the domains would be impossibly time-consuming.

- Grading usually occurs in areas where standardized instruments have been developed. Fitness testing is the major area in elementary physical education where a variety of standardized tests have been developed. Due to the dearth of standardized tests in areas other than fitness, excessive attention is given to fitness testing in some physical education settings.

- Physical education places emphasis on physical fitness and skill performance. Performance in these areas is strongly controlled by genetics, making it difficult for all children to achieve, even when they "give it their best effort." When grades are given for physical fitness, some youngsters feel discouraged because they trained and still did not reach standards of high performance.

Points for Using a Grading System

- Giving grades makes physical education similar to other academic areas in the school curriculum. This gives physical education credibility and gains respect from parents, teachers, and administrators.

- Grades communicate the performance of students to parents.

- When grades are not given, academic respect is lost. Physical education already suffers from the "roll out the ball" misguided perception and a lack of a grading system may make it appear to others that little learning is occurring.

- A grading system provides accountability.

- A grading system rewards skilled students.

If You Choose to Grade, Consider the Following...

If the decision is made to implement a grading system, more difficult issues follow. There are different ways to grade, and many issues have to be examined before developing a grading approach. The following points must be considered when determining how you will assign grades.

Educational Outcomes versus Administrative Tasks

Physical education grading should reflect the outcomes desired: skill development, personal values, and cognitive development. Some grading systems assign weight to each of the areas when compiling a grade. The final grade depends on accomplishment of the established educational objectives. This contrasts with grading on completion of administrative tasks where students earn a part or their entire grade by attendance, participation, and attitude. This latter approach grades students on tasks that have little to do with accomplishment of physical education objectives.

Attitude versus Performance

Should attitude or skill performance be the focal point of grading in physical education? Those who emphasize attitudes stress the importance of students leaving school with warm and positive feelings toward physical activity. The assumption is that students who feel positive about physical activity will be willing to be active throughout their lifetime. These teachers assign grades based on the process of trying rather than reaching skill outcomes. Students who receive higher grades may not be the most skilled but have shown good behavior and a positive attitude throughout the semester.

Teachers who believe in the product camp focus primarily on student accomplishment and see effort as something that is laudable but not part of the grading process. Their philosophy might be stated as follows: "I don't really care whether students like me or physical education. What is ultimately important is their performance."

This is a difficult problem to resolve in physical education and is always hotly debated. One point of view is that students should learn how society works from the grading system. People are not rewarded in life based on how hard they try, but rather, on their performance.

A possible solution is to grade on performance while teaching in a manner that focuses on the student's attitude toward physical activity and skill learning.

Relative Improvement

Some physical educators believe that effort, or "just doing the best that you can," should be the most important factor in assigning grades. To reward effort, these teachers base student grades on the amount a student improves. This involves pre-testing and post-testing to determine the amount of progress made throughout the grading period. This approach contrasts with basing the grade on absolute performance; it is quite possible that the best performer in the class will not receive the highest grade because of lack of improvement.

Grading on improvement is time-consuming and requires that the same test be given at the beginning and end of the semester or unit. The test may or may not be a valid reflection of what has been learned in the class and may not be sensitive enough to reflect improvement made by both poor and outstanding performers.

Students learn quickly that if they perform too well on the pre-test, they will be penalized at post-test time. Thus they understand it is important to perform at a low level in order to demonstrate a higher degree of improvement on the post-test. A related problem is that improvement is sometimes easier at beginning levels of skill than at high levels of performance.

Grading on Potential or Effort

Some teachers choose to grade on whether students reach their potential. These teachers may lower a student's grade because the student did not reach their potential because they felt there was a lack of effort. On the other hand, a grade may be raised because the teacher felt that student didn't have much ability but did reach their potential. How can any teacher really know the absolute potential of any student? When grades are based on a teacher's subjective beliefs rather than on criteria that can be measured and evaluated, grades become difficult to defend. To be defensible, grading systems need to be based on tangible data gleaned from observable behavior and performance.

Negative versus Positive Grading

To make the grading system defensible and concrete, some teachers use point systems. In most point systems, both performance objectives and administrative factors are listed as grade components. A student earns a grade through performance, attitude, and knowledge.

Some teachers use positive methods where the student gains points for successful completion of objectives, and others use a negative method where they deduct points from the total for lack of performance. In a positive system, students can behave in a positive manner to earn points. Teachers are constantly rewarding positive behavior, which fosters positive feelings toward physical education and teachers. A negative system tends to focus teachers on what students cannot do, rather than on what they should or can do. Students do not respond well to this approach. Threatening to lower the grade of a student who does not like physical education or school in general only further alienates the student and is based on a system of negative reinforcement. The grading system should positively encourage students to perform.

Letter Grades versus a Student Progress Report

Letter grades do not report progress or performance related to other students at a similar developmental level. A student progress report gives parents more information and helps to communicate goals of the program to parents. Examples of progress reports are included in this chapter.

Since using a progress report takes more time than assigning letter grades, such a report can't be sent home as often as a simple letter grade. Most elementary school physical education teachers are responsible for 350 to 600 students or more. Completing a progress report for each student four times a year would be an unrealistic expectation because of the inordinate amount of time it takes to complete. A solution is to offer a comprehensive progress report once a year or once every second year.

EVALUATING INSTITUTIONAL OUTCOMES

Institutional outcomes are goals that the state, school district, superintendent, school board, and parents want to reach. They are referred to as accountability outcomes or "what is it that the physical education program should contribute to the total school environment?" To evaluate institutional goals, it is necessary to use a test that is valid and respected both in and out of the school setting.

Health-Related Fitness

Physical fitness testing has occurred for decades in physical education. Some experts make an argument for placing less emphasis on fitness testing and more on activity evaluation (Pangrazi, 2004). Currently the Fitnessgram System (2004) is a popular test used to measure health-related physical fitness and is the recommended test for the AAHPERD.

The focus of the Fitnessgram is on teaching students about the importance of activity for good health. Students are not compared to one another but are given feedback about their fitness and whether it meets the minimum standard for good health.

The Fitnessgram is based primarily on exercise behaviors rather than students' attempts to demonstrate that they are the "best." The Fitnessgram program acknowledges and commends performance; however, it places its highest priority on the development and reinforcement of health-related behaviors that are attainable by all students.

Fitnessgram Test Items

- *Aerobic Capacity.* The PACER (Progressive Aerobic Cardiovascular Endurance Run) test is an excellent alternative to the mile—it involves a 20-meter shuttle run and can be performed indoors.

- *Body Composition.* Body composition is evaluated using percent body fat, which is calculated by measuring the triceps and calf skinfolds or body mass index (calculated using height and weight).

- *Abdominal Strength.* The curl-up test uses a cadence (1 curl-up every 3 seconds). The maximum limit is 75.

- *Upper-Body Strength.* The push-up test is done to a cadence (1 every 3 seconds) and is an excellent substitute for the pull-up. A successful push-up is counted when the arms are bent to a 90-degree angle.

- *Trunk Extensor Strength and Flexibility.* The trunk lift test is done from a face-down position. This test involves lifting the upper body 6 to 12 inches off the floor using the muscles of the back. The position must be held until the measurement can be made.

- *Flexibility.* The back-saver sit and reach is similar to the traditional sit-and-reach test except that it is performed with 1 leg flexed to avoid encouraging students to hyperextend. Measurement is made on both the right and left legs.

CRITERION-REFERENCED HEALTH STANDARDS

A major reason for health-related fitness evaluation is to provide students, teachers, and parents with information about good health. The Fitnessgram (2004) uses criterion-referenced health standards that represent good health instead of traditional percentile rankings. These standards represent a level of fitness that offers some degree of protection against diseases resulting from sedentary living. The Fitnessgram uses an approach that classifies fitness performance into two categories: needs improvement and healthy fitness zone (HFZ). Criterion-referenced health standards do not compare students against each other, as do percentile rankings. Instead, youngsters are concerned with personal fitness and minimizing possible health problems by trying to score within the healthy fitness zone.

Criterion-referenced health standards for aerobic fitness are based on a study by Blair et al. (1989). A significant decrease in risk of all-cause mortality occurred when people were active enough to avoid classification in the bottom 20% of the population. The risk level continues to decrease as fitness levels increase, but not significantly when compared to moving out of the least active group.

The aerobic performance minimums (mile run or PACER) for the Fitnessgram HFZ require achieving a fitness level that is above the least active portion (bottom 20%) of the population.

Criterion-referenced health standards for percent of fat are calculated from equations reported by Slaughter et al. (1988). Williams et al. (1992) reported that students with body fat levels above 25% for boys and 30 to 35% for girls are more likely to exhibit elevated cholesterol levels and hypertension. In other words, students who have higher levels of body fat may be at risk for future health problems.

Criterion-referenced health standards have not been established for abdominal strength, upper-body strength, and flexibility. The standards reflect a reasonable expectation for students who are sufficiently active.

Effective Uses of Fitness Tests

Fitness tests are designed to evaluate and educate students about the status of their physical fitness. In spite of continued research and improvement, fitness tests have limitations and usually show low validity. The 3 major ways to use fitness tests are: (a) to teach personal self-testing, (b) to establish personal best fitness performances, and (c) to evaluate institutional fitness goals. The personal self-testing program is advocated in the elementary school physical education program. It can be completed quickly in class, is educational, and can be done in an unthreatening manner. In addition, little instructional time is lost, and students learn how to evaluate their fitness, a skill that will serve them for a lifetime.

Personal Self-Testing. The personal self-testing program is an approach that is student-centered, concerned with the process of fitness testing, and places emphasis on learning to self-evaluate. When using this technique, students can work individually or find a friend with whom they would like to self-test.

Personal-Best Testing. The personal-best testing approach appeals to gifted performers and to students who are motivated by achieving a maximum performance. The objective is to achieve a maximum score in each of the test items. This approach has been used for years with most fitness tests. In addition, several awards (President's Council on Physical Fitness and Sports, 2004) are issued to high-level performers. This is a formal testing program as compared to the self-testing approach discussed previously.

Institutional Evaluation. The institutional evaluation program involves examining the fitness levels of students to see if the institution (school) is reaching its desired objectives. Institutional objectives are closely tied to the physical education curriculum.

Physical Activity

Another way to evaluate the effectiveness of the institution is to monitor the amount of physical activity students accumulate on a daily basis. Fortunately, today there are accurate instruments available for measuring the amount of physical activity students accumulate (for an in-depth discussion of physical activity monitoring and promotion, see Chapter 12). Using pedometers to measure the physical activity levels of youth is now an accepted instructional and research methodology (Beighle, Pangrazi, & Vincent, 2001; Crouter et al., 2003; Kilanowski, et al. 1999).

Walk4Life pedometers (www.walk4life.com) have a function that measures activity time. Every time a person moves, the pedometer starts accumulating time. When the person stops moving, the timing function stops. This function shows the total hours and minutes of activity time accumulated throughout the day.

Research has shown that gathering 4 days of physical activity will give an accurate indication of a student's average activity level. A set of pedometers can be rotated between classrooms to establish the average level of activity for each classroom.

The President's Council on Physical Fitness and Sports has an award for students who accumulate at least 60 minutes of physical activity almost everyday for 6 weeks. The award is called the ***Presidential Active Lifestyle Award***. Students can sign up on the web and log their activity into the website on a daily basis at www.presidentschallenge.org. This is an excellent way to promote physical activity outside the school day.

Children's Attraction to Physical Activity (CAPA)

The CAPA instrument is a 15-item pencil-and-paper measure used to assess children's (ages 8 to 12) attraction to physical activity (Brustad, 1993). This instrument is unique in that it focuses on dimensions that have been specifically identified by children as being important. These dimensions affect their choices regarding physical activity behavior (Brustad, 1993). The instrument is scored on a 1-to-4 point scale with 4 reflecting the most positive attitude toward physical activity.

The CAPA can be used to evaluate how students feel about physical activity. Since this is a standardized instrument, the results can be used to see whether the physical education program is having a positive impact on the affective domain of students.

EVALUATING INSTRUCTIONAL EFFECTIVENESS

Self-evaluation is a key to improving teaching ability. Self-evaluation is recommended because feedback reviewed in the privacy of one's office is easier to digest and less threatening. The teacher can then set personal goals and chart their performance privately. Instruction should be evaluated to assess the quality of instruction. A variety of techniques can be used: checklists, rating scales, systematic observation with or without computer analysis, and videotape analysis. Teachers are encouraged to make this an integral part of teaching behavior to continually think about ways to improve. Teacher behavior and effectiveness can be evaluated by observing instructional time, management time, practice time, dead time, time on task, response latency, student performance, and instructional feedback. This section offers methods for evaluating teaching behavior that are observable and therefore measurable.

Instructional Time

It is important to know the amount of instruction you offer students. To analyze instructional time, the number of instructional episodes and the length of each episode are recorded. Generally, instructional episodes should be kept to 30 seconds or less.

Management Time

Management time is defined as episodes that occur when students are moved into various formations, when equipment is gathered or put away, and when directions are given relative to these areas.

Practice Time (Time on Task) and Dead Time

To learn physical skills, students must have an opportunity for productive skill practice. Practice time, or time on task, has also been referred to as ALT-PE or Academic Learning Time in Physical Education. Practice time is the amount of time students spend practicing skills that result in accomplishment of program objectives.

Dead time occurs when students are off task or are doing something unrelated to practice, management, or instruction.

Response Latency

Response latency is the amount of time it takes for students to respond when commands or signals are given. Response latency occurs when instructions are given to begin or stop an activity. The average duration of response latency should be 5 seconds to stop the class.

Student Performance

The placheck (planned activity check) observation technique can be used to observe the behavior of a class. The evaluator can observe student effort, on-task behavior, or participation.

Instructional Feedback

Feedback given to students strongly affects the instructional presentation.

Praise and Criticism

When students are involved in activity, feedback related to student performance should be given. Feedback can be positive and constructive or negative and critical in nature.

General versus Specific Feedback

Feedback to students can be general or specific. General feedback can be positive or negative; it does not specify the behavior being reinforced. In contrast, specific feedback identifies the student by name and reinforces an actual behavior. It might also be accompanied with a valuing statement. First names are important in personalizing feedback and directing it to the proper individual.

Corrective Instructional Feedback

Effective teachers inspire students to achieve higher levels of performance. Corrective feedback focuses on improving the performance of the participant.

Nonverbal Feedback

Nonverbal communication is meaningful to students and may be equal to or more effective than verbal forms of communication. Examples are: a pat on the back, a wink, a smile, a nod of the head, the thumbs-up sign, clapping hands, etc. Negative nonverbal feedback includes: frowning, shaking the head in disapproval, walking away from a student, etc.

Active Supervision and Student Contact

Effective instructors actively supervise students. Active supervision means moving among students and offering them personalized feedback.

EVALUATING YOUR PROGRAM

Program evaluation should be a regular activity to assess program goals, philosophy, and objectives of your school/district. The results, including program strengths and weaknesses, can be shared with administrators or used by teachers to evaluate a program they have developed. Four areas that can be evaluated are: program philosophy; instructional procedures; curricular offerings; facilities, equipment and supplies.

INSTRUCTIONAL FORMATS

The material in this chapter may be presented using the lecture style and the Power Point/overhead transparencies to provide your students with an overview of the chapter. The instructor may also use the Guided Discovery method of teaching to introduce and review the materials read by the students. In this style, the instructor asks questions guiding the students toward one answer. The instructor rephrases the questions until the students discover the answer to the question. The introduction/review of the chapter may be followed by cooperative learning assignments that provide active learning and critical thinking activities for the student. In the cooperative learning groups, the students will discuss the materials listed on the Cooperative Learning Task Sheet and/or other topics you may assign. Each group can become a "content expert" for sections of the Task Sheet. Oral summary reports of the group may be presented to the entire class covering all or part of the discussion items.

KEY TERMS

process of learning	anecdotal record	nonverbal feedback
outcomes	sheets	duration recording
product outcomes	time on task	active supervision
placheck recording	response latency	criterion-referenced
instructional time	instructional feedback	health standards
skill refinement	Fitnessgram	
management time	specific feedback	
CAPA		

REFLECTION AND REVIEW QUESTIONS

How and Why

1. In a music or art class, would you want to be evaluated based on the product or the process? Why? How does this relate to your grading as a physical educator?

2. How is giving a child "on the spot" feedback regarding performance a form of evaluation?

3. How are you evaluated as a college student? Do you feel you are evaluated fairly? Explain your answer.

4. How can progress reports be more effective tools for communicating with parents?

5. Would you rather self-evaluate a lesson yourself using videotape or have a peer evaluate you during the lesson? Why?

6. Why might the ability to be self-critical be important for physical education teachers and physical education curriculum designers?

Content Review

1. What is the significance of focusing on the process in physical education? Include comments about how physical education and other academic areas differ with respect to evaluation.

2. Identify and describe several methods of assessing performance outcomes.

3. What are the advantages and disadvantages of a grading system?

4. State the steps to implementing a grading system.

5. How can teachers use self-evaluation of themselves?

6. Identify and explain 4 areas of teaching that can be evaluated. Within your comments, describe how to assess the specific areas.

7. What are the elements of a physical education program evaluation form?

DISCUSSION TOPICS

1. Discuss the value of systematic instructional observation techniques and how they can improve teaching and learning.

2. Present a videotape of a quality teacher utilizing the DPE model of teaching. Evaluate the instructor on several of the key areas identified in this chapter: instruction time, management time, practice time, specific feedback, nonverbal feedback, teacher movement, etc. You may use the tapes available from Benjamin Cummings demonstrating the DPE model of teaching.

3. Discuss the value of anecdotal record sheets versus checklists.

4. Discuss the pros and cons of grading students in physical education.

5. Discuss the pros and cons of using progress reports rather than report cards for student evaluation.

SAMPLE WRITTEN ASSIGNMENTS

1. Develop an anecdotal record sheet.

2. Develop a self-check self-evaluation sheet that can be used by students.

3. Ask the class or groups to create a grading scale/formula using both process and product evaluation.

4. Using a computer, the Teacher Evaluation Program, and a videotape of a lesson, apply systematic observation to evaluating the class.

5. Develop a self-evaluation form that can be used by a teacher.

An article on student self-evaluation can be read at this site:

http://www.ncrel.org/sdrs/areas/issues/methods/assment/as5selfe.htm

Physical education assessment and grading ideas can be found at:

 www.pelinks4u.org
 www.pe4life.org
 http://www.pecentral.org/assessment/assessment.html

COOPERATIVE LEARNING TASK SHEET

Chapter 8: Evaluation

Directions: Your cooperative learning group will become the content experts by finding the answers to the items listed below. Discuss the following items with your group and be ready to report on one or all of them at the end of the class period.

1. Discuss the differences between process and product evaluation. Give examples of each type of evaluation. Discuss the value of each type of evaluation. What is the significance of focusing on the process in physical education? Include comments about how physical education and other academic areas differ with respect to evaluation.

2. What are the advantages and disadvantages of a grading system?

3. Discuss the pros and cons of traditional grading versus progress reports.

4. What are recommended items in which to grade physical education?

5. What items are not recommended to use in grading students in physical education?

6. Create a grading procedure to use in Developmental Level I, II, and III classes.

7. Identify methods of instructional analysis of teacher behavior. Describe the elements being evaluated in each method. Have each member of the group explain the proper use of a different instructional analysis form shown in the textbook.

8. Explain methods to self-evaluate instructional behavior. Use a videotape of an individual and describe how you would apply self-evaluation techniques to evaluate yourself if that tape were of your own teaching.

9. Identify and explain 4 areas of teaching that can be evaluated. Within your comments, describe how to assess the specific areas.

10. Describe the CAPA instrument.

11. Describe health-related fitness.

12. Discuss the methods available to evaluate institutional outcomes.

13. What is a pedometer and how can it be used in physical education classes?

14. Briefly describe the Fitnessgram test items.

15. Describe personal self-testing and the values of its use.

16. Describe personal-best testing.

17. Discuss effective uses of fitness testing.

18. Describe inappropriate uses of fitness testing.

19. On what are criterion-referenced health standards based?

20. List three guidelines that can be used to contribute to the improvement of quality instruction.

21. Conduct an Internet search to identify microcomputer software programs that can assist in the analysis and reporting of fitness and motor performance scores, nutritional information, and record keeping. Assign two members of the group to practice a selected program and describe it to the group.

    To begin, refer to the Fitnessgram site:
    http://www.americanfitness.net/Fitnessgram

22. Explain several uses for and the value of computer-assisted instruction in physical education.

CHAPTER 9

Legal Liability, Supervision, and Safety

SUMMARY

This chapter explains the various legal terms and situations associated with physical education, and describes instructional and administrative procedures common to the responsible and prudent conduct of the physical education program. It is a teacher's legal responsibility to create a safe environment in which risk and the opportunity for injury are minimized and to provide a standard of care that any reasonable and prudent professional with similar training would apply under the given circumstances. Safety instruction is designed to prevent accidents and should be included in lesson plans to ensure coverage. A comprehensive safety checklist is included to assure beginning teachers understand how to establish an accident-free environment.

STUDENT OUTCOMES

- Upon completion of the reading of this chapter, the student will:

- Define tort, negligence, liability, malfeasance, misfeasance, nonfeasance, and other terms common to legal suits brought against educators.

- List major points that must be established to determine negligence on the part of the teacher.

- Explain how to examine all activities, equipment, and facilities for possible hazards and sources of accidents.

- Identify common defenses against negligence.

- Describe supervisory responsibilities expected of all teachers.

- List guidelines for the proper supervision of instruction, equipment, and facilities.

- Describe aspects of sport programs that often give rise to lawsuits.

- Understand how to assure safety focusing on prevention.

- Outline an emergency care plan.

MAIN CONCEPTS

School district personnel, including teaching and nonteaching members, are obligated to exercise ordinary care for the safety of students. This duty is manifested as the ability to anticipate reasonably foreseeable dangers and the responsibility to take necessary precautions to prevent problems from occurring. Purchasing safe and appropriate equipment is also an area of which personnel need to be cognizant.

Many companies sell safe equipment, this is just one example of a company with information available on the Internet:

 http://www.playdesigns.com

Physical education is particularly vulnerable to accidents and resultant injuries. More than 50% of all accidents in the school setting occur on the playground and in the gymnasium.

Go to this site to read guidelines on making playgrounds safe for children:

 http://www.parenthood.com/articles.html?article_id=6606

Courts have ruled that teachers owe their students a duty of care to protect them from harm. Teachers must offer a standard of care that any reasonable and prudent professional with similar training would apply under the given circumstances.

This Internet site will provide you with a legal definition of "duty of care:"

 http://www.nohsc.gov.au/OHSLegalObligations/DutyOfCare/dutycare.htm

Liability is an obligation to perform in a particular way that is required by law and enforced by court action. Teachers are bound by contract to carry out their duties in a reasonable and prudent manner.

TORTS

A tort is concerned with the teacher-student relationship and is a legal wrong that results in direct or indirect injury to another individual or to property.

NEGLIGENCE AND LIABILITY

Liability is usually concerned with a breach of duty through negligence.

Determination of Liability

1. Duty. The first point considered is that of duty owed to the participants. When examining duty or breach of duty, the court looks at reasonable care that a member of the profession in good standing would provide.

2. Breach of duty. A teacher must commit a breach of duty by failing to conform to the required duty. After it is established that a duty was required, it must be proved that such duty was not performed.

3. Proximate cause. The failure of the teacher to conform to the required standard must be the proximate cause of the resulting injury. It must be proved that the injury was caused by the teacher's breach of duty. It is not enough to prove simply that a breach of duty occurred. It must simultaneously be shown that the injury was a direct result of the teacher's failure to provide a reasonable standard of care. The plaintiff's expert will try to convince the court that there was a requisite standard and that standard was not met. In contrast, the defendant will try to show that they met the proper standard of care.

4. Damages. Actual harm must occur if liability is to be established. If no injury or harm occurs, there is no liability. It must be proved that the injured party is entitled to compensatory damages for financial loss or physical discomfort. Actual damages can be physical, emotional, or financial, but the court will only award financial remuneration.

Go to this site for specific reading on legal liability and safety in physical education:

 http://www.kin.sfasu.edu/finkenberg/kin511/Liability.html

Foreseeability

A key to the issue of negligence is foreseeability. Courts expect that a trained professional is able to foresee potentially harmful situations.

TYPES OF NEGLIGENCE

Negligence is defined by the court as conduct that falls below a standard of care established to protect others from unreasonable risk or harm.

Malfeasance occurs when a teacher does something improper by committing an act that is unlawful and wrongful, with no legal basis.

Misfeasance occurs when a teacher follows proper procedures but does not perform according to the required standard of conduct.

Nonfeasance is based on lack of action in carrying out a duty. This is usually an act of omission: The teacher knew the proper procedures but failed to follow them.

Contributory Negligence. Improper behavior by the injured party that causes the accident is usually ruled to be contributory negligence, because the injured party contributed to the resulting harm.

Comparative or Shared Negligence. Under the doctrine of comparative negligence, the injured party can recover only if found to be less negligent than the defendant (teacher).

Search this site for more information on this subject:
 http://insurance.cch.com/rupps/comparative-negligence.htm

COMMON DEFENSES AGAINST NEGLIGENCE

Negligence must be proved in a court of law.

Act of God

The act of God defense places the cause of injury on forces beyond the control of the teacher or the school.

Proximate Cause

The defense attempts to prove that the accident was not caused by the negligence of the teacher.

Assumption of Risk

Physical education is a high-risk activity when compared with most other curriculum areas. The participant assumes the risk accompanying the activity when choosing to be part of that activity.

By going to this site, you can read more about physical education and liability:
 http://www.kin.sfasu.edu/finkenberg/kin511/Liability.html

Contributory Negligence

Contributory negligence is often used by the defense in an attempt to convince the court that the injured party acted in a manner that was abnormal. A key point in the defense is whether the activity was suitable for the age and maturity level of the participants.

> Go to this website to read a school district's measures to prevent accidents:
> http://www.guildhallchambers.co.uk/Resources/PICN_Seminar_Reports/PI_IP_22_MARCH_01.html

AREAS OF RESPONSIBILITY

A two-tiered approach for analyzing injuries is useful for determining responsibility. The first tier for determining responsibility includes duties the administration must assume in support of the program. The second tier defines duties of the instructor or staff member charged with teaching or supervising students. For the responsibilities that are described in the following sections, both administrative and instructional duties are presented.

Supervision

All activities in a school setting must be supervised, including recess, lunch times, and field trips. The responsibilities of the school are critical if supervision is to function properly.

Administration

There are two levels identified in supervision: general and specific. General supervision refers to broad coverage. A supervision plan should be kept in the principal's office that covers rules of conduct governing student behavior. Rules should be posted prominently on bulletin boards, especially in classrooms.

Staff

General supervision is necessary during recess, before and after school, during lunch hour break, and during certain other sessions where instruction is not offered. The general supervisor is concerned primarily with student behavior, focusing on the student's right to a relaxing recreational experience.

Specific supervision requires that the instructor be with a certain group of students.

When teaching, arrange and teach the class so that all students are in view. This implies supervising from the perimeter of the area. If you are at the center of the student group with many students behind you, it will be impossible to supervise a class safely and effectively.

Do not agree to supervise activities where you are unqualified to anticipate possible hazards.

Five recommendations to assure that adequate supervision occurs:

1. The supervisor must be in the immediate vicinity.

2. If the supervisor must leave, the supervisor must have an adequate replacement in place before departing.

3. Supervision procedures must be preplanned and incorporated into daily lessons.

4. Supervision procedures should include what to observe, listen for, where to stand for the most effective view, and what to do if a problem arises.

5. Supervision requires that age, maturity, and skill ability of participants must always be considered, as must be the inherent risk of the activity.

Instruction

Instructional responsibility rests primarily with the teacher, but administrative personnel have certain defined functions.

Administration

The curriculum should be reviewed regularly by the administration and teaching staff to assure that it is current and updated. Administrators are obligated to support the program with adequate finances.

Instructional Staff

Teachers have a duty to protect students from unreasonable physical or mental harm. The major area of concern involving instruction is whether the student received adequate instruction before or during activity participation. Teachers are educated, experienced, and skilled in physical education and must be able to foresee situations that could be harmful.

The age and maturity level of students play an important role in the selection of activities.

Written curriculum guides and lesson plans can offer a well-prepared approach that withstands scrutiny and examination by other teachers and administrators.

Proper instructions demand that students not be forced to participate.

Making students perform physical activity for misbehavior is indefensible under any circumstance.

Points to assure safe instruction:

1. Sequence all activities in units of instruction and develop written lesson plans.

2. Scrutinize high-risk activities to assure that all safety procedures have been implemented.

3. Activities used in the curriculum must be within the developmental limits of the students.

4. If students' grades are based on the number of activities in which they participate, some students may feel forced to try all activities.

5. Include in written lesson plans how equipment should be arranged for safety and where the instructor will carry out supervision.

6. If a student claims injury or brings a note from parents asking that the student not participate in physical activity, the request must be honored.

7. Make sure activities included in the instructional process are in line with the available equipment and facilities.

8. If spotting is required for safe completion of activities, it should always be done by the instructor or by trained students.

9. If students are working independently at stations, distribute carefully constructed and written task cards to help eliminate unsafe practices.

10. Have a written emergency care plan posted in the gymnasium.

SITUATIONAL LEGAL EXAMPLES

The Need for a Curriculum and Lesson Plan

A former gymnast who is now an elementary school physical education teacher decides to teach her classes gymnastics. The school does not have a curriculum guide and the teacher does not write lesson plans. The teacher decides to have students try a headspring over a tumbling mat. A student is seriously hurt (severe neck injury that causes paralysis) and the parents of the student file a 1.5 million dollar lawsuit. What argument would you use to defend yourself in this situation? Would it help if you could say that gymnastics was part of the school curriculum? What if the plaintiff's lawyer brings in an expert witness who says the instructional sequence was inappropriate? Can you show your written lesson plan that delineates the proper instructional sequence based on what expert instructors recommend? Can you be an expert in every activity you teach or do you need to rely on other experts for the proper sequence of activities to teach?

Running for Punishment – The Right Choice?

Youngsters are participating in a physical education class and are unruly. They are talking when they shouldn't and generally not cooperating. The teacher, in a fit of controlled anger, tells two students to go run laps around a large field until they decide to behave. It is a hot fall day and after 15 minutes of running, one of the students falls and goes into convulsions on the far side (a third of a mile away) of the field. The teacher doesn't see the child go down until a student tells him about it. Is this malfeasance? Is running an acceptable choice for punishment? Were the weather conditions considered? Did the youth have some pre-existing health condition? Were the students under the watchful eye of the teacher or out of sight? Could you defend yourself in this situation?

EQUIPMENT AND FACILITIES

School responsibility for equipment and facilities is required for both noninstructional and class use.

Administration

The principal and the custodian should oversee the fields and playground equipment that are used for recess and outside activities.

Proper installation of equipment is critical. A reputable firm that guarantees its work should install equipment that must be hung or anchored.

The use of equipment that is appropriate for the growth and developmental levels of students can enhance safe participation in an activity.

Any piece of equipment or apparatus that has been left unsupervised is considered so attractive to children that they could not be expected to avoid it is called an ***attractive nuisance***. Teachers are liable if attractive nuisances are not removed from unsupervised areas.

Instructional Staff

The physical educator should make regular safety inspections of instructional facilities and equipment before children are allowed in the area. If corrective action is needed, the principal or other designated administrator should be notified in writing.

Give students instruction in the proper use of equipment and apparatus before they are issued to the students and used. Safety instruction should be included in the written lesson plan to ensure that all points are covered.

Equipment should be purchased on the basis of quality and safety as well as potential use. Many lawsuits occur because of unsafe equipment and apparatus.

THE SPORTS PROGRAM

Hiring qualified coaches for an elementary school sports program is a common problem. Incompetent individuals should be removed from coaching duties. When students are involved in extracurricular activities, the teachers/coaches are responsible for the safe conduct of activities.

Mismatched Opponents

A common error that gives rise to lawsuits is the mismatching of students on the basis of size and ability. Students need to be matched according to height, weight, and ability.

Waiver Forms

Participants in extracurricular activities should be required to sign a responsibility waiver form. The form should explain the risks involved in voluntary participation and discuss briefly the types of injuries that have occurred in the past during practice and competition.

Medical Examinations

Medical examinations are necessary for participants of extracurricular activities. Records should be kept on file.

Preseason Conditioning

Preseason conditioning should be undertaken in a systematic and progressive fashion.

Transportation of Students

Whenever students are transported, teachers are responsible for their safety both en route and during the activity.

SAFETY

It is estimated that over 70% of injuries in sport and related activities could be prevented through proper safety procedures. Some accidents occur despite precaution, and proper emergency procedure should be established to cope with any situation.

Learning to recognize high-risk situations is an important factor in preventing accidents.

Guidelines for Safety:

1. In-service sessions in safety should be administered by experienced and knowledgeable teachers.

2. Medical records should be reviewed at the start of the school year. Students with disabilities should be identified and noted within each class listing before the first instructional day.

3. Throughout the school year, safety orientations should be conducted with students.

4. Safety rules for specific units of instruction should be discussed with students at the onset of each unit.

5. If students are to serve as instructional aides, they should be trained for the duties they will assume.

6. Students in competitive situations should be matched by size, maturity, and ability. Proper instruction necessary for safe participation should occur prior to activity.

7. An inventory of equipment and apparatus should include a safety checklist.

8. When an injury occurs, it should be recorded and a report placed in the student's file.

9. Teachers need up-to-date first aid and CPR certification.

The Safety Committee

Safety should be publicized regularly throughout the school, and a mechanism should exist that allows students, parents, and teachers to voice concerns about unsafe conditions.

The Emergency Care Plan

Establish procedures for emergency care and notification of parents in case an injury occurs. This demonstrates a high standard of care for students. All physical education teachers should have first aid training and proper equipment at hand to administer it should an accident occur.

PERSONAL PROTECTION: MINIMIZING THE EFFECTS OF A LAWSUIT

In spite of proper care, injuries do occur and lawsuits may be initiated.

For further information, go to these websites:

http://www.kin.sfasu.edu/finkenberg/kin511/Liability.html
http://www.nils.com/rupps/comparative-negligence.htm
http://www.schoolsecurity.org

Liability Insurance

Teachers should protect themselves to counteract the effects of a lawsuit should one be initiated. One way is to purchase a liability insurance policy. They are available at a reasonable price from AAHPERD.

Record Keeping

Keep complete records of accidents. Write accident reports immediately after an injury.

Safety and Liability Checklists:

Supervision and Instruction

1. Are teachers adequately trained in all of the activities that they are teaching?

2. Do all teachers have evidence of a necessary level of first aid training?

3. When supervising, do personnel have access to a written plan of areas to be observed and responsibilities to be carried out?

4. Have students been warned of potential dangers and risks, and advised of rules and the reasons for the rules?

5. Are safety rules posted near areas of increased risk?

6. Are lesson plans written? Do they include proper instruction, sequence of activities, and safety? When a new activity is introduced, are safety precautions and instructions for correct skill performance always communicated to the class?

7. Are the activities taught in the program based on sound curriculum principles?

8. Do the methods of instruction recognize individual differences among student and are the necessary steps taken to meet the needs of all students, regardless of gender, ability, or disability?

9. Are substitute teachers given clear and comprehensive lesson plans so that they can maintain the scope and sequence of instruction?

10. Is the student evaluation plan based on actual performance and objective data rather than on favoritism or arbitrary and capricious standards?

11. Is appropriate dress required for students?

12. When necessary for safety, are students grouped according to ability level, size, or age?

13. Is the class left unsupervised for teacher visits to the office, lounge, or bathroom?

14. If students are used as teacher aides or to spot, are they given proper instruction and training?

Equipment and Facilities

1. Is all equipment inspected regularly and kept on a written form that is sent to an administrator?

2. Is a maintenance record kept? Are repairs made as needed?

3. Are "attractive nuisances" eliminated from the gymnasium and playing field?

4. Are specific safety rules posted on facilities and near equipment?

5. Are the fields and related equipment checked regularly and maintained?

Emergency Care

1. Is there a written procedure for emergency care?

2. Is a person properly trained in first aid available immediately following an accident?

3. Are emergency telephone numbers readily accessible?

4. Are telephone numbers of parents available?

5. Is an up-to-date first aid kit available?

6. Are health folders maintained regarding each child's restrictions?

7. Are health folders reviewed by instructors?

8. Are students participating in extracurricular activities required to have insurance?

9. Is there a plan utilizing paramedics for treating injuries?

10. Are accident reports filed promptly and analyzed regularly?

Transportation of Students

1. Have parents been informed that their students will be transported off campus?

2. Are detailed travel plans approved by the site administrator and kept on file?

3. Are school vehicles used?

4. Are drivers properly licensed?

5. If teachers or parents use their vehicles to transport students, are the students, driver, and car owner covered by insurance?

REFLECTION AND REVIEW QUESTIONS

How and Why

1. Should teachers have professional insurance?

2. How can effective classroom management help teachers avoid legal issues?

3. How can teachers protect themselves from lawsuits?

4. Why is a safety and liability checklist important?

Content Review

1. What is a tort?

2. Identify four major points that must be established to determine if a teacher is negligent. Also, discuss the importance of foreseeability.

3. List and explain types of negligence.

4. Describe the common defenses against negligence.

5. Discuss the importance of supervision and instruction when examining responsibility.

6. Who is responsible for equipment and facilities? Explain your answer.

7. What are some issues related to sports programs that often result in lawsuits?

8. Briefly describe several guidelines for safety in physical education.

9. Explain the importance of an emergency care plan and discuss the steps in the plan.

INSTRUCTIONAL FORMATS

The material in this chapter may be presented using the lecture style and the overhead transparencies/Power Point presentations providing students an overview of the chapter. The instructor may also use the Guided Discovery method of teaching to introduce and review the materials read by the students. In this style, the instructor asks questions guiding the students toward one answer. The instructor rephrases the questions until the students discover the answer to the question. The introduction/review of the chapter may be followed by cooperative learning assignments, which provide active learning and critical thinking activities for the student. In the cooperative learning groups, the students will discuss the materials listed on the Cooperative Learning Task Sheet and/ or other topics you may assign. Each group can become a "content expert" for sections of the Task Sheet. Oral summary reports of the group may be presented to the entire class covering all or part of the discussion items.

KEY TERMS

foreseeable dangers	act of omission	negligence
malfeasance	breach of duty	general supervision
liability	contributory negligence	attractive nuisance
misfeasance	proximate cause	specific supervision
tort	comparative negligence	mismatched opponents
nonfeasance	foreseeability	waiver form
duty	act of God	

DISCUSSION TOPICS

1. Invite an attorney or legal advisor to a school or school district in to your class to discuss the basic area of legal issues and liability as it applies to the public school teacher.

2. Invite an "expert witness" to discuss cases that he/she has been involved in and what areas they found to be appropriately or inappropriately handled by the teacher or administration.

3. Have students identify a possible hazardous sample situation and discuss the possible legal implications of the given teacher behavior.

4. Visit a local public or private elementary school. Walk through the facilities and make a safety inspection. Note any attractive nuisances and areas of concern. Report the findings to the school and in class.

5. Have students develop an emergency care plan for:

   - The physical education class setting.

   - The coaching/athletic team situation.

SAMPLE WRITTEN ASSIGNMENTS

1. Conduct a literature search in the library or Internet for case studies pertaining to lawsuits against physical educators. Turn in a typed report summarizing the case. Include your comments whether or not you agree with the final decision of the court.

2. Write safety rules that pertain to all activities to be posted in a hallway, locker room, or gym. Write the rules on poster board in a colorful, animated manner.

3. Create a sample public relations letter to be sent home to parents. The letter will explain the physical education program you will be teaching and the requirements of the course. Parents may review the document and sign it indicating understanding and agreement to support their youngster in following the rules.

4. Write a sample responsibility waiver for participation in extracurricular activities. Have a place for both the parent and student to sign and date the document.

ACTIVITY SESSION EXPERIENCES

Lead the students through the following activities:

- Teach a lesson demonstrating improper procedures that could have legal implications. Discuss the elements you purposely demonstrated in the model lesson.

- Have the students peer teach and demonstrate inappropriate behavior that could have legal implications. Discuss the behaviors that were inappropriate and how they could have been corrected.

COOPERATIVE LEARNING TASK SHEET

Chapter 9: Legal Liability, Supervision, and Safety

Directions: Your cooperative learning group will become the content experts by finding the answers to the items listed below. Discuss the following items with your group and be ready to report on one or all of them at the end of the class period.

1. Define tort, negligence, liability, malfeasance, misfeasance, nonfeasance, and other terms common to legal suits brought against educators. Give examples of each situation.

2. Discuss the several major points that must be established to determine negligence on the part of the teacher. Give an example of negligence in your discussions and state the type of negligence that was displayed.

3. List and explain the types of negligence described in this chapter.

4. Explain how to examine all activity areas, equipment, and facilities in general for possible hazards and sources of accidents. Identify several types of attractive nuisances.

5. State common defenses against negligence.

6. Describe several supervisory responsibilities expected of all teachers. Describe a situation that may demonstrate a teacher being liable for an accident.

7. List guidelines for the proper supervision of instruction, equipment, and facilities.

8. Describe several aspects of sport programs that often give rise to lawsuits.

9. Outline an emergency care plan. Write an emergency plan that could be implemented where you work.

10. Identify areas of risk that you could encounter when teaching. Create a set of safety rules that could be posted near areas of risk.

CHAPTER 10

Facilities, Equipment, and Supplies

SUMMARY

This chapter presents procedures associated with the design, purchase, maintenance, and construction of physical education facilities, equipment, and supplies. The term "equipment" refers to items that are more or less fixed in nature. Equipment has a relatively long life span, needs periodic safety checks, and requires planned purchasing. Supplies are nondurable items that have a limited period of use. When resources are limited, much equipment can be constructed. A comprehensive section on how to build equipment and supplies is offered.

STUDENT OUTCOMES

Upon completion of the reading of this chapter, the student will:

- Identify standards to follow in the construction of outdoor and indoor physical education facilities.

- Understand that safety is an essential consideration in facility design.

- List recommended equipment for indoor and outdoor physical education areas.

- Outline a systematic plan for the storage of physical education equipment and supplies.

- Describe procedures for the care and repair of physical education equipment and supplies.

- Be able to construct selected physical education equipment and supplies.

- Illustrate floor lines and markings that enhance management potential and increase ease of instruction.

- List essential equipment and supplies for physical education in the elementary school.

MAIN CONCEPTS

There are two categories for physical education facilities: outdoor and indoor. In addition, to meet the needs of students with disabilities, another indoor play area, separate from but close to the regular indoor facility is needed.

OUTDOOR FACILITIES

Standards for outdoor play areas call for a minimum of 10 acres for the school, with an additional acre for each 100 pupils in the maximum projected enrollment. Usually, outdoor space provides enough room for several classes to work simultaneously. For indoor spaces, a minimum of one indoor teaching station is needed for every eight classrooms.

Outdoor facilities should include field space for games, a track, hard-surfaced areas, apparatus areas, play courts, age-group specific play areas, covered play space, and a jogging trail.

Go to this website to review AAHPERD's recommended equipment and outdoor facilities:
http://www.aahperd.org/naspe/pdf_files/pos_papers/instructional_mat.pdf

The hardtop area should be marked for a variety of games, such as tetherball, volleyball, and basketball courts. Four-square courts, hopscotch layouts, and circles for games are examples of other markings that can be put on these surfaces.

Hard surfaces under outdoor climbing, sliding, swinging apparatus should be covered with protective material such as pine bark nuggets, shredded hardwood bark, shredded tires, sand or outdoor interlocking tiles for dense synthetic turf. The purpose of the protective material is to cushion the impact of falling.

> This Internet site describes equipment available to pad a surface in prevention of accidents related to falls off equipment:
> http://www.safeguardsurfacing.com

SAFETY ON THE PLAYGROUND

60 to 70% of injuries on the playground are caused when children fall from apparatus and strike a hard underlying surface. The type of surface under the equipment is a major factor affecting the severity of injuries associated with falls from apparatus. Safety rules are established in this chapter.

OUTDOOR APPARATUS AND EQUIPMENT

Outdoor equipment should support the emphasis on physical fitness. The following types of movement should be encouraged: climbing, swinging, elevating the body, running games, balancing, throwing, hopping, and jumping activities. Equipment should cover both the upper body and lower body development.

Equipment for Sport Skills

- Basketball goals

- Volleyball standards

- Softball backstops

- Tetherball courts

- Track and field equipment

  Go to these sites for information on purchasing equipment:
   http://www.flaghouse.com
   http://www.palossports.com

INDOOR FACILITIES

The gymnasium must be well planned for maximum use. A combination gymnasium-auditorium-cafeteria facility leaves much to be desired and creates more problems than it solves. Indoor teaching facilities work best if designed for physical education and sports activities. Lines should be painted on the floor for boundaries and games. Walls should have a smooth surface for a distance of 8 to 10 feet up from the floor. Ceilings should have acoustical treatment.

Lighting should be appropriate for playing, and fixtures should be recessed to prevent damage.

Windows should be placed high on the long sides of the gymnasium.

A motor-driven system of backboards and baskets should be installed.

Adequate storage space and organizational shelves and bins are necessary.

An area for students to work on lessons utilizing technology and media should be planned and provided.

EQUIPMENT AND SUPPLIES

Equipment refers to items of a fixed nature that last a long period of time.

Supplies are considered to be nondurable items that have a limited period of use.

> Go to this site for a source to purchase equipment and supplies:
> http://www.gophersport.com

PURCHASING POLICIES

The purchase of supplies and equipment involves careful study of need, price, quality, and material. The safety of the children who will use the equipment is a concern.

Physical education must be given an adequate budget to purchase equipment and supplies annually.

Sufficient equipment should be available so that children do not waste practice time waiting for a turn.

An accurate inventory of equipment should be undertaken at the start and end of each school year.

INDOOR EQUIPMENT

Tumbling mats are basic equipment for any physical education. At least eight should be present. Individual mats are also important to have. Other equipment that should be available to the teacher includes:

- A CD player, tape recorder, and record player with variable speed.

- Six balance beam benches.

- Climbing ropes, a chinning bar, and jumping boxes.

- Volleyball standards and a supply cart.

- A portable chalkboard.

- Additional equipment and basic supplies are described in depth in the chapter.

- A system for storing and repairing broken equipment.

- Procedures and guidelines for constructing equipment and supplies are described in detail in this chapter.

REFLECTION AND REVIEW QUESTIONS

How and Why

1. Do the school facilities in your area meet the standards of outdoor facilities?

2. How might teachers have to adapt because of the many "non-P.E." uses of the indoor facilities?

3. Why would "homemade" equipment be necessary for some schools? Identify equipment that can be made by teachers.

4. How can teachers ensure appropriate maintenance of equipment?

Content Review

1. Present several standards for outdoor facilities. Include comments regarding playgrounds.

2. Identify four pieces of each of outdoor equipment for upper body development, lower body development, and balance skills.

3. Discuss the standards for indoor facilities for physical education.

4. What is the difference between equipment and supplies? Provide examples of each.

5. List several pieces of equipment that are primarily used indoors.

6. Discuss the importance of purchasing policies, storage plans, and maintenance for equipment.

INSTRUCTIONAL FORMATS

The material in this chapter may be presented using the lecture style and the Power Point and overhead transparencies providing students an overview of the chapter. Slides and videotapes of a variety of equipment storage rooms, and purchased and "homemade" equipment can be shown to describe the chapter material. The introduction/review of the chapter may be followed by cooperative learning assignments, which provide active learning and critical thinking activities for the student. In the cooperative learning groups, the students will discuss the materials listed on the Cooperative Learning Task Sheet and/or other topics you may assign. Each group can become a "content expert" for sections of the Task Sheet. Oral summary reports of the group may be presented to the entire class covering all or part of the discussion items.

KEY TERMS

equipment	supplies	indoor facilities
outdoor facilities	outdoor apparatus	

DISCUSSION TOPICS

1. Describe the guidelines for school facility outdoor space versus the size of the schools in your neighborhood. What can be done to rectify the situation if there is a large discrepancy?

2. Visit schools in your neighborhood. Report the outdoor apparatus/facilities you observed and any indoor facilities you observed.

3. Decide on which types of equipment would be most appropriate to purchase and which ones school personnel, teachers, or parents might construct. Discuss the legal liability implications of the decision.

SAMPLE WRITTEN ASSIGNMENTS

1. Make a piece of physical education equipment described with construction specifications in the textbook.

2. Make a list of equipment/facilities recommendation you could offer the school you visited in item #2 above.

3. Gather equipment order forms from a variety of schools. Evaluate each form and create one that you feel is ideal.

4. Write an inclement weather, indoor, limited space lesson plan.

COOPERATIVE LEARNING TASK SHEET

Chapter 10: Facilities, Equipment, and Supplies

Directions: Your cooperative learning group will become the content experts by finding the answers to the items listed below. Discuss the following items with your group and be ready to report on one or all of them at the end of the class period.

1. Describe the standards listed in the chapter to follow for the construction of outdoor and indoor physical education facilities.

2. Describe safety items that are essential to consider in facility design. Discuss items that might need to be added to many facilities for safety purposes.

3. Identify four pieces each of outdoor equipment for upper body development, lower body development, and balance skills.

4. Create what you consider to be an ideal model for location of equipment in a teaching facility.

5. Diagram a systematic plan for the storage of physical education equipment and supplies.

6. Describe procedures and plans necessary for the care and repair of physical education equipment and supplies.

7. With your group, construct (or discuss the construction of) a selected piece of physical education equipment or supplies.

8. Illustrate floor lines and markings that enhance management potential and increase ease of instruction.

9. List essential equipment and supplies for physical education in the elementary school. State how many of each item you would like to have as the teacher of the students.

10. Discuss how you might obtain the equipment listed in item #9 above, if funding is inadequate.

11. Visit a school and make a list of current equipment and facilities. Make a list of items you would recommend for the school to obtain to improve their teaching situation.

CHAPTER 11

Integrating Academic Concepts

SUMMARY

In physical education integration involves incorporating concepts learned in the classroom into the physical education lesson to reinforce the concepts or teach them from a different perspective. Although research findings do not suggest that increasing the physical activity levels of children increases their academic performance, integrating academic content into physical education may help clarify concepts students are having difficulty with, or simply strengthen the child's understanding of the concept. In addition, by assisting classroom teachers in the form of integrating academic content, physical education teachers build goodwill with classroom teachers and improve the overall climate of the schools to that of cohesion with all teachers working toward the betterment of all students.

STUDENT OUTCOMES

Upon completion of the reading of this chapter, the student will:

- Define integration and explain its importance

- Understand the role of integration in physical education

- Explain the benefits and limitations of integration in physical education

- Discuss the relationship between physical activity and learning

- Present models of integration and discuss how they can be used

- Describe several activities that integrate either math, science, language arts, and/or social studies into a quality physical education lesson

MAIN CONCEPTS

During their time in school students are often taught concepts that combine two seemingly unrelated academic areas. Physical education offers an outstanding setting for integration with minimal impact on the integrity of the physical education curriculum. For instance, teachers often have students time their stretching exercises by counting from 1 to 10. To integrate a foreign language, students can count in a different language; to integrate spelling students can spell out vocabulary words for the week; and to integrate math, skip count by 4s. Physical education instruction should not be centered on academic integration. Academic integration is a secondary outcome for physical education as contrasted to the six primary NASPE outcomes discussed in Chapter 1. It is important to remember that physical education is the only area in the school where youngsters are taught how to care for the physical side of their body. Integrate academic concepts when possible, but not at the expense of physical activity and health for students. When integrating academic concepts, a series of instructional activities are planned to assure physical education outcomes are reached.

WHY INTEGRATE ACADEMIC CONCEPTS?

Education is always seeking strategies and research to support methods for effectively teaching concepts. One such method is integration. Although there are relatively few studies to support the integration of academic content into physical education as an effective strategy for teaching, many experts believe this practice should be promoted.

Related to the need for research on the effectiveness of integration, is research on the impact of physical activity on learning. Researchers in this area want to know if physically active children learn better and perform better academically than physically inactive children. In a statistical review of numerous studies on children, Sibley and Etnier (2003) concluded that physical activity and cognition are positively related and physical activity may aid in cognitive development. Tomporowski (2003) suggests that physical activity may improve cognitive performance. This paper also suggested that behavior improves following activity bouts. Similarly, Pellegrini, Huberty, & Jones (1995) found that recess spread throughout the day, thus allowing short and regular bouts of physical activity, may help children's attention and behavior.

If the research is not definitive, why incorporate academic concepts into the physical education lesson? In short, integration serves as a marketing tool for physical educators. In an area of accountability where classroom teachers are under great pressure to increase academic achievement by increasing high-stakes test scores, physical educators can build goodwill with classroom teachers by offering to supplement the classroom content.

Integration in physical education has benefits and limitations. The benefits include building goodwill in the school, helping students who are kinesthetic learners, teaching content in a new setting through a different method, showing physical educators are educators too, and increasing the activity level of students when classroom teachers integrate physical activity into their instruction. The limitations most often cited are: finding the time to develop the lessons, planning for integration that does not sacrifice the physical education lesson, and feeling uncomfortable teaching outside an area of expertise.

TYPES OF INTEGRATION

Several models can be used when planning integration activities. These models range from the physical education teacher working alone, to a group of teachers working together to develop learning experiences in a variety of settings.

For the partner model, the physical education teacher collaborates with a classroom teacher. This collaboration could be as simple as the physical education teacher asking the classroom teacher for the vocabulary words for the week. The model can be as complex as two teachers developing a yearly calendar that has similar concepts taught during the same time.

Group collaboration may involve a single classroom teacher and a physical education teacher, but it is more likely to involve a group of classroom teachers from a common grade level. In this model, a considerable amount of planning is involved and it usually centers on a theme.

HOW TO INTEGRATE ACADEMIC CONTENT

Integrating academic content must be carefully and thoughtfully planned to ensure the activity is a quality learning experience and to maintain the integrity of the physical education curriculum.

Steps to follow:

1. Decide on the integration model

2. Ask about students who could use additional support

3. Ask teachers what concepts they will be teaching

4. Ask how concepts are being taught

5. Show classroom teachers what is being taught during physical education

6. Reflect

    a. Did the integration activity sacrifice any of the activity planned for the physical education lesson?

    b. Could I have integrated the concept with less interference?

    c. Did the students understand the academic content?

    d. How could I change the integrated activity to make it more effective?

    e. Would the integrated concept fit better in another part of the lesson or in another lesson?

ACADEMIC INTEGRATION ACTIVITIES

This chapter presents ideas for integrating academic concepts through physical education instruction. All of the activities are designed to be implemented with *Dynamic Physical Education Curriculum Guide* (2007) lessons. The areas of ideas presented in the chapter are:

*   Math

*   Language Arts

*   Science

*   Social studies

REFLECTION AND REVIEW QUESTIONS

How and Why?

1. Why should physical education teachers integrate academic content into their lessons?

2. How can physical education teachers go about integrating academic content?

3. Why might physical education teachers be apprehensive about integrating academic content?

Content Review

1. Discuss the models of integration available to physical educators.

2. Explain some of the issues a physical educator should consider when deciding whether to integrate academic content.

3. List and discuss strategies teachers should use when integrating in physical education.

4. Discuss several ways to integrate math into physical education.

5. Explain three strategies or activities that can be used to integrate science into physical education.

6. Provide four ways to integrate language arts into physical education.

7. Describe several methods of integrating social studies into physical education.

INSTRUCTIONAL FORMATS

This chapter should be presented with lecture, Power Point slides, guided discovery, and activity sessions. A videotape, if available, could be shown demonstrating activities that integrate academic material into physical education and vice versa.

KEY TERMS

integration   partner model
individual model

SAMPLE WRITTEN ASSIGNMENTS

1. Write a sample lesson plan to be conducted in a limited space setting, integrating math into physical education.

2. Interview a physical education specialist and describe the activities the individual interviewed has successfully implemented integrating physical education into the academic setting.

3. Write lesson plan ideas on a specific topic that you could share with a classroom teacher to integrate physical education topics into the curriculum.

ACTIVITY SESSION EXPERIENCES

Lead the students through the following activities:

- An activity integrating math concepts into physical education.

- A lesson integrating science concepts into physical education.

COOPERATIVE LEARNING TASK SHEET

Chapter 11: Integrating Academic Concepts

Directions: Your cooperative learning group will become the content experts by finding the answers to the items listed below. Discuss the following items with your group and be ready to report on one or all of them at the end of the class period.

1. Discuss why physical education teachers should integrate academic content into their lessons.

2. Discuss the ways in which physical education teachers go about integrating academic content into lessons.

3. Why might physical education teachers be apprehensive about integrating academic content? Discuss this topic within your group.

4. Explain some of the issues a physical educator should consider when deciding whether to integrate academic content.

5. List and discuss strategies teachers should use when integrating in physical education.

6. Discuss several ways to integrate math into physical education.

7. Explain three strategies or activities that can be used to integrate science into physical education.

8. Provide four ways to integrate language arts into physical education.

9. Describe several methods of integrating social studies into physical education.

10. Write a lesson plan integrating history into physical education.

CHAPTER 12

Promoting and Monitoring Physical Activity

SUMMARY

This chapter explains the differences between physical fitness and physical activity. It also explains how different students will choose one outcome over the other based on their personal needs. The physical activity pyramid gives students a concrete explanation of how they should plan for and incorporate physical activity into their daily lifestyles. The focus is on adding at least 60 minutes or more of moderate to vigorous activity to their daily routine.

Pedometers are an important tool for promoting adequate amounts of physical activity. Pedometers are accurate when students learn how to find the best placement point on their body. Goal setting can be easily done using pedometers that measure either steps or activity time. Students can set personal goals that are within reach to assure continued motivation.

Walking is the "real" lifestyle activity. It can be done anywhere with a minimum of equipment and the vast majority of students are capable of walking for activity. Walking is also an effective tool for teaching students to deal with weight management issues. A school-wide walking program can be implemented to help create an "active school."

STUDENT OUTCOMES

Upon completion of the reading of this chapter, the student will:

- Describe why activity is just as effective as fitness for ensuring health.

- Know the different parts of the physical activity pyramid and why each level is important for optimal health.

- Understand how to identify moderate to vigorous physical activity.

- Know how to incorporate pedometers into physical education lessons.

- Help students learn where to place the pedometer for highest accuracy.

- Help students design personal goals for activity.

- Understand why pedometers can be used to measure program activity outcomes.

- Express the role of physical activity in maintaining proper body weight.

- Implement a school-wide walking program.

MAIN CONCEPTS

Physical activity or physical fitness? Which of these outcomes should physical education focus upon in the quest to better serve students? The answer is that it depends on each student's needs and desire. In the 1950s there was a focus on fitness testing. Fifty years later, when teachers are asked to show a measure of accountability for their program, the majority will fall back on fitness testing. Sadly, this approach to children's health has been a failure. Today's youth are showing the same deficits in personal health as their parents did years earlier. The percentage of youth who are overweight has more than tripled in the past 30 years (USDHHS, 2002) and fitness levels show little if any improvement. Students who are overweight, unskilled, or not predisposed to physical fitness do all they can to avoid physical education classes when they are old enough to make personal choices. It is becoming clear that physical education is not meeting the needs of those who need it most – the overweight, the unskilled, and the inactive. Could it be that fitness testing youth in front of others twice a year and labeling those who don't score adequately as unfit has undermined their desire to be active? Is it possible that schools are failing the youth we want to help the most?

It is clear that students have different needs and are driven by different personal goals. Some students want to develop their personal fitness to the highest level possible in order to improve their skill performance (skill-related fitness). Others want to improve their appearance. However, the majority of students wants to enjoy moderate to vigorous activity and are not concerned about achieving a high fitness level. They will probably mature into adults who want to be active but are motivated by appearance and health motives rather than performance. They will be better served by developing a lifestyle that includes physical activity on a daily basis.

Physical activity is defined as bodily movement that is produced by the contraction of skeletal muscle and that substantially increases energy expenditure (NASPE, 2004). Physical activity is an umbrella term that looks at the process of moving.

Physical fitness is a set of attributes that people have or achieve relating to their ability to perform physical activity (USDHHS, 1996). Whereas physical activity is a process-oriented outcome related to behavior and lifestyles, physical fitness is a product outcome with an emphasis on achieving a higher state of being. Physical fitness has a strong genetic component that regulates the level of fitness that can be achieved.

Most students who are non-athletes are not interested in the product of physical fitness but are receptive to learning to enjoy their bodies through lifestyle physical activities.

The National Association for Sport and Physical Education (NASPE) has developed activity guidelines for elementary school children (2004). The guidelines call for 60 minutes or more of physical activity (total volume) for children and youth. Adult recommendations (30 minutes a day) are based primarily on the energy expenditure necessary to reduce risk of chronic disease associated with what is commonly called aerobic or cardiovascular fitness.

Guidelines for Youth Physical Activity

1. Children should accumulate at least 60 minutes, and up to several hours, of age-appropriate physical activity on all, or most days of the week. This daily accumulation should include moderate and vigorous physical activity of which the majority is intermittent in nature. It is recommended that an accumulation of steps per day be 11,000 and 13,000 steps for girls and boys, respectively.

2. Children should participate in several bouts of physical activity lasting 15 minutes or more each day. Much of a child's daily activity will be in short bursts and accumulated throughout the waking hours.

3. Children should participate each day in a variety of age-appropriate physical activities designed to achieve optimal health, wellness, fitness, and performance benefits. See the Physical Activity Pyramid for suggested guidelines.

4. Extended periods (periods of two hours or more) of inactivity are discouraged for children, especially during the daytime hours. This includes time watching TV, playing video games, and working on the computer. Research suggests that people (including children) who watch excessive amounts of

television, play computer games, work on computers for extended periods of time, or engage in other low-energy expenditure activities will likely fail to meet guidelines 1, 2, and 3. There is evidence to show that reducing the average amount of daily sedentary time is effective in counteracting weight problems in children (Epstein, 1995).

Moderate to Vigorous Activity

METS (resting metabolic rate) are used to quantify activity. One MET equals calories expended at rest (resting metabolism). Two METS is activity that is twice as intense. Three METS requires three times the energy as compared to being at rest, and so on. Activities of three METS or less are considered to be light activities. Examples are strolling (slow walking), slow stationary cycling, stretching, golf with a motorized cart, fishing (sitting), bowling, carpet sweeping, and riding a mower (Pate et al., 1995). Moderate activities would range in the area of 4 to 6 METS. Examples of moderate activities would be shoveling, sweeping, and walking at 2.5 mph. Activity that expends more than six times the energy expended at rest (more than six METS) is considered to be vigorous (high intensity) in nature. Examples of activity at this level are brisk walking, running, stair climbing, and rope jumping.

Moderate to vigorous activity of all types is beneficial to students and adults because it contributes to health.

The lifestyle activity prescription for children (see Table 12.2) covers a broad range of moderate to vigorous activities, including those that can be done as part of work or normal daily routines as well as during free time. Frequency, intensity, and time are used to define lifestyle activity but they differ from physical fitness prescription, which requires high intensity activity (training zone heart rates).

THE PHYSICAL ACTIVITY PYRAMID

The Physical Activity Pyramid (Figure 12.1) is a visual approach to a model for activity prescription for good health. The pyramid depiction helps students understand how much and what type of activity they need.

The primary reason for arranging the pyramid into six categories and four levels is associated with the benefits that result from each activity type. Those activities having broad general health and wellness benefits for large numbers of people are placed at the base of the pyramid.

Lifestyle Activities are placed at the base of the pyramid because scientific evidence indicates that inactive people who begin regular exercise have the most to gain. The Surgeon General's Report on Physical Activity and Health (USDHHS, 1996) points out that our nation could reap great health and economic benefits if the 24 percent of the U.S. population who are totally sedentary would begin modest amounts of regular physical activity.

Level 2 contains more vigorous activities. Scientific reports suggest that for those people who are already active, active aerobics and active sports and recreation provide health and fitness benefits in addition to those provided by regular lifestyle activity. For those with little free time, regular activity from Level 2 can substitute for lifestyle activity, though participation at both levels is encouraged.

Level 3 exercises are designed to build flexibility and muscle fitness. Performing exercises of either type builds physical fitness that contributes to improved performance in various jobs and in active sports. Muscle fitness has also been associated with reduced risk of osteoporosis (Shaw and Snow-Harter, 1995), and both types of exercises when prescribed and performed appropriately are thought to contribute to reduced rate of injury and less risk of back problems (Plowman, 1993).

Activity Recommendations for Children

Level 1: Lifestyle Physical Activities

Lifestyle activities for this age include active play and games involving the large muscles of the body. Climbing, tumbling, and other activities that require lifting the body or relocating the body in space are desirable activities when they can be performed safely.

Level 2: Active Aerobics

The second level of the pyramid includes active aerobic activities. Aerobic activities are those performed at a pace for which the body can supply adequate oxygen to meet the demands of the activity. Examples of popular moderate-to-vigorous active aerobics are jogging, brisk walking, moderate-to-vigorous swimming, and biking. Participation in some aerobic activities is appropriate if children are not expected to participate in them continuously for long duration. More appropriate are intermittent aerobic activities such as recreational swimming, family walking, or aerobic activities that are included in the lifestyle activity category such as walking or riding a bicycle to school or in the neighborhood.

Level 2: Active Sports and Recreational Activities

Some examples of active sports are basketball, tennis, soccer, and hiking. Like active aerobics, this type of activity is typically more vigorous than lifestyle physical activity. Sports often involve vigorous bursts of activity with brief rest periods.

When young children choose to be involved in sports it is appropriate that sports be modified to meet their developmental level. In general, active sports should not comprise the major proportion of activity for Developmental Levels I and II children. It is important that children at Developmental Levels I and II have time to learn basic skills that are prerequisite to performing sports and other recreational activities such as catching, throwing, walking, jumping, running, and striking objects.

Developmental Level III youngsters are often involved in active sports. For this reason a greater amount of time may be dedicated to this type of activity. Lead-up games and emphasis on skill development are necessary to make the activities suitable for this age. An emphasis on conditioning for sport is unnecessary for this age group.

Level 3: Flexibility Exercises

Flexibility exercises are included at the third level of the pyramid. They are referred to as exercises because they are done specifically to build the part of physical fitness called flexibility. Flexibility is the ability to use joints through a full range of motion as a result of having long muscles and elastic connective tissues. Stretching exercises are best to increase flexibility.

More time is spent teaching and performing flexibility exercises at Developmental Level III. Children, especially boys, begin to lose flexibility at this age. Some regular stretching is appropriate either in the form of age appropriate flexibility exercises or activities that promote flexibility such as tumbling and stunts.

Level 3: Strength and Muscular Development Exercises

Exercises and physical activities designed and performed specifically to increase strength (the amount of weight one can lift) and muscular endurance (the ability to persist in muscular effort) are included in this category. Modified fitness activities are an excellent way to help youngsters learn about exercises in a positive, non-failing manner. Formal resistance training is usually not recommended, particularly in a group setting.

Youngsters at Developmental Level III participate in strength development activities that require them to move and lift their body weight. Participation in active play and games and sports that require muscle overload are desirable for these youngsters. Exercises using body weight are appropriate when alternative exercises are offered to allow all children to be successful. It is important to show children the relevance of these exercises. Formal exercises and conditioning programs as part of youth sports or other activity programs should not typically constitute a major part of activity periods, though highly motivated children may benefit from exposure to these activities.

Level 4: Rest and Inactivity

At the top of the pyramid are rest and inactivity. Some types of inactivity are not necessarily detrimental to health. For example, adequate amounts of sleep are needed and after vigorous exercise rest is important.

USING PEDOMETERS TO MONITOR PHYSICAL ACTIVITY

Pedometers measure the daily amount of physical activity a person accumulates. They do not measure the intensity of physical activity, only the quantity of physical activity. Pedometers measure the number of steps a person takes. Counting steps is an effective way to measure how active a person is throughout the day, even though pedometers can't measure all types of activity. Using pedometers to measure the physical activity levels of youth is now an accepted instructional and research methodology (Beighle, Pangrazi, & Vincent, 2001; Crouter et al., 2003; Kilanowski, et al. 1999).

Walk4Life pedometers have a function that measures activity time as well as steps. Every time a person moves, the pedometer starts accumulating time. When the person stops moving, the timing function stops. This function shows the total hours and minutes of exercise time accumulated throughout the day in addition to the steps completed.

For more information on Walk4Life pedometers, go to this site:
 www.walk4life.com

The Accuracy of Pedometers

Activity recommendations in terms of daily minutes of physical activity for youth (NASPE, 2004) and adults (USDHHS, 2000) have created an interest in accurately measuring personal movement. With children, some type of objective measuring tool is helpful for documenting activity levels because it avoids dependency on recollection and reading of questionnaires. The pedometer is an objective way to measure physical activity and its validity and reliability have been studied by a number of researchers.

A limitation of pedometers is that they are less accurate when people move slowly (less than 4 km/h) or walk with an uneven gait (Crouter et al., 2003). Pedometers depend on a fairly consistent up and down motion with each step, and an uneven or slow gait may not create enough movement for the pedometer to measure. Pedometers overestimate distance covered at slower speeds and underestimate actual distance at higher speeds.

Teaching Students about Pedometer Placement and Accuracy

Pedometers are designed to be worn at the waistline directly in line with the midpoint of the front of thigh and kneecap. The first thing that students need to be taught about pedometers is a placement point where the pedometer measures most accurately.

Guidelines for Pedometer Placement

1. Place the pedometer on the waistband in line with the midpoint of the thigh and kneecap. The pedometer must be parallel with the body and upright. Teach students to open their pedometer (without removing it from the waist band) and reset it to zero steps. Have them walk at their normal cadence while counting the number of steps they are taking. Ask them to stop immediately when 30 steps are reached. If the step count is within plus or minus two steps of 30, this placement is an accurate location for the pedometer.

2. This step involves moving the pedometer on the waistband until an accurate position is found. Adjust the pedometer so it is positioned slightly closer to the belly button or the hip. Open the pedometer, clear it, and take 30 steps as described in step 1. Again, if the step count is within plus or minus two steps of 30, this new placement is accurate and they should always position the pedometer in that position. If not, try another placement and repeat the step test.

3. If it is difficult to find an accurate measuring position, consider using a specially made *Walk4Life* Velcro belt for attachment to assure that the pedometer is maintained in an upright position.

Pedometers and Personal Goal Setting

A standard for youth that is often mentioned is 11,000 steps/day for girls and 13,000 steps/day for boys. This standard is used for the Presidential Active Lifestyle Award (PCPFS, 2005), which is awarded to students who meet these daily standards over a six-week period.

The problem with a single standard goal is that it doesn't take into account the substantial individual differences between people of all ages and gender. "One size fits all" doesn't work with fitness goals.

The approach recommended in this textbook is the baseline and goal-setting technique (Pangrazi, Beighle, & Sidman, 2003). This method requires that individuals identify their average daily activity (baseline) level. For preadolescent youth, 4 days of monitoring step counts (or activity time) are required to establish an average activity level (Trost, et al., 2000). Baseline data can be entered in a chart demonstrated in this chapter.

After the baseline level of activity has been established, each individual has a reference point for setting a personal goal. The personal goal is established by taking the baseline activity level and adding 10 percent more steps (or time in whole minutes) to that level.

A third way to establish step levels for youth is to define a healthy activity zone (HAZ). In this method, there is not one standard that each youngster has to reach. This approach has been utilized by the Fitnessgram (2004) for specifying a range of scores (the healthy fitness zone) where students should score on fitness test items. Some of the Fitnessgram test items (e.g., PACER run and skinfolds) are based on health-related criteria, while others are based on improvement due to training. Applied to physical activity, a range of steps (or activity time) can be established for each gender that would serve as the HAZ. This method requires further research, but may be an acceptable way to establish a range of scores that can apply to the vast majority of children and adults. It is also possible that a combination of methods such as baseline/goal setting and HAZ standards will ultimately be the best solution.

Using Pedometers in a Class Setting

A set of 36 pedometers will cost in the area of $400.00 to $800.00 depending on the type and accompanying materials. Many schools have been successful in asking parent-teacher groups to fund pedometers.

Using pedometers in physical education requires teaching proper protocol to students. Here is an example of procedures that seem to minimize pedometer handling time, resulting in maximum instructional time. Number each of the pedometers and store no more than six pedometers in each container. Make sure you have the same number of pedometers in each container so it is easy to see when a pedometer (and which student has it) is missing.

Students should be taught to enter the teaching area, pick up their assigned pedometer, and put it on while moving around the area. When all students have their pedometers on, freeze the class and have students reset their pedometers. Class then begins, as usual. At the end of class, students remove their pedometers, put them back in the proper container, record their steps or activity time on the sheet next to their container, and prepare to exit class.

Program Ideas for Integrating Pedometer Lessons

- **Moving across the State or U.S.:** Students accumulate steps and measure their stride length so they can do the math to see how far they have traveled on a state or U.S. map. As they reach different checkpoints, class discussions about foods, art, and various cultural sites can be conducted.

  To view an interesting website *WalkSmart! Active Schools*, go to the following website:
  http://www.walksmartactiveschools.com/default_pages/default_home.aspx

- **Active or Inactive:** Students can participate in a variety of physical education lessons and try to predict which lessons are high-activity and which are low-activity. An enjoyable related activity is to try and guess how many steps they will take in the activity.

- **A Safe Walk to School:** Walking to school can add 1,000 to 2,000 steps each to a student's activity level. This is a good activity for teaching students about safe walks, walks that increase the distance (and steps), and walks that avoid traffic.

- **School Steps Contest:** This is a school-wide contest with all classes participating. The step counts of all students in each class, including the teacher, are added and then divided by the number of students. Finding the average number of steps for the entire class makes this a group competition and avoids putting down students who are less active.

- **Presidential Active Lifestyle Award (PALA):** The President's Council on Physical Fitness and Sports sponsors the Presidential Active Lifestyle Award (PALA). If students accumulate 60 minutes or 11,000 (girls) to 13,000 steps (boys) for most of the days of the week for 6 weeks, they can earn the PALA.

  For more information on the PALA, go to:
  http://www.presidentschallenge.org/index.aspx

- **Estimation or How Many Steps Does it Take?** Measure off a distance that is exactly one-eighth or one-fourth mile in length. Students put on their pedometers, clear them at the starting line and walk at a normal pace to the end of the distance. Depending on whether they walked a one-eighth or one-fourth mile distance, they multiply the number of steps they accumulated by 8 or 4. That is the number of steps it takes them to walk one mile.

Pedometers and Program Accountability

A common issue for physical education teachers is to find criteria for which they can be held accountable. Teachers have chosen fitness or skill development as outcomes they are willing to use as a measure of their success. Such tests may not be a good choice because the increase in obesity among today's youth decreases fitness test performance. The ability to respond to training is strongly affected by genetics (Bouchard, 1999) with some individuals showing little or no improvement with training. Therefore, fitness testing for accountability is not a good criterion.

Skill development is an important assessment outcome for physical education. However, a large part of skill performance is genetically endowed, much in the same way that some students are born better artists or musicians. Additionally, physical skills can be difficult to evaluate due to time constraints and the overall numbers of students seen by the physical education teacher. Perfection is never reached in the performance of physical skills. Why not base program success on an average school increase in physical activity? What could be more important for health and wellness than increasing the amount of activity students accumulate on a daily basis? All students can move and be physically active in settings both in and out of school. Most parents would be delighted if their youngsters were taught to live an active lifestyle.

Pedometers can be used to evaluate the baseline activity levels of students at or near the start of the school year. This can be followed up with regular monitoring a number of times throughout the school year. Goals for increasing daily physical activity can be increased by all students regardless of genetic predisposition. A program designed to increase the amount of physical activity students accumulate on a daily basis makes a valuable contribution to all students in the school environment.

WALKING: THE "REAL" LIFETIME ACTIVITY

Walking is an activity that almost all people can do. In fact, it forms the basis for all lifestyle physical activity. Therefore, a strong focus of physical education should be to teach the joy of moving and walking and trying to accumulate physical activity.

Benefits of Walking

- Weight management. When combined with a healthy approach to eating, walking is a lifetime approach to weight management.

- Blood pressure management. Physical activity strengthens the heart and makes it more efficient so it pumps more blood with less effort.

- Boosting high-density lipoproteins (HDL), which help reduce low-density lipoproteins (LDL) or "destructive cholesterol." LDL increases plaque buildup in the arteries, which is a major cause of heart attacks.

- Reducing the risk of type 2 diabetes, which is increasing at an alarming rate among young people. People at high risk of diabetes cut their risk in half by combining walking with lower fat intake and 5% to 7% decrease in weight.

- Decreasing the risk of heart attack. Three hours of walking a week was associated with a 30% to 40% lower risk of heart disease in women.

- Walking has the advantage of not requiring any special equipment and of having a low injury rate. Walking, probably more than any other activity, will be done by students when they reach adulthood.

For Maximum Benefit When Walking, Remember:

1. Walk at a brisk pace with a comfortable stride and a good arm swing.

2. Students' walking pace should allow them to carry on a conversation without difficulty.

3. The walking program in school is a great place to coordinate pedometer use. Students can begin to see how many steps they typically gather in a specified amount of time.

Walking and Weight Management

Currently, it is estimated that nearly 16 percent of youth are overweight. Another 15 percent are "at risk" for becoming overweight (Beals, 2003). It is estimated that 70 percent of overweight adolescents will grow to be overweight adults making it important that activity be increased in the elementary school years. Unfortunately, energy expenditure through physical activity has decreased over the last 10 years while energy intake has increased. The super-sized fast-food meals and high fat content foods have certainly contributed to this increase in caloric consumption.

Walking is probably the activity of choice for overweight students. It is easy on the joints, doesn't overly stress the cardiovascular system, and is not painful to perform. The old adage, "no pain, no gain" makes absolutely no sense for overweight students. Many of these students have already been turned off to physical activity because of negative past experiences.

A question often asked is "does walking really make a difference in weight management?" The answer is "yes, it makes a difference, but, of course it is always possible to outeat the number of calories expended." Consider the following. The number of calories burned during exercise depends on a number of factors, among them the speed of walking and body size being two of the more important. Table 12.3 shows the number of calories burned during a 30-minute walk based on body weight.

Recently, walking (or trekking) poles (similar to ski poles) have come in vogue and they may be a boon for Developmental Level III students who are overweight. They have been used for years in the Scandinavian countries and research has shown that 25 to 30 percent more calories are burned as compared to walking without poles (Church, et al., 2002). The poles increase heart rate by 10-15 beats and put more than 90% of the body's muscle mass to work. Additionally, they help absorb some of the impact on the knees and ankles, which results in an increase in upper body strength and decrease in hip, knee, and foot injures. Adding walking poles to a physical education program is another way to motivate students, reduce joint injuries in overweight children, and realize greater results from their walking.

Go to the following websites to learn about walking/trekking poles:
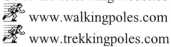 www.walkingpoles.com
www.trekkingpoles.com

Implementing a School Walking Program

When initiating a program, the walking should be done where all students are in view of the teacher. If approved by the administration, walking courses around the school neighborhood can be established so students become familiar with many different walking paths and the time required to complete the circuit. All walking paths should be designed and mapped by the teacher prior to allowing students to follow them.

Safety guidelines to consider are:

1. Always use the sidewalk. If a sidewalk is not available, walk on the left side of the roadway facing traffic.

2. Stipulate that students must walk with another person or in a small group. If someone is injured or needs help, one member of the group can return to the school for help.

3. Running from aggressive dogs only makes the problem worse. Teach students to stop, face them, and give them a stern, "no!"

4. Have students sign out, listing which path they are walking or assign the group the path. If someone is missing, it will be much easier to locate such students.

5. If students have a serious health problem, they should be cleared by the school nurse. Also, they should be required to wear a "medical tag" in case of an accident requiring emergency care.

6. Encourage parents to purchase walking or running shoes for their youngsters with reflective tape built into them.

7. Warm up students before the walk and teach them to cool down when they have finished walking. Walk a short distance, stop and stretch the arms, legs, and back (see Chapter 13 for suggested stretches). When you have finished your walk, stretch one more time.

8. Drink plenty of water whether it is cold or hot. Drink eight ounces of water 15 minutes before the walk. If it is hot and dry, drink six ounces every 15 to 20 minutes during the walk. At the end of the walk, drink another 8 to 16 ounces of water.

9. In cold weather, teach students about layering clothing so a layer can be removed if it gets too hot. Layers of lighter clothing are much more useful than one heavy layer. Wear a hat, gloves, and scarf if necessary. In hot weather, wear loose, light-colored clothing, a hat, and sunglasses. Remember to put on sunscreen regardless of heat or cold; ultraviolet sunrays will quickly cause sun damage.

Suggested Walking Activities

1. "I Spy." Students take a scorecard with them on their walk. The card has a challenge on it. For example, "Identify as many different makes of cars as possible." Or, "List as many different birds and animals as you can." Different cards can be designed to create varying challenges. When the students complete their walks, the items they have identified can be discussed.

2. "Mixed-Up Walks." Add some variations for limited amounts of time (e.g., backwards; sideways slide with a left shoulder lead; then a right shoulder lead; skipping; galloping). For example, start with a backwards walk for one minute, then regular walk for one minute, then skip for one minute, then regular walking, and so on. Tasks assigned can be different types of movement tasks or varying challenges like "Complete your walk by making 10 left turns on your route." The location of where students made a turn must be documented.

3. "Interval Walk." Set up a walking circuit with stretching and strength activities at each corner of the football field. For example, walk a lap, then do a standing stretch for 30 seconds, then walk half of a lap to a sitting stretch, then walk another lap, then do some abdominal activities, then walk to a push-up station.

4. "Cross-Country Walking." Set up a cross-country walking race with teams in the class. Have a map set up for the walking course so there is a nice variety of walking areas. Students try to walk as fast as possible and receive a number at the finish line. The team with the lowest number of points is the winner. This is a competitive activity, but it can be approached in a positive and fun manner for students' efforts to walk fast.

5. "Walking Golf." Set up a walking "golf" tournament with hula-hoops for holes and a tennis ball to be thrown by each student. Set the course up around your teaching space with cones for the tees and hoops for the holes. Students throw the ball and then walk with their group to the hoop. Students use a scorecard to keep track of the number of throws for each hole.

6. "Treasure Hunt." Set up a walking course with a set of clues to follow to 10 sites. At the sites you can tape a set of words that can be found and later arranged in a particular order to come up with a popular saying or jingle. Examples of the clues to follow could include a place for extra points on the south side; a place for H_2O; fans sit here on the west side; long jumpers take off here; stand under this for the score of the game; a place for trash.

7. "Poker Walk." Set out several decks of cards at various locations around the teaching area. Students walk to the areas and pick up one card without looking at the card. They walk to as many areas as possible within a time limit and then add up the points. Have a prize for high- and low-point totals and then change the rules each time. Set it up so anyone can win by just walking to the card areas, picking up the card, and then adding up the points at the end of the time limit.

8. "Know your Community." Have the class take different walks and identify different types of businesses and professional offices along their route. Different challenges can be listed asking students to find different businesses or locations.

9. "Weekly Walking Calendar." Each week students can be given a 5-day calendar that stipulates different types of things to do on their walk. For example, Monday: Walk with a friend; Tuesday: Walk with walking poles; Wednesday: Walk, stop, and stretch periodically; Thursday: Walk 15 minutes in one direction and return to the starting spot by retracing your path; Friday: Walk and use a pedometer to count your steps.

10. "Learn about Your Friend." Give students a series of questions on a card that will help them get to know a friend better. The goal is to walk and discover new things about a friend while moving.

11. "Off-Campus Walks." Students can gain extra credit by taking walks outside of the school day. This can be an excellent opportunity to use pedometers to track their walks. They can record their steps and activity time and report back to class on both measures.

Go to the following websites for more walking program ideas:
www.americaonthemove.org
www.steptracker.com

INSTRUCTIONAL FORMATS

The material in this chapter may be presented using the lecture style and the Power Point/overhead transparencies providing students an overview of the chapter. The instructor may also use the Guided Discovery method of teaching to introduce and review the materials read by the students. In this style, the instructor asks questions guiding the students toward one answer. The instructor rephrases the questions until the students discover the answer to the question. The introduction/review of the chapter may be followed by cooperative learning assignments that provide active learning and critical thinking activities for the student. In the cooperative learning groups, the students will discuss the materials listed on the Cooperative Learning Task Sheet (CLTS) and/or other topics you may assign. Each group can become a "content expert" for sections of the CLTS. Oral summary reports of the group may be presented to the entire class covering all or part of the discussion items. You may want to distribute the CLTS the class before the discussion or post them on a website for students to preview. Some of the items may require reviewing a website prior to completion.

KEY TERMS

high-density lipoproteins	active aerobics	MET
low-density lipoproteins	healthy activity zone	Fitnessgram
pedometer	lifestyle activities	Physical Activity Pyramid

REFLECTION AND REVIEW QUESTIONS

How and Why?

1. What are the levels of the Physical Activity Pyramid?

2. How much time should be spent on each of the components on a weekly basis?

3. What level in the activity pyramid forms the foundation for good health?

4. How can students be taught to change their activity habits to meet the minimum activity requirements?

5. What can pedometers measure?

6. Which of the measurements is most accurate and useful for the majority of students? Why?

7. What are the steps to follow when teaching students to develop personal goals? When should the goals be reset?

DISCUSSION TOPICS

1. What is the impact of adding at least 60 minutes of daily physical activity to your lifestyle?

2. What are the three most common areas physical educators use to establish the accountability of their program? Which of the three might be most meaningful to choose as a program outcome? Why?

SAMPLE WRITTEN ASSIGNMENTS

1. Write a walking program applicable for a Developmental Level III program.

2. Write a walking program that can be implemented at home with the student and family.

ACTIVITY SESSION EXPERIENCES

Lead the students through the following activities:

*   Placing the pedometer on correctly.

*   Walking with the pedometer and observing the number of steps taken in a given time.

*   Allow the student to wear the pedometer home for several days. Ask if having the pedometer motivated her/him to increase their activity level.

*   Allow the students in class to participate in "I Spy" written earlier in the chapter. Ask for evaluation of the experience.

*   Direct small groups of students to work together to create a walking activity integrating the pedometer and walking the school facility.

COOPERATIVE LEARNING TASK SHEET

Chapter 12: Promoting and Monitoring Physical Activity

Directions: Your cooperative learning group will become the content experts by finding the answers to the items listed below. Discuss the following items with your group and be ready to report on one or all of them at the end of the class period.

1. Discuss the impact of adding at least 60 minutes of daily physical activity to one's lifestyle.

2. Describe the levels of the Physical Activity Pyramid. How much time should be spent on each of the components on a weekly basis?

3. Discuss how students can be taught to change their activity habits to meet the minimum activity requirements described in the physical activity pyramid for good health.

4. Describe what pedometers can measure. Which of the measurements is most accurate and useful for the majority of students? Why?

5. Discuss the value of using pedometers in a physical education class or school-wide physical activity program.

6. What are the three most common areas physical educators use to establish the accountability of their program? Which of the three might be most meaningful to choose as a program outcome?

7. Describe why walking is often called the "real" lifetime activity.

8. Discuss how walking can play an important role in weight management.

9. What are the basic steps to follow when implementing a walking program in physical education?

10. Describe activities that can be done to encourage student physical activity outside of the school environment.

11. Create three walking activities that can be assigned to students for after-school physical activity.

12. Create two walking activities that can be used in a physical education class and that were not described in the chapter.

CHAPTER 13

Physical Fitness

SUMMARY

The value and the importance of teaching lifetime physical fitness are discussed in this chapter. An understanding of the difference between health-related and skill-related fitness helps clarify the need for emphasizing lifetime activity. High-level fitness performance is no longer an objective for the majority of children. Instead, the goal is to increase the activity and general fitness level of all students in order to improve their health status. Fitness activities for children can be moderate in intensity and still offer many health benefits. Suggestions for developing a fitness module, motivating children to maintain fitness, and developing positive attitudes toward activities are included. A variety of exercises and proper performance techniques are described so a health-related program that meets the needs of all students can be offered.

STUDENT OUTCOMES

Upon completion of the reading of this chapter, the student will:

- Differentiate between skill-related and health-related physical fitness.

- Describe the fitness status of youth in the United States.

- Explain the role that a broad program of physical fitness and activity plays in the elementary school curriculum.

- Identify the various components of health-related versus skill-related physical fitness.

- List guidelines for developing and maintaining physical fitness.

- Develop a fitness module.

- Cite strategies and techniques to motivate children to maintain physical fitness.

- Discuss the importance of fitness testing and cite several tests that could be used to measure fitness in children.

- Categorize various exercises by the muscle group involved.

- Characterize isotonic, isometric, and isokinetic exercises.

- Identify harmful physical activities and exercises.

- Plan and demonstrate numerous activities and exercises that can improve the physical fitness of children.

MAIN CONCEPTS

DEFINITIONS OF PHYSICAL FITNESS

Physical activity is a process that involves accumulating a wide variety of movement. Many experts believe that if there is enough physical activity accumulated, then physical fitness will take care of itself. *Physical fitness* is a product that is often measured to see if there is an adequate standard in place to ensure good health. The general definition of physical fitness is, "a set of attributes that people have or achieve relating to their ability to perform physical activity" (U.S. Department of Health & Human Services, 1996). An alternative definition of physical fitness is "a state of well-being with a low risk of premature health problems and energy to participate in a variety of physical activities" (Howley & Franks, 2003).

There are two types of physical fitness most often identified: (1) health-related physical fitness and (2) skill-related physical fitness. The differentiation between physical fitness related to functional health (or health-related fitness), and physical performance related to athletic ability (or skill-related fitness) makes it easier to develop proper fitness objectives and goals for youngsters. The components of health-related physical fitness are a subset of skill-related fitness components.

Health-related fitness is characterized by moderate and regular physical activity as discussed in Chapter 12. People who are generally unwilling to exercise at high intensities should aim for health-related fitness. Health-related fitness activities can be integrated into regular everyday activities that are often characterized as lifetime activities. In contrast, *skill-related physical fitness* includes the health-related components, but also covers components that are related to genetic limitations that control physical performance. Skill-related fitness is the right choice for people who can and want to perform at a high level, but is less acceptable for the majority of people because it requires training and exercising at high intensities.

Health-Related Physical Fitness

Health-related fitness should be a priority in physical education. The benefit of health-related fitness is that all students can improve their health status through daily physical activity. Health-related fitness is one of the few areas where all students can succeed regardless of ability level and genetic limitations. This contrasts with skill-related fitness, which is performance-oriented and influenced by genetic traits and abilities. A primary reason for teaching health-related fitness is that it leaves students with positive lifetime activity habits.

Health-related physical fitness includes those aspects of physiological function that offer protection from diseases related to a sedentary lifestyle. It can be improved and/or maintained through regular physical activity. Specific components include cardiovascular fitness, body composition (ratio of leanness to fatness), abdominal strength and endurance, and flexibility. These components are all measured in the Fitnessgram test (Cooper Institute, 2004) as described in Chapter 8. The Fitnessgram uses an approach that classifies fitness performance into two categories: needs improvement and healthy fitness zone (HFZ). All students are encouraged to score in the HFZ; however, there is little advantage to scoring beyond the healthy fitness zone. Criterion-referenced health standards do not compare students against each other. The goal is for all students to achieve and move their personal performance into the HFZ. The following are the major components of health-related fitness.

Cardiovascular Endurance

Aerobic fitness offers many health benefits and is often seen as the most important element of fitness. Cardiovascular endurance is the ability of the heart, the blood vessels, and the respiratory system to deliver oxygen efficiently over an extended period of time.

Body Composition

Body composition is an integral part of health-related fitness. Body composition is the proportion of body fat to lean body mass.

Flexibility

Flexibility is the range of movement through which a joint or sequence of joints can move. Inactive individuals lose flexibility, whereas frequent movement helps retain the range of movement. Through stretching activities, the length of muscles, tendons, and ligaments is increased.

Muscular Strength and Endurance

Strength is the ability of muscles to exert force. Most activities do not build strength in areas where it is needed—the arm-shoulder girdle and the abdominal-trunk region. *Muscular endurance* is the ability to exert force over an extended period.

Skill-Related Physical Fitness Components

Whereas health-related fitness is primarily sought for functional health, skill-related fitness is necessary for athletic accomplishment. It is strongly influenced by genetic factors. The primary fitness test for teachers today is the President's Challenge Youth Fitness Test (2005). Because skill-related fitness is strongly influenced by one's natural or inherited traits, it is difficult for the majority of students to achieve. In contrast to health-related tests, skill-related fitness tests often use norm-referenced standards where students are compared in terms of where they rank compared to their peers. For some students, the goal becomes trying to do better than other students rather than learning to do the best they can regardless of peer scores. Where it is possible for all students to perform adequately in health-related fitness activities, it is difficult, if not impossible, for a large number of youngsters to excel in this area of fitness. Asking students to "try harder" only adds to their frustration if they lack native ability, because they see their more-skilled friends perform well without effort. When skill-related fitness is taught, it should be accompanied by an explanation of why some students can perform well with a minimum of effort, whereas others, no matter how hard they try, never excel.

Skill-related physical fitness includes the health-related items listed above plus the following:

- **Agility**

  Agility is the ability of the body to change position rapidly and accurately while moving in space. Wrestling and football are examples of sports that require agility.

- **Balance**

  Balance refers to the body's ability to maintain a state of equilibrium while remaining stationary or moving.

- **Coordination**

  Coordination is the ability of the body to perform smoothly and successfully more than one motor task at the same time.

- **Power**

  Power is the ability to transfer energy explosively into force. To develop power, a person must practice activities that are required to improve strength, but at a faster rate involving sudden bursts of energy. Skills requiring power include high jumping, long jumping, shot putting, throwing, and kicking.

- **Speed**

  Speed is the ability of the body to perform movement in a short period of time. Usually associated with running forward, speed is essential for the successful performance of most sports and general locomotor movement skills.

ARE TODAY'S CHILDREN FIT?

A commonly held point of view among physical education teachers is that children today are less fit than children in previous generations. This opinion is used as a justification for more physical education time in the schools. Research (Corbin & Pangrazi, 1992) suggests, however, that the fitness of today's youngsters has not degenerated, showing they do quite well when compared to past students. When data from the last four national surveys of youth fitness conducted by AAHPERD and/or the President's Council on Physical Fitness and Sports were compared, children and youth today appeared to be as fit as they were in the past. It is difficult to compare youngsters from different eras because the only items that were used in all four surveys were pull-ups and the flexed-arm hang. Currently, 16% of youth 6 through 19 years (1999-2002) are overweight and another 31% are at risk for overweight (85th percentile of sex-specific BMI-for-age growth charts) (Hedley, et al., 2004). This large increase in obesity takes its toll on fitness scores. Common sense would dictate that if someone can do 50 push-ups at normal weight, putting 20 lbs. of sand on their back would decrease the number of push-ups they are able to perform. Body fat is dead weight and does not contribute to muscular or cardiovascular performance. Thus, all strength and aerobic performance scores decrease as obesity increases among youth at a rapid rate.

Why Can't All Children Meet Established Standards of Fitness?

Is it realistic to expect all children to reach specified standards of fitness? What factors control fitness performance, and how much control do youngsters have over their fitness accomplishments? Payne and Morrow (1993) reviewed 28 studies examining training and aerobic performance in children and concluded that improvement is small to moderate in prepubescent children. They state that the relatively small-to-moderate increase in pre- to post-aerobic improvement and the weak relationship between type of training program and effect size lead to questions concerning traditional practices when dealing with children and their fitness. Are we expecting too much from traditional physical education or fitness programs?

Research has shown that differences in "trainability" are strongly influenced by genetic predisposition (Bouchard et al., 1992). Trainability means that some individuals receive more benefit from training (regular physical activity) than do others. For example, assume two youngsters perform the same amount of activity (workload) throughout a semester. Child A shows dramatic improvement immediately, while child B does not. Child A simply responds more favorably to training than does child B; child A inherited a system that is responsive to exercise. Child A not only improves her fitness and scores well on the test but also gets feedback that says, "the activity works—it makes me fit." Child B scores poorly, receives negative or no feedback, and concludes that, "activity doesn't improve my fitness, so why bother?" The truth is that child B may improve in fitness (to a lesser degree than child A), but it will take longer to show improvement. Child B will probably never achieve the fitness level attained by child A because of genetic limitations.

Another factor that impacts fitness performance is physical maturation. If two youngsters are the same age and sex, but one is physiologically older (advanced skeletal maturation), the more mature youngster usually performs better on tests than does the less mature child.

Studies have shown that the relationship between physical fitness and physical activity among children is low (Pate, Dowda, & Ross, 1990; Pate & Ross, 1987; Ross, Pate, Caspersen, Damberg, & Svilar, 1987). When teachers make the mistake of assuming that a child is inactive because of scores on a fitness test, this can create unforeseen problems.

Why Are the Majority of Children Labeled Unfit?

For years, the only available fitness test for teachers was the Youth Fitness Test (1976, 1987), which is currently available as one component of The President's Challenge (President's Council on Physical Fitness and Sports, 2005). This test measures skill-related fitness and awards the Presidential fitness award to youngsters performing at the 85th percentile or better in all test items. Data from the National School Population Fitness Survey (Reiff et al., 1987) showed that only one-tenth of 1 percent of boys and three-tenths of 1 percent of girls could pass a battery of six tests at the 85th percentile. Why are the standards so high? A probable explanation is that it compares with academic standards and test developers felt that physical education standards should be set at a similar level.

Because many physical educators and parents felt that the 85th percentile standard is unrealistically high, a second award was created—the National Fitness Award. To earn this award, youngsters must pass the same battery of test items at the 50th percentile or better.

Another reason people continue to believe that youngsters are unfit is because the definition of physical fitness has changed over the years. Newer fitness tests are focusing on health-related fitness and its relationship to good health and feelings of well-being. High performance on fitness test items is not necessary for good health. Evidence shows that moderate amounts of health-related physical fitness are enough to contribute to good health (Blair et al., 1989; U.S. Department of Health and Human Services, 1996). When health-related fitness test items are used to evaluate fitness, today's children perform as well as (and better than) those in years past. Health-related fitness standards reveal that the majority of children are fit.

Finally, it is likely that many physical education teachers have chosen to believe that youngsters are unfit so that a strong case can be made for employing physical education teachers. This belief is counterproductive because the fitness of children has been measured for over 40 years and the fitness levels of youth have neither substantially improved nor declined over the last four decades (Corbin & Pangrazi, 1992).

FITNESS TESTING ISSUES

Consider a number of issues before implementing a testing program. The overriding consideration is to be sure the testing experience is positive and educational. Children can learn about their personal fitness and how to develop a lifestyle that maintains good health without being turned off by the testing experience. Many schools have tested children twice a year throughout their school career with the result that some have been labeled unfit for an entire school career. How could this practice possibly encourage inactive children who require the most motivation?

Skill-Related or Health-Related Fitness Test?

Students should understand the difference between the types of fitness so they understand the purposes of each. Skill-related fitness helps improve performance in motor tasks related to sport and athletics. The ability to perform well on skill-related tests is influenced by predetermined genetic skills.

In contrast, health-related physical fitness focuses on how much activity is required for good health. Emphasis is placed on the process of activity and participation rather than on the product of high-level physical skill performance. Health-related fitness batteries use criterion-referenced health standards in contrast to skill-related fitness tests that use percentile scores standards. Criterion-referenced standards relate to how much activity is required for good health.

Should Performance Recognition Awards be Used?

Award systems have been used to recognize students who demonstrate high levels of fitness performance. The intent of the award systems was to motivate youngsters to improve their level of fitness. However, research shows that performance awards usually only motivate youngsters who feel they have the ability to earn them (Corbin, Lovejoy, & Whitehead, 1988; Corbin, Lovejoy, Steingard, & Emerson, 1990). Many students find it impossible to earn such awards and often feel as though there is no use in making the effort only to fail again. Fitness awards focus on a single episode of accomplishment, making the act of participating in daily activity less important than earning an award.

Reward systems that focus on improvement look at short-term changes. Fitness award systems ask students to look at their immediate health status. There is evidence to show that youngsters who achieve at an elite level do so because they are genetically gifted (Bouchard et al., 1992). If gifted students can pass the test without training, it leads them to believe they do not have to exercise regularly. If awards are used, it is best to reward for participation in regular activity (behavior) rather than fitness performance. The role of the physical education teacher is to encourage behavior that lasts a lifetime. When the focus is on long-term behaviors, instruction is focused on participation in regular and moderate activity.

Awards are not recommended because children should be taught in a way that their intrinsic motivation is not undermined. Awards are extrinsic rewards that are not available to all children, thus they may undermine intrinsic motivation. However, if awards are used, consider and incorporate the following:

1. Base awards on achievement of goals that are challenging, yet attainable (Locke & Lathan, 1985).

2. If fitness goals do not seem attainable to youngsters, "learned helplessness" sets in (Harter, 1978). This phenomenon occurs when children believe there is no use trying to reach the goals and their efforts are in vain. Learned helplessness often occurs when performance rather than participation or effort is rewarded. Difficult-to-achieve goals teach youngsters who need to be motivated that there is no use in trying.

3. If an award system is used to motivate children's activity, the system should be phased out as soon as possible. Awards do motivate primary-grade children; however, by the age of 9 or 10 years, children start to see the rewards as bribery to do something (Whitehead & Corbin, 1991). Other children find achievement of the awards to be hopeless; they are not motivated but are discouraged by the rewards being given to others. Gradually removing awards helps students learn that participation is done for intrinsic and personal reasons.

4. An alternative and long-term approach that focuses on behavior rather than a single outcome are awards to recognize students for regular participation in activity. This places the rewards in reach of all youngsters and helps establish activity habits that last a lifetime. In addition, this approach supports the research cited in the report of the Surgeon General on the benefits of moderate to vigorous physical activity (U.S. Dept. of Health and Human Services, 1996).

CREATE POSITIVE ATTITUDES TOWARD FITNESS

Teachers can do a number of things to increase the possibility of students being "turned on" to activity. Fitness activity is neither good nor bad. Rather, how fitness activities are taught determines how youngsters feel about making fitness a part of their lifestyle. The following strategies help make physical activity a positive learning experience.

Go to the following websites for more information on physical activity and fitness assessment:

🏃 www.cooperinst.org/ftgmain.asp

🏃 www.presidentschallenge.org/home_kids.aspx

Physical Activity Reports can be read at the following sites:

🏃 www.cdc.gov/nccdphp/dnpa/physical/recommendations/index.htm

🏃 www.health.gov/healthypeople

🏃 www.actionforhealthykids.org

Personalize Fitness Activities

Students who find themselves unable to perform exercises are not likely to develop a positive attitude toward physical activity. Fitness experiences should allow children to determine their personal workloads. Use time as the workload variable and ask children to do the best they can within a time limit.

Expose Youngsters to a Variety of Fitness Activities

Presenting a variety of fitness opportunities decreases the monotony of doing the same routines week after week and increases the likelihood that students will experience fitness activities that are personally enjoyable. Youngsters are willing to accept activities they dislike if they know there will be a chance to experience routines they enjoy in the near future.

Give Students Positive Feedback about Their Effort

Teacher feedback contributes to the way children view fitness activities. Immediate, accurate, and specific feedback regarding effort encourages continued participation. Provided in a positive manner, this feedback can stimulate children to extend their participation habits outside the confines of the gymnasium. Reinforce all children, not just those who perform at high levels.

Teach Physical Skills and Fitness

Physical education programs should concentrate on skill development as well as fitness. Some states mandate fitness testing, which causes teachers to worry that their students will not pass. Unfortunately, the skill development portion of physical education is often sacrificed to allow for an increased emphasis on teaching fitness. Physical education has two major objectives: fitness and skill development. Skills are the tools that many adults use to maintain personal fitness. These individuals maintain fitness through various skill-based activities such as tennis, badminton, swimming, golf, basketball, aerobics, bicycling, and the like. People have a much greater propensity to participate as adults if they feel competent in an activity. School programs must graduate students with requisite entry skills in a variety of activities.

Be a Role Model

Appearance, attitude, and actions speak loudly about teachers and their values regarding fitness. Teachers who display physical vitality, take pride in being active, participate in activities with children, and are physically fit will positively influence youngsters to maintain an active lifestyle. It is unreasonable to expect teachers to complete fitness routines nine times a day and five days a week. However, teachers must exercise with a class periodically to assure students that they are willing to do what they ask others to do.

Care about the Attitudes of Children

Attitudes dictate how youngsters participate in activity. Too often, adults want to force fitness on children in an effort to make them all physically fit. This results in insensitivity to the feelings of participants. Training does not equate to lifetime fitness. When youngsters are trained without concern for their feelings, the result will be fit children who may hate physical activity. Once a negative attitude is developed, it is difficult to change. This does not mean that youngsters should avoid fitness activity. It means that fitness participation must be a positive experience. Youngsters should not all be funneled into one type of fitness activity. For example, running may be detrimental to the health of obese children, and lean, uncoordinated students may not enjoy contact activities. The fitness experience works best when it is a challenge rather than a threat. Keep fitness goals within the realm of challenge. A final note: whether an activity is a challenge or a threat depends on the perceptions of the learner, not the instructor. Listen carefully to students rather than telling them they "should do it for their own good."

Start Easy and Progress Slowly

Fitness development is a journey, not a destination. No teacher wants students to become fit and then quit being active. A rule of thumb to follow is to allow students to start at a level that they can accomplish successfully. This usually means self-directed workloads within a specified time frame. Don't force students into heavy workloads too soon. Start easy, assure success, and gradually increase the workload. This avoids the discouragement of failure and excessive muscle soreness. When students successfully accomplish activities, they develop a system of self-talk that looks at their exercise behavior in a positive light. This minimizes the practice of self-criticism where students fail to live up to their own or others' standards.

Use Low-Intensity Activity

Make activity appropriate for the developmental level of the youngster. The amount of activity needed for good health is dictated by two variables—the intensity of the activity and the duration of the activity. Most children participate in high-volume–low-intensity activity because they have opportunities for activity sporadically all day. This naturally occurring activity is consistent with the developmental level of children. In contrast, most adults are involved in high-intensity–low-volume activity because they have little time throughout the day to be active. This contrast of activity styles leads adults to believe that children need to participate in high-intensity activities to receive health benefits. They often view children as unfit because youngsters don't like to participate in high-intensity fitness activities. This focus on high-intensity activity causes some children to become discouraged and burned out at an early age. Youngsters are the most active segment of society (Rowland, 1990), and it is important to maintain and encourage this trait. When regular activity is reinforced, fitness follows to the extent possible for each child, given heredity and maturation level.

DEVELOP AN UNDERSTANDING OF PHYSICAL FITNESS PRINCIPALS

Physical education instruction should teach habits that carry over to out-of-school activities. Regardless of how often youngsters participate in physical education, time spent teaching physical fitness knowledge and physical activities is necessary. When youngsters are not taught fitness activities, they learn that such activities are unimportant or not valued by teachers and the school. Youngsters are experiential; that is, they learn from participation and develop perceptions based on those experiences. If physical activities are taught in school, youngsters begin to learn that daily activity is an important habit for a healthy lifestyle. Teaching students different ways to develop and maintain fitness (even if only one day per week) demonstrates that the school values health and exercise as part of a balanced lifestyle. Consider the following for integrating knowledge of fitness into the physical education program.

1. Provide basic explanations of rudimentary anatomy and kinesiology. Children can learn the names and locations of major bones and muscle groups, including how they function in relation to selected joint action.

2. Provide an understanding of how fitness is developed. Explain the value of the procedures followed in class sessions so children understand the purpose of all fitness developmental tasks. In addition, teach children the basic components of a personal fitness program for life.

3. Bring the class together at the end of a lesson to discuss key fitness points to promote a clear understanding of why fitness is important. Learning the values of being physically fit, how to apply the principles of exercise, and how fitness can become part of one's lifestyle can positively alter students' views of physical activity. To share cognitive information, establish a muscle of the week, construct educational bulletin boards to illustrate fitness concepts, or send home handouts explaining principles of fitness development.

4. Develop cognition of the importance of fitness for wellness. Help students understand how to perform fitness activities and why these activities should be performed. They need to know the values derived from maintaining a minimal fitness level.

5. Place bulletin boards in the teaching area to explain components of the physical education program to parents and students. Bulletin boards can explain skill techniques, motivational reminders, and fitness activities that will be upcoming in class. Classroom teachers are required to develop bulletin boards for their classes; in similar fashion, when physical education teachers design visual aids for the gymnasium, credibility is enhanced.

6. Exploit the use of audiovisual aids. Audiotapes of fitness routines increase the motivation of youngsters. Exercise videotapes are an excellent medium for beginning a new fitness activity.

7. Help children understand the values of physical fitness and the physiology of its development and maintenance. Homework dealing with the cognitive aspects of fitness development communicates to parents that their children are gaining knowledge for a lifetime.

8. Emphasize self-testing programs that teach children to evaluate their personal fitness levels. In self-evaluation programs, children assess their fitness without concern for others judging them. Fitness and activity are personal for most adults and should be considered a personal matter for youngsters as well.

AVOID HARMFUL PRACTICES AND EXERCISES

The following points contraindicate certain exercise practices and should be considered when offering fitness instruction.

The following techniques (Macfarlane, 1993) should be avoided when performing abdominal exercises that lift the head and trunk off the floor:

- Avoid placing the hands behind the head or high on the neck. This may cause hyperflexion and injury to the discs when the elbows swing forward to help pull the body up.

- Keep the knees bent. Straight legs cause the hip flexor muscles to be used earlier and more forcefully, making it difficult to maintain proper pelvic tilt.

- Don't hold the feet on the floor. Having another student secure the feet places more force on the lumbar vertebrae and may lead to lumbar hyperextension.

- Don't lift the buttocks and lumbar region off the floor. This also causes the hip flexor muscles to contract vigorously.

Two types of stretching activity have been used to develop flexibility. *Ballistic stretching* (strong bouncing movements) formerly was the most common stretching used, but this has been discouraged for many years because it was thought to increase delayed onset muscle soreness. The other flexibility activity, *static stretching*, involves increasing the stretch to the point of discomfort, backing off slightly to where the position can be held comfortably, and maintaining the stretch for an extended time. Static stretching has been advocated because it was thought to reduce muscle soreness and prevent injury. One study (Smith et al., 1993) disputed the muscle soreness and tissue damage theory with findings that showed ballistic and static stretching both produced increases in muscle soreness. In fact, the static stretching actually induced significantly more soreness than did ballistic stretching. Static stretching is an excellent choice, but ballistic stretching is probably not as harmful as once thought.

- If forward flexion is done from a sitting position in an effort to touch the toes, the bend should be from the hips, not from the waist, and should be done with one leg flexed. To conform to this concern, the Fitnessgram backsaver sit-and-reach test item is now performed with one leg flexed to reduce stress on the lower back.

- Straight-leg raises from a supine position should be avoided because they may strain the lower back. The problem can be somewhat alleviated by placing the hands under the small of the back, but it is probably best to avoid such exercises.

- Deep knee bends (full squats) and the duck walk should be avoided. They may cause damage to the knee joints and have little developmental value. Much more beneficial is flexing the knee joint to 90 degrees and returning to a standing position.

- When doing stretching exercises from a standing position, the knees should not be hyperextended. The knee joint should be relaxed rather than locked. It is often effective to have students do their stretching with bent knees; this will remind them not to hyperextend the joint. In all stretching activities, participants should be allowed to judge their range of motion. Expecting all students to be able to touch their toes is an unrealistic goal. If concerned about touching the toes from this position, do so from a sitting position with one leg flexed.

- Activities that place stress on the neck should be avoided. Examples of activities in which caution should be used are the Inverted Bicycle, Wrestler's Bridge, and abdominal exercises with the hands behind the head.

- Avoid the so-called hurdler's stretch. This activity is done in the sitting position with one leg forward and the other leg bent and to the rear. Using this stretch places undue pressure on the knee joint of the bent leg. Substitute a stretch using a similar position with one leg straight forward and the other leg bent with the foot placed in the crotch area.

- Avoid stretches that demand excessive back arching. An example: While lying in prone position, the student reaches back and grabs the ankles. By pulling and arching, the exerciser can hyperextend the lower back. This places stress on the discs and stretches the abdominal muscles (not needed by most people).

IMPLEMENT A YEARLONG FITNESS PLAN

Plan carefully to offer a variety of fitness experiences to learners. Good planning allows for progression and ensures that youngsters receive a well-rounded program of instruction. Plan physical fitness instruction in a manner similar to skill development sequences. *The Dynamic Physical Education*

Curriculum Guide: Lesson Plans for Implementation (2007) offers a yearly sequence of fitness units for all three developmental levels.

When organizing a yearly plan for fitness instruction, consider the following. Fitness units should vary in length depending on the age of the youngster. Children need to experience a variety of routines that maintain a high level of motivation. During the elementary school years, exposure to different types of activities is more important than progressive and demanding fitness routines. Adhere to one principle: There are many methods for developing fitness, none of which is best for all children.

IMPLEMENTING FITNESS ROUTINES

Fitness routines are exclusively dedicated to the presentation of a variety of fitness activities. The following are suggestions for successful implementation of the fitness routines.

1. Precede fitness instruction with a 2- to 3-minute warm-up period. Introductory activities are useful for this purpose because they allow youngsters an opportunity to prepare for strenuous activity.

2. The fitness portion of the daily lesson, including warm-up, should not extend beyond 10 to 13 minutes. Some might argue that more time is needed to develop adequate fitness. However, the reality is that most teachers are only allowed a 20- to 30-minute period of instruction. Because skill instruction is part of a balanced physical education program, compromise is necessary to ensure that all phases of the program are covered.

3. Use activities that exercise all body parts and cover the major components of fitness. Children are capable performers when workloads are geared to their age, fitness level, and abilities.

4. A variety of fitness routines comprising sequential exercises for total body development is the recommended alternative to a yearlong program of regimented calisthenics. Use a diverse array of activities that appeal to the interest and fitness level of children to replace the traditional approach of doing the same routine day in and day out.

5. Assume an active role in fitness instruction. Children respond positively to role modeling. When you actively exercise with children, hustle to assist those youngsters having difficulty, and make exercise fun, your actions instill in children the value of an active lifestyle.

6. When determining workloads for children, the available alternatives are time or repetitions. Base the workload on time rather than on a specified number of repetitions so youngsters can adjust their workload within personal limits. Beginning dosages for exercises should start at a level at which all children will succeed. The best way to ensure success is to allow students to adjust the workload to suit their capabilities. Using a specified amount of time per exercise allows less gifted children to perform successfully. All children should not be expected to perform exactly the same workload.

7. Take advantage of interval training with youngsters. Alternate stretching and strength development exercises with aerobic exercises. This gives youngsters a chance to recover from an aerobic activity while stretching. It also allows time for recovery from strength-development activities. Most routines are effective in 30-second intervals. Beyond this length of time, students will start to fatigue or become bored and go off-task.

8. Use audiotapes to time fitness activity segments so you are free to move throughout the area and offer individualized instruction. The easiest way to time segments is to alternate 30-second intervals of music and silence. When music is playing, it signals that students are to perform an aerobic activity. When the silence interval is on, it signals stretching or strength-development activity.

9. Never use fitness activities as punishment. Such a practice teaches students that push-ups and running are things you do when you misbehave. The opportunity to exercise should be a privilege as well as

an enjoyable experience. Think of the money adults spend to exercise. Take a positive approach and offer students a chance to jog with a friend when they do something well. This allows them the opportunity not only to visit, but also to exercise with a positive feeling. Be an effective salesperson; sell the joy of activity and the benefits of physical fitness to youngsters.

Fitness Activities that Ensure a Successful Experience

The remainder of the chapter describes appropriate fitness activities for each developmental level student. Fitness activities for young children have the potential to teach components of physical fitness and exercise the various body areas. Fitness routines and games are listed in this chapter that are appropriate to each development level student. Examples listed are:

Squad Leader Exercises

Squad leader exercises give students an opportunity to lead exercises in a small group. This approach is an effective method for teaching students how to lead others and to help them learn to put together a well-balanced fitness routine. A student within each squad is given a task card that has exercises and activities grouped by how they impact different parts of the body.

Exercises to Music

Exercises to music add another dimension to developmental experiences. Many commercial CD sets with exercise programs are available. Using a homemade tape/CD with alternating intervals of silence and music signals time for exercises and aerobic activity. For example, if doing Random Moving, students could run/walk as long as the music is playing and stretch when the silent interval occurs. Having the music pretaped frees you from having to keep an eye on a stopwatch.

Continuity Exercises

Children are scattered, each with a jump rope. They alternate between rope jumping and exercises. A specified time period governs the length of the rope-jumping episode. At the signal to stop rope jumping, children drop the ropes and take the beginning position for the exercise selected. Many of the exercises use a 2-count rhythm. When children are positioned for the exercise, the leader says, "Ready!" The class completes one repetition of the exercise and responds "One, two!" This repeats for each repetition.

Challenge Courses

Challenge Courses are popular as a tool for fitness development in the elementary schools. Students move through the course with proper form rather than run against a time standard. The course is designed to exercise all parts of the body through a variety of activities.

Aerobic Fitness Routines

Aerobics is a fitness activity for people of all ages that develops cardiorespiratory fitness plus strength and flexibility.

Partner Resistance and Aerobic Fitness Exercises

Partner resistance exercises combined with aerobic fitness routines make an excellent fitness activity. Partner resistance exercises develop strength but offer little aerobic benefit. Combining them with aerobic fitness routines offers a well-balanced program.

Sport-Related Fitness Activities

Many sport drills can be modified to place fitness demands on students. An advantage of sport-related fitness activities is that many children are highly motivated by sport activities. Thoughtful preplanning and creative thinking can result in drills that teach sport skills as well as provide fitness benefits.

Walking and Jogging

Jogging and walking, fitness activities for all ages, can lead to regular activity habits and to a lifelong exercise program. Jogging is defined as easy, relaxed running at a pace that can be maintained for long distances without undue fatigue or strain.

Fitness Orienteering

Students work together as members of a team. Eight to ten stations are placed around the area in random fashion. Each squad is given a laminated "map" card of exercise stations. Each of the maps has the stations in different order so that there is only one squad at a "landmark." The team members exercise together (each member performing at their own pace) and "hunt" for the next exercise station listed on their map card when signaled. When they complete the station activity, one member of the squad picks up a letter from the "checkpoint" and the team moves to the next station. The goal is to complete the fitness orienteering stations, pick up a letter at each station, and return to the original starting point to unscramble "the secret word." Intervals of music (30 seconds) and silence (15 seconds) signal when to exercise and when to change to a new station. Examples are listed in the chapter.

All-Around Jackpot Fitness

Three different "jackpots" (boxes) are filled with fitness exercises and activities are placed around the teaching area. One jackpot is filled with a variety of strength development activities written on small index cards. A second jackpot is filled with flexibility activities. The third jackpot contains aerobic activities. Students can work individually or with a partner. They begin at one of the jackpots of choice and randomly pick out an activity to perform. If with a partner, they take turns selecting the card from the box. The only stipulations are that they must rotate to a different box each time and cannot select an activity they previously performed.

Partner Interval Fitness

Students pair up with a partner and perform activities that are designed so one partner performs aerobic activity while the other is stretching or doing strength development activities.

Interval Training

All fitness routines in this chapter take advantage of interval training principles. Interval training is effective with elementary school children because they fatigue and recover quickly. Interval training involves alternating work and recovery intervals. Intervals of work (large muscle movement dominated by locomotor movements) and recovery (dominated by nonlocomotor activity or walking) are alternated at regular timed intervals.

Partner Fitness Challenges

Partner challenges are fitness activities that can be used with intermediate-grade youngsters. They can be used to develop aerobic endurance, strength, and flexibility. Another advantage of partner challenges is that they can be performed indoors as a rainy-day activity.

Go to the following websites for additional information on physical activity and fitness concepts.

- www.americanheart.org
- www.cdc.gov/HealthyYouth/publications/index.htm
- www.nlm.nih.gov/medlineplus/exerciseforchildren.html
- www.pe4life.com
- http://www.eatsmartmovemorenc.com/index.htm

INSTRUCTIONAL FORMATS

The material in this chapter may be presented using the lecture style and the Power Point/overhead transparencies providing students an overview of the chapter. The instructor may also use the Guided Discovery method of teaching to introduce and review the materials read by the students. In this style, the instructor asks questions guiding the students toward one answer. The instructor rephrases the questions until the students discover the answer to the question. The introduction/review of the chapter may be followed by cooperative learning assignments that provide active learning and critical thinking activities for the student. In the cooperative learning groups, the students will discuss the materials listed on the Cooperative Learning Task Sheet (CLTS) and/or other topics you may assign. Each group can become a "content expert" for sections of the CLTS. Oral summary reports of the group may be presented to the entire class covering all or part of the discussion items. You may want to distribute the CLTS to the class before the discussion or post them on a website for students to preview. Some of the items may require reviewing a website prior to completion. Additionally, for the material in this chapter activity sessions are appropriate to demonstrate the types of physical activity described in the chapter.

KEY TERMS

skill-related fitness	flexibility	coordination
health-related fitness	muscular endurance	power
body composition	isotonic exercises	isokinetic exercises
muscular strength	isometric exercises	physical activity

REFLECTION AND REVIEW QUESTIONS

How and Why

1. Why are America's youth perceived as being unfit and inactive?

2. Why must physical education teachers understand various concepts related to physical fitness?

3. Why do so many students fail fitness tests? Defend your answer.

4. How can teachers make fitness fun?

DISCUSSION TOPICS

1. Should awards be used for fitness testing?

2. Should physical education teachers be physically fit? Explain.

SAMPLE WRITTEN ASSIGNMENTS

1. Create a developmentally appropriate fitness routine. Make a CD/tape to be used with the routine. Be sure to identify the developmental level that will use the routine.

2. Write guidelines for promoting fitness for children that could be used school-wide.

ACTIVITY SESSION EXPERIENCES

Lead the students through the following activities:

*   Interval training

*   Partner challenges

*   Rope-jumping routines

*   Continuity exercises

*   Exercises to music

*   Squad leader exercises

*   All-around jackpot fitness exercises

*   Fitness orienteering

*   Racetrack fitness

*   Walking and jogging activities

*   Sports-related fitness activities

*   Partner resistance

*   Aerobic fitness exercises

*   Challenge courses

*   Astronaut exercises

*   Hexagon hustle

*   Circuit training

COOPERATIVE LEARNING TASK SHEET

Chapter 13: Physical Fitness

Directions: Your cooperative learning group will become the content experts by finding the answers to the items listed below. Discuss the following items with your group and be ready to report on one or all of them at the end of the class period.

1. Discuss several major conclusions of the Surgeon General's Report on Physical Activity and Health.

2. Describe health-related fitness.

3. Describe skill-related fitness.

4. Respond to the question: Are American children fit? Explain your answer with examples from the chapter.

5. Discuss why teachers of physical education should understand various concepts related to physical fitness.

6. Discuss the reasons why so many students fail fitness tests. Defend your answer using material from the chapter.

7. Describe ways in which teachers can make fitness fun.

8. Identify the purpose of physical fitness testing.

9. Write the steps to implementing a fitness test battery. Include descriptions of several fitness tests and the fitness component each measures.

10. Describe methods for fostering positive attitudes toward physical fitness.

11. Discuss guidelines for promoting fitness for children.

12. Cite at least three harmful exercises.

13. Create a developmentally appropriate fitness routine for Level I children.

14. Create a developmentally appropriate fitness routine for Level II children.

15. Create a developmentally appropriate fitness routine for Level III children.

16. Discuss the pros and cons of fitness testing awards.

17. Discuss the question: Should physical education teachers be physically fit? Explain.

18. Describe at least three activities and exercises designed to improve the fitness of children.

CHAPTER 14

Active and Healthy Schools

SUMMARY

Weight management problems have increased over the past two decades. The need to promote active and healthy behaviors in youth led to passage of the Child Nutrition and WIC Reauthorization Act of 2004. This act highlights the importance of developing solutions that increase the physical activity of children, provide nutrition education, and ultimately teach youth healthy eating and activity habits that last a lifetime. A sound physical education program is a necessity in schools; however, it is not enough. Even in a daily physical education program children only receive a 30-minute period of instruction that offers about 15 minutes of daily physical activity. The total environment of the school must be changed in a way that encourages children to be active and develop healthy nutritional habits. This chapter will show how to change the structure of a typical school and create an active and healthy school environment.

STUDENT OUTCOMES

Upon completion of the reading of this chapter, the student will:

- Discuss the recommendations of the Child Nutrition and WIC Reauthorization Act of 2004.

- Explain the importance of schools in promoting active healthy behaviors.

- Discuss each component of an Active Healthy School Program.

- Explain how to implement ideas in schools to increase the activity level of students.

- Describe the requirements for implementing and maintaining an Active Healthy School Program.

MAIN CONCEPTS

Descriptions of an active and healthy school environment are described in detail in this chapter. This chapter will show you the many possibilities for changing the environment of a school so that children have the opportunity to accumulate adequate activity and learn about nutrition, proper eating habits, and sun safety.

The health of America's youth (and adults) is a national matter of concern. In an effort to abate the childhood obesity epidemic and improve programs for children, the Child Nutrition and WIC Reauthorization Act of 2004 was passed into law. This act highlights the importance of developing solutions that increase the physical activity of children, provide nutrition education, and ultimately teach youth healthy eating and activity habits that last a lifetime. In short, the law requires all school districts with a federally funded school meals program (which is nearly all public schools) to develop and implement wellness policies that address nutrition and physical activity. The policy must be in place by the start of the 2006-2007 academic school year. Once the wellness policy is in place, it is hoped that most districts will continually evaluate and revise their program each year. The Reauthorization Act recommends (but does not mandate) that schools implement some of the following points in an effort to meet the wellness policy plan:

- Make recess and lunchtime active settings for all students.

- Offer regularly scheduled activity breaks in the classroom of 3-5 minutes to give students a respite from long periods of sitting.

- Design school walking programs that are buddy based or small group based.

- Develop activity contracts for students (teaching students to monitor their daily activity patterns).

- Facilitate programs for parents; share information with parents through newsletters and school-based programs.

- Place point-of-decision prompts in classrooms to encourage healthy eating, physical activity, and other healthy behaviors.

- Encourage students to participate in after-school activities.

- Maintain and strengthen nutritional service programs on campus.

Another important emphasis of the Reauthorization Act is to balance the impact on childhood obesity while maintaining local control for the states and schools. The government recommends that wellness policies address issues that impact childhood obesity, such as physical activity and nutrition. Since each school district has the latitude to develop its own policy, it is likely districts will use local personnel to assist in the development of the wellness plan.

The physical educator should ask to be apart of the wellness policy committee. As a member of the committee it is paramount that physical education teachers be familiar with the requirements of the law. In addition, PE teachers need a plan of action that meets the requirements and serves to address the childhood obesity issues in their districts. The development of an Active and Healthy School Program (AHSP) is an approach that can be coordinated and directed by the physical education teacher.

The remainder of this chapter presents suggested components of an AHSP and numerous strategies for implementing these components. It is understood that not all strategies will be effective at a particular school. However, by selecting and implementing effective strategies, reflecting on their effectiveness, and making alterations, a living AHSP that evolves over time can be created.

COMPONENTS OF AN ACTIVE AND HEALTHY SCHOOL

Quality Physical Education

In most cases, physical education teachers should serve as the physical activity coordinator in a school, specifically in an AHSP. Although they may not actively participate in an event or strategy, it is likely that they will have input into virtually every physical activity-based strategy in an AHSP. For example, a physical education teacher may organize and teach an after-school aerobics class for teachers. In addition, he/she may coordinate a group of teachers that supervise a before-school physical activity club for students. Without a physical education teacher, it is highly unlikely that physical activity will be an integral part of the school day. Thus, the physical education teacher is essential.

A quality physical education program is important for maintaining and increasing student involvement. If physical education is not enjoyable to students, it is difficult to imagine them wanting to participate in AHSP activities. For example, if a typical physical education lesson consists of calisthenics and sitting on the sidelines while half the class plays soccer, it will be difficult to recruit students to come to an after-school program. Children might be thinking, "You want me to stay after school for more of the same?" Thus, to increase participation and ensure that a physical activity coordinator is present, quality physical education is the foundational component of an AHSP.

Active Learning in the Classroom

Research has demonstrated that physical activity may at least be indirectly related to the learning process. When possible, integrating movement into instruction can offer another medium for learning and promote the activity levels of students. Successful implementation of this principle requires overcoming two major barriers. Classroom teachers often do not feel comfortable teaching students in an active setting and do not know how to integrate movement into their lessons.

Areas that must be taken into consideration to integrate movement into the classroom setting:

1. How much space is available? Strategies for addressing this barrier are:

    a. Students can move their desks to the perimeter.

    b. Activities can be performed while in the same position (e.g., behind their desks).

2. Consideration must be given to neighboring teachers, i.e., what is happening next door. In some activities noise can become an issue.

3. As the program director, the physical educator must learn what the "comfort zone" of each classroom teacher is. Would he/she be willing to do a dance with students? Is he/she an outdoors person? Does he/she like team sports? With this information, physical educators can work with classroom teachers to generate effective and active classroom-based learning experiences for students.

Before–and After-School Programs

Usually, after-school hours offer the most opportunity for students to be active. These programs are usually activity-based with students playing in the gymnasium, on the playground, or in a grassy space. After-school programs offer an excellent opportunity to teach students about healthy foods and other healthy behaviors. Before-school hours also offer an opportunity for students to be active. Opening the school grounds and offering activities for students who arrive before school has great potential.

Activity Breaks

In elementary schools, activity breaks are offered in three forms: recess, lunchtime activity time, and mini-breaks offered throughout the school day. Students should be provided with at least two 15-minute activity breaks (recess) per day. Children should be encouraged to be active during this time. One study found that girls average almost 1200 steps and boys 1400 steps during a 15-minute activity break (Tudor-Locke, et al. in press). In just 15 minutes, children can accumulate approximately 10% of the daily physical activity award thresholds for the President's Active Lifestyle Award (2004).

Mini-activity breaks in the classroom allow students to accumulate physical activity in small bouts throughout the day. Typically a mini-break lasts 3-5 minutes and may or may not involve leaving the classroom. Pellegrini, Huberty, and Jones (1995) found that offering activity breaks every hour decreased behavior issues and problems with inattentive students. Other research has found that providing activity breaks, along with journaling activity from the previous day, is effective in increasing the daily physical activity levels of children, particularly girls (Ernst & Pangrazi, 1998; Pangrazi, Beighle, Vehige, and Vack, 2003).

Sun Safety Program

One method of getting students to be more active is to increase the amount of time they spend outdoors (because children are more active when outdoors). This brings additional risk, that of skin damage caused by the sun. In the United States, one in five Americans will develop skin cancer. Children are particularly vulnerable because overexposure to the sun at a young age puts individuals at an increased risk of skin cancer throughout life. An estimated 80 percent of a person's sun exposure occurs before age 18 (Stern, et al., 1986). Blistering sunburns during childhood significantly increase the risk of developing skin cancer later in life (American Academy of Pediatrics, 1999). Children should learn about the sun, the risks associated with exposure to the sun, and how they can be protected from the sun.

The United States Environmental Protection Agency sponsors the The Sunwise School Program designed for educators. Sunwise is a comprehensive program that includes lesson plans, brochures, and letters for parents and workbooks for students. Included in the materials are a number of active games that can be played to teach concepts about sun safety and how to become a Sunwise school.

All the materials for the Sunwise program can be accessed at the following website:
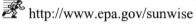 http://www.epa.gov/sunwise

Point-of-Decision Prompts

Point-of–decision prompts are simply signs placed in areas around the school where students and faculty will be making choices regarding healthy behaviors. The signs are as simple as "Be Active," or they provide a list of activities that can be played during activity breaks. Signs can be posted on the playground to encourage students to be active. Nutrition-based point-of-decision prompts can be located in the cafeteria. For example, signs reminding students of healthy food choices can be used. This chapter indicates such examples.

Teacher Involvement

Encouraging faculty to improve their own health through school-based activities is another strategy to consider when developing an AHSP. Students see teachers as models. If they see their teacher eating healthier foods and being active during activity breaks, the potential impact these seemingly small acts may have is tremendous. Physical educators can coordinate walking clubs, after-school aerobics, brief nutrition education presentations at faculty meetings, or even a friendly "steps" competition among teachers.

A school-wide fundraising idea is to sell pedometers to students and parents. The company will award a portion of profit of sales to the school. For more information, go to:
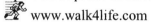 www.walk4life.com

Walking-to-School Events

Walking-to-school programs are becoming more and more popular, with local, state, and national events held throughout the country.

For more information, go to the Center for Disease Control's website:
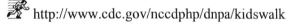 http://www.cdc.gov/nccdphp/dnpa/kidswalk

Parental Involvement

For elementary students, parents/guardians are the most significant adult in their lives. With respect to physical activity, parents have a substantial impact on their child's attitude towards physical activity and their physical activity level (Welk, Wood, & Morss, 2003). Thus, programs that involve parents and get parents to be active with their children can be effective in promoting physical activity not just for children, but an entire family. The following are a few of the ideas that foster parental involvement and can be included in an AHSP.

1. Activity Calendars

2. PE Nights/Demonstration Nights

3. Fun Days: sometimes called Play Days

4. Charity Events

Community Involvement

Every community is full of resources that are of value to an AHSP. These resources may have experience planning events, working with other community organizations, collaborating with schools, or simply the ability to generate funding for programs. Physical educators should constantly seek collaborative, creative involvement from the community.

Organizations That May Participate in the AHSP

- YMCAs, recreation centers, Boys and Girls Clubs

- City/county health agencies

- Businesses

- Youth sports

School Nutrition Environment

When developing an AHSP it is important that physical educators emphasize the importance of the physical activity side of weight management; after all, that is what they are trained to do. However, they must not lose sight of the other side of the equation: calories consumed, or diet. Although physical education teachers are not trained to make decisions regarding school food services, they most certainly can become involved and influence the school nutrition environment.

Below are strategies that can be advocated by physical education teachers to improve the school nutrition environment.

1. All students must have access to nutritious foods.

2. If vending machines are on campus, they must serve only nutritious, healthy choices.

3. In the classrooms, foods should not be given as a reward. Many teachers hand out candy bars, gum, or other sweet treats as rewards for correct answers, good behavior, etc.

4. Children should be provided nutrient-dense meals.

   Recommendations for nutrition standards and instructional materials are available from the United States Department of Agriculture (USDA) at the following website: http://www.nutrition.gov

5. School club sales should be limited to nutritious foods.

6. The eating environment should be clean, safe, and attractive.

7. Lunch should be served as close to noon as possible. More and more schools are serving lunch to students as early as 10 a.m.

8. Use bulletin boards and signs in the cafeteria to compliment the nutrition education, sun safety, and physical activity promotion that are occurring throughout the school.

9. Integrate nutrition education content into physical education activities.

10. Gather feedback from parents and other community members regarding their feelings about the nutrition environment at the school or the changes being made.

GETTING AN AHSP STARTED

One of the toughest tasks for physical educators is getting a program started. The following are suggestions that can help make creating and maintaining an AHSP a series of smaller pieces that can be accomplished in a systematic manner.

1. Form an AHSP Committee.

2. Develop an implementation plan.

3. Reflect and evaluate so the program can progress.

4. Meet with other schools to coordinate efforts.

REFLECTION AND REVIEW QUESTIONS

How and Why

1. Why are Active Healthy Schools important?

2. How can physical educators contribute to an active healthy school?

3. How can community involvement impact the effectiveness of an AHSP?

4. Why is it important to develop an AHSP committee?

Content Review

1. Explain what the Child Nutrition and WIC Reauthorization Act means to physical education teachers.

2. Present several recommendations made by the Child Nutrition and WIC Reauthorization Act.

3. Discuss the purpose of an AHSP.

4. List and describe the components of an Active Healthy School Program.

5. Describe how a physical education teacher can go about starting an AHSP.

INSTRUCTIONAL FORMATS

The material in this chapter can be presented using the lecture style plus the Power Point materials and overhead transparencies providing students an overview of the chapter. The introduction may be followed by cooperative learning assignments that provide active learning and critical thinking activities for the student. In the cooperative learning groups, the students will discuss the materials listed on the Cooperative Learning Task Sheet and/or other topics you may assign. Each group can become a "content expert" for sections of the Task Sheet. Oral summary reports of the group may be presented to the entire class covering all or part of the discussion items.

KEY TERMS

Active Healthy School Program	Child Nutrition and WIC Reauthorization Act of 2004	walking-to-school events point-of–decision prompts

DISCUSSION TOPICS

1. Discuss Active Healthy School Programs in your neighborhood.

SAMPLE WRITTEN ASSIGNMENT

1. Create an Active Healthy School Program for a neighborhood school.

COOPERATIVE LEARNING TASK SHEET

Chapter 14: Active and Healthy Schools

Directions: Your cooperative learning group will become the content experts by finding the answers to the items listed below. Discuss the following items with your group and be ready to report on one or all of them at the end of the class period.

1. Describe an Active Healthy School Program.

2. Why are Active Healthy Schools important?

3. How can physical educators contribute to an active healthy school?

4. Describe how a physical education teacher can go about starting an AHSP.

5. How can community involvement impact the effectiveness of an AHSP? What community groups can be enlisted to assist with the program?

6. Why is it important to develop an AHSP committee?

7. What is the role of the AHSP committee?

8. Define the Child Nutrition and WIC Reauthorization Act.

9. What does this act mean to physical education teachers?

10. Present several recommendations made by the Child Nutrition and WIC Reauthorization Act.

11. List and describe the components of an Active Healthy School Program.

CHAPTER 15

Movement Concepts and Themes

SUMMARY

This chapter is designed to help teachers and students understand movement concepts—the classification and vocabulary of movement. Teachers learn the classification of movement concepts, including body awareness, space awareness, qualities of movement, and relationships. Emphasis at this level is placed on the process of moving rather than on the product of correct performance of a skill. Creativity is rewarded and ingenuity reinforced. Movement themes are designed to integrate the concepts into actual activities on the floor.

STUDENT OUTCOMES

Upon completion of the reading of this chapter, the student will:

- Explain how movement themes are used to develop an understanding of movement concepts.

- Define how human movement concepts are classified into four major categories.

- Explain the purpose of movement themes.

- Define the qualities of movement.

- Teach a variety of movement themes.

- Design a unique movement theme using the four-step approach.

- Specify individual cooperative partner activities and group activities to develop educational movement.

MAIN CONCEPTS

Physical education places emphasis on skill development in the elementary school years. It is important to learn fundamental skills in the early years because they are the building blocks for more sophisticated skills. This chapter explains the vocabulary and classification of human movement and offers teachers a framework for designing lessons that help students understand the relationship between their bodies and movement. There are three major components to learning movement concepts:

1. Know the classification scheme for movement.

2. Understand how to design effective movement themes for instruction.

3. Use movement themes to bring the concepts of movement to life. This step integrates concepts and activities for the purpose of developing a "movement-educated" youngster.

Chapters 15 through 18 cover development of fundamental motor skills. This section forms the foundation for the development of a physically educated youngster. The chapters cover movement concepts, fundamental motor skills, manipulative skills, and body management skills. Even though all the skills and concepts are learned simultaneously they are listed in separate chapters.

With Development Level I children (ages 4 to 9), emphasis is placed on developing an understanding of movement concepts. Less emphasis is placed on skill technique and correct performance of skills.

Emphasis is placed on teaching children the vocabulary of movement. Lessons are designed to help students understand and physically experience the classification of movement concepts, which includes body awareness, space awareness, qualities of movement, and relationships. Instructional objectives are to show children how movements are classified and how movement themes can turn concepts into concrete movements. Emphasis is placed on the process of moving rather than on the product of correctly performing a skill.

Movement themes are categorized according to the movement concept classifications of space awareness, body awareness, qualities of movement, and relationships. As youngsters experience movement, they also learn the vocabulary of movement, in order to increase their understanding of the diversity and openness of movement possibilities.

Movement themes form the foundation of movement experiences necessary for developing more specific fundamental skills. Through this process, children develop an increased awareness and understanding of the body as a vehicle for movement, and acquire a personal vocabulary of movement skills. Movement themes in this text are categorized in the major classifications of space awareness, body awareness, qualities of movement, and relationships.

CLASSIFICATION OF HUMAN MOVEMENT CONCEPTS

The movement concept categories of body awareness, space awareness, qualities of movement, and relationships offer structure and direction for planning new movement experiences. As youngsters experience movement, they learn the vocabulary of movement so they are able to discuss and understand the unlimited possibilities for creative and productive movement.

Body awareness defines what the body can perform; the shapes it can make, how it can balance, and transferring weight to different body parts.

> Go to this website to view a piece of equipment that has been designed to enhance eye-hand coordination and body awareness:
>  http://www.esn.net/howell/touchandspin

Space awareness defines where the body can move, focusing on directions and using a variety of levels including:

- General or personal space

- Direction

- Level

- Pathways

- Planes

These constructs classify how the body moves. The qualities of movement define how the movement will be conducted. Rather than dealing with specific movements, the focus is on how movements are performed, for example, with speed or great force or lightly. These qualities can be applied to many different skills and activities.

1. Time or speed

2. Force

3. Flow: interrupted flow; sustained flow

Relationship

A relationship is defined as the position of the performer to a piece of apparatus or to other performers. Additionally, relationships can define the body parts of a single performer, such as arms together–apart or symmetrical–asymmetrical.

TEACHING MOVEMENT SKILLS AND CONCEPTS

The teacher needs to develop and design movement themes for students to experience. Four steps are suggested in the textbook for creating lessons that teach movement skills and concepts incorporating the problem-solving teaching style.

Step One: Set and Define the Problem

- Define the problem. Use action words.

- State what you want the children to do.

- Describe where you want the students to move.

- State how you want them to move and the force factors you want them to use when moving.

- State with whom or what you want the children to move.

Step Two: Experiment and Explore

Present problems in the form of questions or statements that elicit and encourage depth and variety of movement. Restate the question in a variety of ways to vary the exploration experience. Numerous examples are listed in this section of the chapter.

Step Three: Observe and Discuss Various Solutions

In this step, youngsters observe some of the patterns that others have created.

Step Four: Refine and Expand Solutions to the Problem

This step involves integrating various ideas students have observed and expanding their ideas.

- Challenge youngsters to put the movements together into a combination with transitional movements.

- Incorporate partner and small-group skill decision-making between partners in the creation of movements and/or combinations.

- Teach about symmetrical and asymmetrical movements by creating movement exploration activities.

MOVEMENT SKILLS AND CONCEPTS LESSON PLANS

The accompanying text, *Dynamic Physical Education Lesson Plans for Implementation*, 15th ed., contains lesson plans for teaching movement skills and concepts. Each lesson plan contains a variety of experiences in movement concepts and skills. Each lesson contains the following sections:

1. Movement themes

2. Fundamental skills

3. Manipulative skills

TEACHING MOVEMENT THEMES

Movement themes are used to apply movement concepts and help students learn by moving. Movement themes focus on a movement concept that children use to create movement patterns and sequences. The purposes are to explore and experiment with the concept through movement. Some themes involve only a single principle or factor, while others involve two or more. Themes in this chapter focus on exploring different concepts of movement, but in actuality, isolating a particular factor is difficult. For example, in exploring balance, movement possibilities are expanded through the application of body shape, level, and time factors. The following themes are classified into four major groups of human movement concepts: body awareness, space awareness, qualities of movement, and relationships. Numerous examples are listed in the chapter.

Qualities of Movement Themes (How the Body Moves)

The qualities of time, speed, contrasting movements, force, tension and relaxation, and relationships of movement are detailed in this chapter.

Go to the following websites for further information on movement activities for young children:

www.happalmer.com/articlepg1.htm

www.cfc-efc.ca/docs/cccf/00013_en.htm

www.arepublish.com/BCM.html

www.southernearlychildhood.org/position_arts.html

INSTRUCTIONAL FORMATS

The material in this chapter may be presented using the lecture style and the Power Point/overhead transparencies providing students an overview of the chapter. The instructor may also use the Guided Discovery method of teaching to introduce and review the materials read by the students. In this style, the instructor asks questions guiding the students toward one answer. The instructor rephrases the questions until the students discover the answer to the question. The introduction/review of the chapter may be followed by cooperative learning assignments that provide active learning and critical thinking activities for the student. In the cooperative learning groups, the students will discuss the materials listed on the Cooperative Learning Task Sheet (CLTS) and/or other topics you may assign. Each group can become a "content expert" for sections of the CLTS. Oral summary reports of the group may be presented to the entire class covering all or part of the discussion items. You may want to distribute the CLTS to the class before the discussion or post them on a website for students to preview. Additionally, for the material in this chapter activity sessions are appropriate to demonstrate the types of physical activity described in the chapter.

KEY TERMS

movement themes	space awareness	sustained flow
body awareness	interrupted flow	qualities of movement

DISCUSSION TOPICS

1. Discuss how movement themes are used to develop an understanding of movement concepts.

2. Discuss the purpose of movement theme lessons for Developmental Level I students.

SAMPLE WRITTEN ASSIGNMENTS

1. Using the guidelines in the textbook, write the phrases you would say to a class to develop body awareness and spatial awareness movement exploration.

2. Write a lesson focus covering a movement theme for Level I students. Use an Internet search to help you with new ideas.

3. Write a lesson focus covering a movement theme for Level II students. Use an Internet search to help you with new ideas.

4. Using a small manipulative to motivate movement, write a lesson exploring movement qualities. Suggestions for manipulative equipment to use might be: balloons, ribbons, juggling scarf, beach ball, etc.

ACTIVITY SESSION EXPERIENCES

Lead the students through the following activities:

- Demonstrate a variety of movement concepts and themes described in the textbook.

- Teach model lessons for Developmental Level I and II using the lessons written in the lesson plan book with movement concepts and themes as the lesson focus.

- Have students peer teach a lesson from the lesson plan book using the activities described in this chapter as the lesson focus.

COOPERATIVE LEARNING TASK SHEET

Chapter 15: Movement Concepts and Themes

Directions: Your cooperative learning group will become the content experts by finding the answers to the items listed below. Discuss the following items with your group and be ready to report on one or all of them at the end of the class period.

1. Look through the chapter and identify the words that can be used to elicit movement concepts/ themes. In your group, select a theme and write phrases that you can use with children to elicit movement exploration in your identified theme.

2. Identify a "teacher" in your group. The rest of the group will be role-playing Developmental Level I children. Peer teach the lesson to your cooperative learning group. Upon completion, evaluate the questions asked and modify them if necessary. Allow another member of the group to peer teach. Evaluate the experience as the "doer" and the "teacher."

3. Write a lesson on the theme of weight transfer and moving in general space. Develop all of the questions to be used with the children. Repeat the procedures established in # 2 above.

4. Write and peer teach a lesson using the theme of qualities of movement. Use the guidelines established in #1 and #2 above.

5. In your group, select another movement concept/theme. Write the lesson focus for developing the movement concept/theme. Have one member of the group peer teach the lesson. Then critique the effectiveness of the lesson together.

CHAPTER 16

Fundamental Motor Skills and Introductory Activities

SUMMARY

This chapter contains two major parts: fundamental skills and introductory activities. Fundamental skills in this chapter include two major categories: locomotor and nonlocomotor skills. These skills form the foundation for nearly all physical activities students will choose to participate in throughout life. Locomotor skills define the many ways the body can be moved throughout space. Non-locomotor movements are generally performed without the requirement of movement throughout space. These skills are learned through repetition and refinement with many variations offered to keep students motivated.

The second part of the chapter is introductory activities. The foundation of introductory activities is locomotor movement. These activities are used as activities for starting a lesson. They require little instruction and immediately immerse students in large muscle activities. Beginning a lesson with introductory activities will assure students are warmed up and motivated for the rest of the lesson.

STUDENT OUTCOMES

Upon completion of the reading of this chapter, the student will:

- Understand that teaching fundamental movement is synonymous with providing instruction toward the acquisition of a specific skill.

- Describe the differences between locomotor and nonlocomotor skills.

- Cite stress points, instructional cues, and suggested movement patterns to enhance the learning of locomotor and nonlocomotor skills.

- Specify activities designed to develop locomotor and nonlocomotor motor skills.

- Describe the rationale for including introductory activities in the lesson plan.

- Characterize various features of the opening phase of the lesson.

- Develop an introductory activity that meets established criteria for preparing children physiologically and psychologically.

- Describe the type of fundamental skills used in introductory activities.

MAIN CONCEPTS

Fundamental skills are utilitarian skills that people need for living and being. This group of skills is sometimes labeled basic or functional. The designation *fundamental skill* is used because the skills are necessary for children to function effectively in the environment. Fundamental skills form the foundation of human movement, and are usually identified by a single verb, such as walking, twisting, running, jumping, or stretching. (Most of the fundamental skills end in the suffix -ing.) Learning physical skills develops in a general to specific manner. This chapter is focused on general motor skills that involve large muscle movements. Fundamental skills are the tools that most adults use to participate in leisure activities. Without a learned set of fundamental skills and a positive feeling about being able to perform in activity settings, many people will relegate themselves to a lifetime of inactivity.

Learning fundamental skills requires practicing the basic locomotor and nonlocomotor skills through an unlimited number of repetitions. Repetition under a wide range of conditions and constantly refining performance helps assure the skills will be able to be performed in varying conditions. To help you teach these skills in an efficient manner, important points and instructional cues are listed. These are points of emphasis that will help students learn the skills correctly and quickly. The locomotor movement activities also include a section on rhythmic activities since all locomotor movements are rhythmic in nature. The following skills are grouped for ease of teaching and ease of comprehension by students. Although the skills are presented here individually, they are most often performed in a seemingly infinite number of combinations, depending on the sport or activity.

Fundamental skills are divided into three categories: locomotor, nonlocomotor, and manipulative. Teaching tips for locomotor, nonlocomotor, rhythmic, and manipulative skills are included in detail in the chapter. Pushing, pulling, fleeing, chasing, and tagging activities are also described in this chapter.

INTRODUCTORY ACTIVITIES

Introductory activities represent the first activity youngsters experience when entering the activity area. Such activities incorporate vigorous fundamental motor skills and require minimal instruction. Introductory activities are used during the first two to three minutes of the lesson. They are used to warm children up physiologically and to prepare them for the physical activity that follows. It is a truism in teaching that a lesson that starts well, ends well. Introductory activities allow an opportunity for practicing management skills and focusing on the objectives of the lesson.

Regardless of the introductory activity used, it is most important to be sure a class begins in a well-managed and attentive manner. An excellent "rule of three freezes" can be used to check the disposition of a class and to get them ready for instruction. Have the class enter the teaching area on the move and freeze on signal. Move them a second time and privately correct off-task behavior (while students are on the move). Freeze the class two more times to correct off-task behavior and to see if they are ready to learn. If the class is still not with you after three corrective episodes, don't teach an introductory activity; rather focus on management activity such as moving and freezing on signal. Introductory activities, by their nature, are upbeat and active. They will overly arouse a poorly managed class. Use the highly active and enjoyable activities to reinforce a class that exhibits well-managed behavior.

Introductory activities are used for a number of reasons:

1. To offer youngsters immediate activity when entering the gym. This satisfies their desire to move and offers you an opportunity to establish a positive learning attitude (purposive movement performed under control) for the class.

2. To warm children up physiologically and prepare them for the activity that will follow.

3. To focus youngsters on the objectives of the lesson. Focus students on learning objectives by telling them the "what and why" of activities in the upcoming lesson.

Perform introductory activities at a slow pace in the initial stages for safety reasons and to warm up students. For example, if using Rhythmic Running as an introductory activity, begin by walking. As the class warms up, pick up the pace to a run. If using Group Over and Around, begin by asking students to moderately move over and around each other. After a short period of warming up, perform the activity at full speed.

Examples of numerous introductory activities are described in this chapter. Partner and small group activities are also explained in detail in this chapter.

Go to the following websites for further reading on fundamental motor skills:

    http://rubistar.4teachers.org/index.php

    www.learning.gov.ab.ca/physicaleducationonline

INSTRUCTIONAL FORMATS

The material in this chapter may be presented using the lecture style, Power Point slides and the overhead transparencies providing students an overview of the chapter. A videotape of a lesson demonstrating the teaching of fundamental motor skills for elementary children should be shown. In addition, the instructor using suggested movement patterns listed in this chapter or in the lesson plan book should lead an activity session. The introduction/review of the chapter material and activity session may be followed by cooperative learning assignments, which provide active learning and critical thinking activities for the student. In the cooperative learning groups, the students will discuss the materials listed on the Cooperative Learning Task Sheet and/or other topics you may assign. Each group can become a "content expert" for sections of the Cooperative Learning Task Sheet. Oral summary reports of the group may be presented to the entire class covering all or part of the discussion items.

KEY TERMS

fundamental skills	leaping	twisting
nonlocomotor skills	galloping	locomotor skills
rhythmic activities	skipping	
hopping	sliding	

DISCUSSION TOPIC

1. Contrast the methods used to teach fundamental movement skills versus thematic movement concepts.

SAMPLE WRITTEN ASSIGNMENTS

1. Write a position paper explaining the importance of learning fundamental and specialized skills during the formative elementary school years and the impact the acquisition of such skills may have on future activity participation of the person.

2. Write a creative lesson to explore the basic locomotor skills.

3. Write a lesson covering the development of a thematic lesson.

4. Write a lesson focus covering nonlocomotor skill exploration.

ACTIVITY SESSION EXPERIENCES

Lead the students through the following activities:

- Teach model lessons for each developmental level using the lessons written in the lesson plan book with fundamental movement skills and thematic movement as the lesson focus.

- Have students peer teach a lesson from the lesson plan book using the activities described in this chapter as the lesson focus.

COOPERATIVE LEARNING TASK SHEET

Chapter 16: Fundamental Motor Skills and Introductory Activities

Directions: Your cooperative learning group will become the content experts by finding the answers to the items listed below. Discuss the following items with your group and be ready to report on one or all of them at the end of the class period.

1. Discuss how teaching fundamental movement is synonymous with providing instruction toward the acquisition of a specific skill.

2. Identify the basic fundamental motor skills described in the chapter. Using examples from the chapter, lead your classmates through activities selected from examples in this chapter.

3. Peer teach the locomotor skills described in the textbook using phrases listed in the chapter to elicit movement. Evaluate the lesson within your group.

4. Cite instructional cues and suggested movement patterns to enhance learning fundamental skills. Try out the cues and movement patterns in your group. Evaluate the experience.

5. Follow the directives for suggested movement patterns for locomotor activities listed in the chapter in a peer teaching experience within your group. Evaluate the directives listed based on your experience practicing. Write additional directives to elicit these movement patterns.

CHAPTER 17

Manipulative Skills

SUMMARY

Activities in this chapter develop manipulative skills. A manipulative skill is one in which a child handles an object with the hands, feet, or other body parts. Development of sport skills results from repeating and refining activities in this chapter. Jump rope activities develop specialized motor skills, particularly visual-tactile coordination. Rope-jumping activities in this chapter progress from individual movements using rope patterns, to long-rope jumping with turners, to individual rope-jumping challenges. Rhythmic gymnastic activities combine rhythmic and manipulative skills using a particular piece of manipulative equipment while moving to accompaniment.

STUDENT OUTCOMES

Upon completion of the reading of this chapter, the student will:

- Demonstrate the various stages of development associated with throwing, catching, kicking, and striking.

- Identify instructional procedures related to different types of manipulative skills.

- Identify objects that can be used to help youngsters succeed in manipulative skills.

- Outline skill progressions, activities, and instructional hints associated with using balloons, beanbags, balls, paddles, Frisbees, hoops, jump ropes, parachutes, and other objects to teach manipulative skills.

- Identify beginning, intermediate, and advanced rope-jumping skills and routines using individual and long ropes.

- List progressions to use when teaching rope jumping.

MAIN CONCEPTS

Manipulative activities are characterized by the use of some type of implement, usually with the hands but possibly with the feet or other body parts.

Manipulative activities develop both hand-eye coordination as well as dexterity.

Progressions and movement themes are presented in this chapter as a means to teach manipulative activities.

Skills can be reinforced and enhanced through creative games.

Suggested activities include the following manipulatives: balloons, beanbags, balls, juggling scarves, scoops and balls, bowling activities, paddles and balls, Frisbees, wands, and hoops.

MANIPULATIVE SKILLS

Manipulative skills are basic to a number of specialized sport skills—catching, throwing, striking, and kicking, among others. These are complex motor patterns and general stages of development have been identified, from initial stages through mature patterns of performance.

Throwing

In throwing, an object is thrust into space and is accelerated using movement of the arm and the total coordination of the body to generate force.

Throwing is divided into four stages of development. The stages are:

Stage one: (two- and three-year-old children usually) Arm movement from the rear toward the front of the body. Feet are stationary and shoulder width. Little or no trunk rotation.

Stage two: (three- to five-year-olds usually) Some rotation is developed to increase the force of the throw. A lateral fling of the arm, with some rotation occurring in the trunk. Often children step in the direction of the throw. It may look like a discus throw.

Stage three: (five- and six-year-olds usually). A step is made toward the target with the foot on the same side of the body as the throwing arm. Arm action is nearer to the overhand style of throwing than flinging. There is an increase in hip flexion.

Stage four: (eight or nine years old) Mature form of throwing with force applied to the object being accelerated. Opposition is used. The target is addressed with the nonthrowing side of the body and strides toward the target to shift body weight.

Catching has four stages. Catching is more difficult to learn than throwing because the object must be tracked and the body moved into the path of the object simultaneously. Additionally, the fear of being hurt by the oncoming object adds to the complexity of this skill.

Stage one: A trapping movement, since the arms press the ball against the chest to catch. The arms are held in front of the body, with the elbows extended and palms up until the ball makes contact.

Stage two: The ball is cradled and then pulled into the chest.

Stage three: Contact is made with the hands first and then the object is guided to the chest. The chest is used as a backstop for the ball.

Stage four: Occurs at approximately nine years old; is characterized by catching with the hands.

Kicking also has four stages of learning. The stages described in the textbook are:

Stage one: Body is stationary and the kicking foot is flexed in preparation for the kick. The kicking motion is carried out with a straight leg and with little or no flexing at the knee. Minimal movement of the arms and trunk. All concentration is on the ball.

Stage two: The kicking foot is lifted backwards by flexing at the knee. The child displays opposition of the limbs usually. The kicking leg moves farther forward in the follow-through motion than in stage one.

Stage three: Movement toward the object to be kicked is added. There is an increase in the distance the leg is moved, coupled with a movement of the upper body to counterbalance the leg movement.

Stage four: A preparatory extension of the hip to increase the range of motion is displayed in this mature kicking pattern. A run to the ball and a small leap to get the kicking foot in position is made. As the kicking foot is carried forward, the trunk leans backward, and a small step forward is made on the support foot to regain balance.

Striking occurs when an object is hit with an implement. There are three stages to this skill:

Stage one: Feet are stationary and the trunk faces the direction of the tossed ball (or ball on a tee). Elbows are fully flexed and the force is generated by extending the flexed joints in a downward plane. Little body force is generated by extending the flexed joints in a downward plane. Little body force is generated because there is no trunk rotation and the motion developed is back to front. Generation of forces comes from the arms and wrists.

Stage two: The upper body begins to generate force. The trunk is turned to the side in anticipation of the ball. There is a weight shift from the rear foot to the forward foot prior to contacting the ball. Trunk and hip rotation is used. Extending the flexed joints generates force. Trunk rotation and forward movement are in an oblique plane.

Stage three: Mature striking is characterized by a swing through the full range of motion and a sequential transfer of weight from the rear to the front plane of the body.

MANIPULATIVE SKILL ACTIVITIES

Manipulative skills come into play when children handle an object. Most of these skills involve the hands and feet, but other parts of the body can also be used. The manipulation of objects leads to better hand-eye and foot-eye coordination, which are particularly important for tracking items in space. Manipulative skills form the foundation for many game skills. Propulsion (throwing, batting, kicking) and receipt (catching) of objects are important skills that can be taught by using beanbags and various balls. Rebounding or redirecting an object in flight (such as a volleyball) is another useful manipulative skill. Continuous control of an object, such as a wand or hoop, is also a manipulative activity.

Progression of Instructional Activities

Instructional activities within each unit in this chapter are presented in progression and are organized into major skill groups.

Some teachers ask why activities are grouped around equipment rather than skills. It would certainly be possible to create random practice sessions by using different types of equipment to practice the same skills. However, this makes most lessons equipment-intensive. The single factor that keeps most teachers from teaching certain skills and units is the amount of equipment that is required.

Reinforce Skills with Student-Developed Games

Skills can be reinforced and enhanced through games that students create. Children can be given a brief outline of a game situation on which they can structure a game applying the skills just learned. Specification of the game situation can range from open choice to creativity within guidelines.

ACTIVITIES WITH BALLOONS AND BEACH BALLS

Balloons provide interesting movement experiences and emphasize hand-eye coordination. Success can be achieved with balloons when students are not ready for faster-moving ball skills. Instructional procedures are described in the chapter.

ACTIVITIES WITH BEANBAGS

Activities with beanbags provide valuable learning experiences for elementary school children at all levels. All parts of the body can be brought into play. For tossing and catching, though, the beanbag encourages manipulation with the hands; playground balls lead to arm and body catching. Beanbag activities can be used with older youngsters provided that the activities are carefully selected to challenge students. The more challenging partner activities—juggling, different and unique methods of propulsion, and the Split-Vision Drill —are examples of suitable activities. Instructional procedures are described in the chapter.

ACTIVITIES WITH BALLS

Included in this section are the ball skills in which the child handles balls without the aid of other equipment, such as a bat or paddle. Ball skills are mostly of two types: (a) hand-eye skills, including throwing, catching, bouncing, dribbling (as in basketball), batting (as in volleyball), and rolling (as in bowling); and (b) foot-eye skills, including kicking, trapping, and dribbling (as in soccer). Instructional procedures are described in the chapter.

JUGGLING

Juggling is a novel task that is exciting to elementary school youngsters. It is a challenging task that demands practice and repetition to learn. An excellent medium for teaching beginners is sheer, lightweight scarves that measure 18 to 24 inches square. These move slowly, allowing children to track them visually. Juggling with scarves teaches children correct patterns of object movement; however, it does not transfer easily to juggling with faster-moving objects such as fleece balls, tennis balls, rings, and hoops. Therefore, two distinct sections for juggling are offered: a section dealing with learning to juggle with scarves and a second discussion explaining juggling with balls. Juggling with scarves will bring success to a majority of the class. Youngsters who have mastered the scarves can move to balls and other objects. Instructional procedures are described in the chapter.

ACTIVITIES WITH SCOOPS AND BALLS

Scoops can be purchased or made with bleach bottles or similar containers (see Chapter 10). They are excellent for practicing catching and tossing skills using an implement rather than the hands. Instructional procedures are described in the chapter.

BOWLING ACTIVITIES

Younger children should practice informal rolling. As they mature, the emphasis should change from informal rolling to bowling skills. Bowling skills begin with a two-handed roll and progress to one-handed rolls, alternating between the right and left hand. Various targets can be used, including bowling pins, milk cartons, small cones, blocks, and even people. Instructional procedures are described in the chapter.

ACTIVITIES WITH WANDS

Wands have been used in physical education programs for many years, but only recently have a wide variety of interesting and challenging activities been developed. Wands can be made from 3/4-inch maple dowels or from a variety of broom and mop handles. If two lengths are chosen, make them 36 and 42 inches. Instructional procedures are described in the chapter.

ACTIVITIES WITH HOOPS

Most hoops manufactured in the United States are plastic, but Europeans sometimes use wooden ones. The plastic variety is less durable but more versatile. Extra hoops are needed because some breakage will occur. The standard hoop is 42 inches in diameter, but it is desirable to have smaller hoops (36 inches) for primary-grade children.

ACTIVITIES WITH JUMP ROPES

Rope jumping is an excellent activity for conditioning all parts of the body. It increases coordination, rhythm, and timing, while offering a wide range of challenges. Rope jumping is regarded as an excellent medium for fitness development. It can be designed to suit the activity needs of all individuals regardless of age or condition. Workloads can easily be measured and modified by changing the amount of time jumped or the number of turns. It is a useful activity to teach children, because it offers carryover value for activity in later life.

Rope patterns can be created and a variety of activities can be presented to be performed inside the pattern, as a part of the pattern, or outside the pattern. Locomotor and nonlocomotor activities can be practiced.

Partners can work with one or two ropes, and can do matching, following, or contrasting movements.

Long-rope jumping is an excellent activity for beginning jumpers. Youngsters can concentrate on jumping the rope without learning the skill of turning.

Double Dutch rope jumping is popular on playgrounds and in gymnasiums across the country. This type of jumping requires two rope turners using two long ropes that are turned in opposite directions.

Formation jumping requires four to six ropes with turners. Tasks are given to each set of turners. Formations are described in the chapter.

Go to the following site for more activities involving rope jumping:

 www.worldofropejumping.com

 www.aahperd.org

FOOTBAG ACTIVITIES

Footbag activities involve keeping the bag in the air by means of repetitive foot contact. A combination of lifting and kicking motions are used to keep the bag in the air.

Go to the following site for more activities involving the footbag:

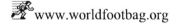www.worldfootbag.org

RHYTHMIC GYMNASTICS

Rhythmic gymnastic activities offer the student the challenge of using selected manipulatives in combination with locomotor movements performed to music. The manipulatives include: hoops, balls, ribbons, and clubs.

INSTRUCTIONAL FORMATS

An overview of the material in this chapter may be presented using the lecture style with the use of the Power Point slides. A videotape of a lesson demonstrating the teaching of manipulative skills to elementary children should be shown. In addition, an activity session should be led by the instructor using suggested movement patterns listed in this chapter or in the lesson plan book. The introduction/review of the chapter material and activity session may be followed by cooperative learning assignments that provide active learning and critical thinking activities for the student. In the cooperative learning groups, the students will discuss the materials listed on the Cooperative Learning Task Sheet and/or other topics you may assign. Each group can become a "content expert" for sections of the Cooperative Learning Task Sheet. Oral summary reports of the group may be presented to the entire class covering all or part of the discussion items.

KEY TERMS

formation jumping	footbag	wands
rhythmic gymnastics	cascading	manipulative skills

DISCUSSION TOPIC

1. Discuss the rationale for teaching skills based on grouping with like equipment.

SAMPLE WRITTEN ASSIGNMENTS

1. Write the instructions for a footbag lesson.

2. Write the directions you would say in leading a Developmental Level I class through hoop exploration activities for an introductory activity.

3. Write a plan for a week of different long rope activities.

4. Write the instructions for an individual rope-jumping routine.

ACTIVITY SESSION EXPERIENCES

Lead the students through the following activities:

- Beach ball, balloon, and beanbag activities.

- Partner activities using beanbags.

- Ball-handling activities including: bouncing, rolling, tossing, catching, and batting experiences.

- Juggling with scarves.

- Activities with scoops and balls.

- Bowling and paddling activities.

- Frisbee basic skills.

- Activities with wands including cooperative activities.

- Hoop activities.

- Individual, long rope, and Double Dutch rope-jumping skills. Include music and routines.

- Footbag activities individually and with a partner.

- Rhythmic gymnastics skills using ball, hoop, rope, and creative floor exercise activities.

- Teach model lessons for each developmental level using the lessons written in the lesson plan book with rope jumping, wands, hoop activities, and rhythmic gymnastics as the lesson focus.

- Have students peer teach a lesson from the lesson plan book using the activities described in this chapter as the lesson focus.

COOPERATIVE LEARNING TASK SHEET

Chapter 17: Manipulative Skills

Directions: Your cooperative learning group will become the content experts by finding the answers to the items listed below. Discuss the following items with your group and be ready to report on one or all of them at the end of the class period.

1. Discuss and then write a lesson incorporating creative opportunities for teaching manipulative skills. You may use ideas presented in the textbook and combine them in a creative manner or develop your own ideas. Try the lesson out on your group, if possible. Then peer teach it to another group, if possible.

2. Outline skill progressions, activities, and instructional hints associated with teaching each of the following: balloons, beanbags, balls, and paddles, to teach manipulative skills. Each person in the group should select one apparatus and peer teach, if possible, within your group the ideas outlined.

3. Outline skill progressions, activities, and instructional hints associated with teaching each of the following: Frisbees, hoops, jump ropes, parachutes, and other objects to teach manipulative skills. Each person in the group should select one apparatus and peer teach, if possible, within your group ideas outlined.

4. Identify the stages of development associated with throwing. Each person in the group should select a stage of throwing and demonstrate it to the group, if possible, to the best of their ability.

5. Identify the stages of development associated with catching. Each person in the group should select a stage of catching and demonstrate it to the group, if possible, to the best of their ability.

6. Identify the stages of development associated with kicking and striking. Each person in the group should select a stage of each activity and demonstrate it to the group to the best of their ability.

7. Read through the section in the chapter on rhythmic gymnastics. Assign each member of the group one apparatus listed in the chapter. That person should try out the movement ideas listed and teach them to members of your group. Try to create a mini routine within your group. You may decide to demonstrate your routines created to another group in class.

8. Identify beginning, intermediate, and advanced rope-jumping skills and routines using individual ropes. Together develop an individual rope-jumping routine.

9. Identify beginning, intermediate, and advanced rope-jumping skills and routines using long ropes. Together develop a long-rope jumping pattern of skills or a routine.

10. List progressions to use when teaching rope jumping. Try the progressions out in your group.

CHAPTER 18

Body Management Skills

SUMMARY

Body management skills are required for control of the body in a variety of situations. Body management skills require an integration of agility, coordination, strength, balance, and flexibility. Activities in this chapter help students learn to control their bodies while using a wide variety of apparatus. This chapter offers organizational hints, instructional strategies, and activities for helping youngsters develop body management skills.

STUDENT OUTCOMES

Upon completion of the reading of this chapter, the student will:

- Know how to help students develop body management skills using large and small apparatus.

- Apply proper instructional procedures to a wide variety of apparatus activities.

- Design a safe environment when teaching large apparatus activities.

- Teach a variety of activities on large apparatus, including climbing ropes, benches, balance beams, and jumping boxes.

- .Teach activities using small apparatus, including magic ropes, individual mats, tug-of-war ropes, and gym scooters.

MAIN CONCEPTS

Body management skills are an important component of movement competency. Efficient movement demands integration of a number of physical traits, including agility, balance, strength, flexibility, and coordination. In addition, youngsters must develop an understanding of how to control their bodies while on large apparatus, such as beams, benches, and jumping boxes. A basic understanding of movement concepts and mechanical principles used in skill performance is necessary for quality movement.

For further reading on body management skill development, go to these sites:

http://www.extension.iastate.edu/Publications/PM1359B.pdf

http://www.uen.org/Lessonplan/preview.cgi?LPid=945

http://www.mpsaz.org/tafttest/programdescrip.html

Youngsters must develop an understanding of how to control their body while on large apparatus such as beams, benches, and jumping boxes.

A basic understanding of movement concepts and mechanical principles used in skill performance is necessary for quality movement.

The focus of this chapter is on developing body management skills using large and small apparatus.

This site allows you to see how one district approaches this topic:

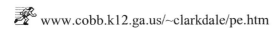 www.cobb.k12.ga.us/~clarkdale/pe.htm

Large apparatus activities include climbing ropes, benches, balance beams, and jumping boxes. These activities offer the opportunity to learn body management skills while free of ground support.

Small apparatus activities help develop body control in space and on the ground. These activities include: magic ropes, individual mats, and gym scooters.

The safe and effective use of this apparatus is described in detail in this chapter.

SAFE AND EFFECTIVE USE OF APPARATUS

Apparatus is often set up when youngsters arrive in class. The children need to be taught that they cannot use the equipment until the instructor has given approval for its use. Establish instructional procedures for setup, storage, and safe use of apparatus and mats. Youngsters should be taught they are not to use the equipment until instructor approval has been given.

Return Activities

Return activities increase the movement potential of apparatus. Return activities require students to perform a movement task after they have performed on the apparatus. This reduces the time children stand in line waiting for another turn after completion of their task on the apparatus.

ACTIVITIES WITH CLIMBING ROPES

Climbing ropes offer high-level developmental possibilities for the upper body. Activities for their use are described in detail in this section of the chapter.

ACTIVITIES ON BALANCE BEAMS AND BENCHES

Balance beam activities contribute to control in both static and dynamic balance situations. Balance beam benches are appropriate to use in the elementary school. Activities for their use are described in detail in this section of the chapter.

ACTIVITIES WITH JUMPING BOXES

Jumping boxes provide opportunities for children to jump from a height and propel the body through space. Activities for their use are described in detail in this section of the chapter.

ACTIVITIES WITH INDIVIDUAL MATS

Individual mats are the basis for many exploratory and creative movements. Activities for their use are described in detail in this section of the chapter.

ACTIVITIES WITH MAGIC ROPES

Magic rope activities originated in Germany. Each rope is similar to a long rubber band. Activities for their use are described in this section of the chapter.

ACTIVITIES WITH PARTNER TUG-OF-WAR ROPES

Partner tug-of-war rope activities offer good possibilities in movement exploration. Activities for their use are described in this section of the chapter.

Partner Resistance Activities

Partner resistance activities involve controlled pulling, not tugging a partner. The partner should not be compelled to move out of position. Partners are instructed to work together, both in the same position. Activities for their use are described in this section of the chapter.

ACTIVITIES WITH GYM SCOOTERS

Gym scooters make excellent devices for developmental activity. Safety rules must be established before their use. Activities for their use are described in detail in this section of the chapter.

INSTRUCTIONAL FORMATS

An overview of the material in this chapter may be presented using the lecture style. A videotape of a lesson demonstrating the teaching of body management activities using large and small apparatus to elementary children should be shown. In addition, an activity session should be led by the instructor using suggested movement patterns listed in this chapter or in the lesson plan book. The introduction/review of the chapter material and activity session may be followed by cooperative learning assignments that provide active learning and critical thinking activities for the student. In the cooperative learning groups, the students will discuss the materials listed on the Cooperative Learning Task Sheet and/or other topics you may assign. Each group can become a "content expert" for sections of the Cooperative Learning Task Sheet. Oral summary reports of the group may be presented to the entire class covering all or part of the discussion items.

KEY TERMS

body management skills	small apparatus activities	partner tug-of-war ropes
return activities	jumping box	partner resistance activities
large apparatus activities	magic rope	

DISCUSSION TOPIC

1. Create a position paper that a physical education department could present to a school board to receive support for purchasing and installing climbing ropes and gym scooters for the district.

SAMPLE WRITTEN ASSIGNMENTS

1. Write a lesson focus concentrating on body management skills.

2. Create a combination of partner tug-of-war rope activities that could be used in a lesson focus.

ACTIVITY SESSION EXPERIENCES

Lead the students through the following activities:

- Balance beam activities combined with return activities.

- Climbing rope activities.

- Balance beam challenge stunts.

- Bench activities combined with return activities.

- Jumping box activities.

- Individual mat experiences.

- Magic rope activities.

- Partner tug-of-war activities.

- Partner resistance activities.

- Gym scooter experiences.

- Teach a model lesson for Developmental Level I students using the lessons written in the lesson plan book with body management skills as the lesson focus.

- Have students peer teach a lesson using body management skills as the lesson focus.

COOPERATIVE LEARNING TASK SHEET

Chapter 18: Body Management Skills

Directions: Your cooperative learning group will become the content experts by finding the answers to the items listed below. Discuss the following items with your group and be ready to report on one or all of them at the end of the class period.

1. Using a partner tug-of-war rope describe and then practice the skills listed in the chapter.

2. Create a series of partner tug-of-war activities. Try them out in your group. Teach them to another group.

3. Create a game using gym scooters. Write up the rules. Try it out within your group. Try it out on another group.

4. Create a game using jumping boxes. Write up the rules. Try it out within your group. Try it out on another group.

5. Develop a set of partner resistance activities. Try them out within your group. Write down the directions for the activities onto a task sheet that children could follow.

6. Write a lesson focus using a theme/concept to develop body management skills for Level I children.

CHAPTER 19

Rhythmic Movement Skills

SUMMARY

Activities in this chapter are selected for the purpose of developing rhythmic movement skills. The activities are listed in progression of easy to more complex and by developmental level. The development of social skills and a positive self-concept occur when rhythmic activities are taught in a sensitive and educational manner. Rhythmic activities should be scheduled in the same manner as other phases of the yearly physical education program. Most dances employ skills and steps, which are learned in a sequential manner.

STUDENT OUTCOMES

Upon completion of the reading of this chapter, the student will:

- Know where to find sources of rhythmic accompaniment.

- Understand the inherent rhythmic nature of all physical activity.

- Outline components of the yearly rhythmic movement program and identify accompanying activities and skill progressions.

- Describe instructional procedures and ideas to facilitate implementation of rhythmic movements into the yearly program.

- Cite creative rhythms, movement songs, folk dances, and other dance activities that are used as learning experiences in physical education.

- Describe dance progressions that are appropriate for the various levels of development that children exhibit.

MAIN CONCEPTS

Rhythm is the basis of music, dance, and movement in general. All body movements tend to be rhythmic — the beating of the heart, swinging a tennis racquet, running, throwing a ball. Rhythmic activities are particularly appropriate for younger children. A large portion of the Developmental Level I program is devoted to such activities.

There are a large variety of rhythmical activities available to teach youngsters. If the teacher prepares properly, he will become comfortable with rhythms and find that these activities are a favorite of children.

An important component of children's dance is fundamental rhythms. Instruction begins with and capitalizes on locomotor skills that children already possess — walking, running, hopping, and jumping.

Rhythmic activities provide a vehicle for expressive movement. Youngsters have a chance to create unique rhythmic responses within action songs and dances.

IMPLEMENTING THE RHYTHMIC MOVEMENT PROGRAM

The rhythmic program should be balanced and include activities from each of the categories of rhythmic movement. Recommended skill progressions are presented for each developmental level in this section.

Developmental Level I

Youngsters in Developmental Level I focus on creative rhythms and movement songs.

Developmental Level II

At this level, greater practice on folk dances and line dances include combinations of locomotor skills, such as the step-hop, and the grand right and left. Marching, basic tinikling steps, and introductory square dancing steps are taught as skill improves. All the activities are taught with an emphasis on mastering simple locomotor skills rather performing the dances with perfection.

Developmental Level III

Developmental Level III students begin to learn some of the more difficult steps such as the grapevine step, schottische, polka, intermediate tinikling steps, two-step, advanced tinikling step, square dancing, and all steps introduced at earlier levels. Developmentally, these students are not comfortable moving with partners of the opposite sex, so activities are modified to allow for individual activity.

Understanding Rhythmic Accompaniment

Children should be taught to recognize, understand, and appreciate the basic characteristics of music: tempo, beat, meter, accent, intensity, phrasing, and measures.

Sources of Rhythmic Accompaniment

Essential to any rhythmic program is accompaniment that encourages desired motor patterns and expressive movement. If children are to move to a rhythm, it must be stimulating, appropriate for the expected responses, and appealing to the learners.

CREATIVE RHYTHMS

Creativity should be part of all dance and rhythmic activities, with the scope of the activity determining the degree of freedom. Creative rhythms, however, provide a special program area in which creativity is the goal and functional movement is secondary. The emphasis is on the process and not on the movement outcomes.

Instructional Procedures

1. Appropriate music or rhythmic background is important; otherwise, movement can become stilted. An atmosphere of creative freedom must be established.

2. When analyzing the setting, ask, "What is the basic idea? What expressive movements can be expected? What are the guidelines or boundaries of movement? What space are the children to use?"

3. Listening is an important element, because children must understand the mood or sense of the rhythmic background. Some questions that can be posed to children are, "What does the music make us think of?" and "What does the music tell us to do?"

4. Use action-directing statements such as, "Let's pretend we are . . . ," "Let's try being like . . . ," "Try to feel like a . . . ," and "Make believe you are. . . ."

5. In some lessons, the initial focus may be on the selection of appropriate rhythmic background. In this instance children formulate a creative rhythm of the dramatic type and then seek suitable music for their dance.

6. Give children time to develop and try their ideas. This is an open-ended process that has a variety of solutions.

Expressive Movement

Children can express moods and feelings and show reactions to colors and sounds by improvising dances or movements that demonstrate different aspects of force, or gestures that depict different feelings. A piece of music is played and is followed by a discussion of its qualities and how it makes the children feel. Children may interpret the music differently. Moods can be described as happy, lighthearted, sad, brave, fearful, cheerful, angry, solemn, silly, stately, sleepy, funny, cautious, bold, or nonchalant.

Identification

There are endless subject sources for identification and interpretation. Children can take on the identity of a familiar character, creature, or object. The following ideas should be useful.

1. Animals—elephants, ducks, seals, chickens, dogs, rabbits, lions, and others

2. People—soldiers, firefighters, sailors, nurses, various kinds of workers, forest rangers, teachers, cowboys and cowgirls, and so on

3. Play objects—seesaws, swings, rowboats, balls, various toys, and many other common articles with which children play

4. Make-believe creatures—giants, dwarfs, gnomes, witches, trolls, dragons, pixies, fairies, and so on

5. Machines—trains, planes, jets, rockets, automobiles, bicycles, motorcycles, tractors, elevators, and the like

6. Circus characters—clowns, various trained animals, trapeze artists, tightrope performers, jugglers, acrobats, and bands

7. Natural phenomena—fluttering leaves, grain, flowers, rain, snow, clouds, wind, tornadoes, hurricanes, volcanoes, and others

Dramatization

Dramatization and rhythm are useful vehicles for group activity. Suitable background music or rhythmic accompaniment is a necessary ingredient. Excellent recordings are available, from short numbers lasting a minute or two to more elaborate productions such as those found in the Dance-a-Story series (RCA Victor).

FOLK DANCES

A folk dance is defined as a traditional dance of a particular culture. In this concept, a definite pattern or dance routine is usually specified and followed. Folk dancing is one phase of a child's education that can assist in bringing about international understanding. A country's way of life and many other habits are often reflected in its folk music. From these dances, children gain an understanding of why people from certain countries act and live as they do, even though modern times may have changed their lifestyle from that of days gone by.

Go to this site to read a brief history of square and round dancing:

 http://www.dosado.com/articles/hist-sd.html

By going to this website you will view a wealth of information on dances from Mexico:

 http://www.alegria.org/rgndance.html

Teaching New Dances Successfully

The underlying goal of folk dancing is to learn to move rhythmically. Techniques for successfully teaching dances include:

1. Slow down the music.

2. Use the whole-teaching approach. If it is a longer dance with several different parts, use the part–whole
    method and teach one part at a time.

3. Introduce a new dance with students placed in scattered formation. Circles and formations cause some students to feel others are looking directly at them.

4. Avoid the use of partners when teaching a new activity. Partners add a degree of complexity to many dances and should be added only after the basic steps have been mastered.

5. Avoid the left-right and clockwise-counterclockwise orientation when introducing a new dance. Anytime students are asked to move in a specified direction, it increases the possibility of error. Allow students to choose the direction they would like to move when learning new steps.

6. To avoid stressing students, perform a dance once or twice in a daily lesson. Presenting a number of dances, rather than one or two in depth, gives students who are having difficulty a chance to start with a clean slate on a new dance.

7. Teach rhythmic activities in the same way sport skills are taught.

8. Dances that emphasize strong movements such as hand clapping and foot stomping appeal to boys.

Modifying Rhythmic Activities

Folk dances can be modified to increase student interest and increase the ease of learning.

If you would like to purchase videotapes to help visualize dances of a variety of styles that you may teach, click on the site below. This site is a comprehensive resource to available videotapes:

 http://www.activevideos.com

This site will provide you with dance teaching ideas:

 http://pecentral.org/lessonideas/dance/danceindex.asp

Levels of rhythmic skills are described in this site:

 http://www.edb.utexas.edu/coe/depts/kin/Faculty/slacks/crpac/rhythms_levels.html

CULMINATING EVENTS FOR THE RHYTHMS UNIT

Culminating events and school-wide festivals for a rhythms unit are described in-depth in this chapter.

INSTRUCTIONAL FORMATS

An overview of the material in this chapter may be presented using the lecture style. A videotape of a lesson demonstrating the teaching of rhythms to elementary children at each developmental level should be shown. In addition, an activity session should be led by the instructor using suggested rhythms patterns listed in this chapter or in the lesson plan book. The introduction/review of the chapter material and activity session may be followed by cooperative learning assignments that provide active learning and critical thinking activities for the student. In the cooperative learning groups, the students will discuss the materials listed on the Cooperative Learning Task Sheet and/or other topics you may assign. Each group can become a "content expert" for sections of the Cooperative Learning Task Sheet. Each group may be asked to present a dance to the entire class for each or a selected developmental level.

KEY TERMS

tempo	accent	creative movement
beat	intensity	dramatization
measure	phrase	folk dance

DISCUSSION TOPICS

1. Identify and discuss the societal stigmas that may occur when teaching rhythms.

2. Discuss the rhythm and dance qualities exhibited in sports.

3. Discuss the carry over value in sports and other activities to learning rhythm.

SAMPLE WRITTEN ASSIGNMENTS

1. Research the background and history on several dances listed in the chapter.

2. Write an introduction that can be used on a Rhythms Day Festival.

3. Write ideas for multicultural experiences using dance/rhythms as the theme.

ACTIVITY SESSION EXPERIENCES

Lead the students through the following activities:

- Identifying a beat in music.

- Locomotor movements to a drum and/or tambourine beat.

- Nonlocomotor movements to a tambourine or a variety of instruments including music.

- Creative movement experiences to themes.

- Dramatizations.

- Manipulatives with rhythms.

- Techniques for introducing folk dance lessons.

- Teach an example of a Developmental Level I, II, and III dance.

- Teach the management "games" that are used to create partner and common formations for the dances listed in the textbook.

- Have the students peer teach a lesson using rhythms as the lesson focus.

COOPERATIVE LEARNING TASK SHEET

Chapter 19: Rhythmic Movement Skills

Directions: Your cooperative learning group will become the content experts by finding the answers to the items listed below. Discuss the following items with your group and be ready to report on one or all of them at the end of the class period.

1. Experiment using rhythm instruments such as a drum, tambourine, maracas, sand paper blocks, triangles, etc. Exchange instruments within your group. Listen to the drumbeat of each group member. Give feedback as to strength and quality of the drum accompaniment.

2. Discuss the inherent rhythmical nature of all physical activity. Identify sports movements that demonstrate rhythmical movements.

3. Outline components of the yearly rhythmic movement program and identify accompanying activities and skill progressions that could be used.

4. Select two manipulatives. Create a rhythms lesson using those manipulatives. Try the lesson out on your group. Try it out on another group and ask for feedback from the other group.

5. Re-read the sections in the chapter on creative rhythms and expressive movements. Guide your group through a variety of creative movement explorations using rhythms at the motivation for movement creation.

6. Select a storybook that could be used to dramatize in Developmental Level I. Read the storybook to each other and discuss the areas in the book that are best to use for the dramatization. Try the lesson out in your group. Discuss the experience.

7. Read the section in the chapter that describes partners and formation. Using management "games" to try to make the formations described in the chapters.

8. Select a dance listed in Developmental Level I. Together, stand up and try to analyze the dance steps that are written in the instructions. Obtain the music and try to put the dance steps to the music. Together try to perform the dance. Teach it to another group. Evaluate the experience.

9. Select a dance listed in Developmental Level II. Together stand up and try to analyze the dance steps written. Obtain the music and try to put the dance steps to the music. Together try to perform the dance. Teach it to another group. Evaluate the experience.

10. Select a dance listed in Developmental Level III. Together stand up and try to analyze the dance steps written. Obtain the music and try to put the dance steps to the music. Together try to perform the dance. Teach it to another group. Evaluate the experience.

CHAPTER 20

Gymnastic Skills

SUMMARY

Gymnastic activities make a significant contribution to the overall physical education experience for children in elementary schools. Gymnastic activities develop body management skills without the need for equipment and apparatus. Flexibility, agility, balance, strength, and body control are outcomes that are enhanced through participation in gymnastics. Specialized motor skills such as body rolling, balance skills, inverted balances, and tumbling skills are learned through these activities. Various partner and group activities offer opportunity for social interaction and cooperation. Positive learning experiences in gymnastic activities are dependent on progression. When teaching activities, developing a positive attitude and overcoming personal limitations is more important than performing with perfect technique. Safety is foremost in the gymnastic program.

STUDENT OUTCOMES

Upon completion of the reading of this chapter, the student will:

- List progressions and developmental level placements for gymnastic activities.

- Understand the techniques of spotting when teaching gymnastic activities.

- Organize a comprehensive lesson of gymnastic activities that includes the six basic groups: a) animal movements, b) tumbling and inverted balances, c) balance stunts, d) individual stunts, e) partner and group stunts, and f) partner support activities.

- Identify effective management techniques when teaching gymnastic activities.

- Cite safety considerations essential to the gymnastic program.

- Describe tumbling activities that are appropriate for elementary school children.

MAIN CONCEPTS

Gymnastics activities are an important part of every child's overall experience in physical education and can make a significant contribution to the goals of physical education. Through the gymnastics program, personal characteristics such as dedication and perseverance can be furthered since stunts are seldom mastered quickly.

Go to this website to read about a variety of ways to approach teaching gymnastics:

 http://www.geocities.com/Colosseum/Stadium/7261/DEVGYM2.HTM

Since much of gymnastics is individual, children face challenges to develop resourcefulness, self-confidence, and courage. When a challenging stunt is mastered, satisfaction, pride of achievement, and a sense of accomplishment contribute to improved self-esteem.

Social interplay is developed through partner and group stunts requiring cooperative effort. The social attributes of tolerance, helpfulness, courtesy, and appreciation for the ability of others grow out of the lessons when the methodology is educationally sound.

Go to this website to read a variety of lesson plans:

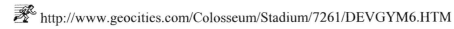 http://www.geocities.com/Colosseum/Stadium/7261/DEVGYM6.HTM

Body management skills, coordination, flexibility, and agility are enhanced in gymnastics. Stunts demanding support by the arms provide development of the often weak musculature of the arm-shoulder girdle.

PROGRESSION AND DEVELOPMENTAL LEVEL PLACEMENT

Progression of instruction is extremely important for safety reasons as well as skill development in gymnastics. The appropriate progressions are listed in this chapter and should be reasonably maintained to avoid safety problems.

The Developmental Level I instruction relies on simple stunts with a gradual introduction to tumbling stunts classified as lead-ups or preliminaries to more advanced stunts. The Developmental Level II and III programs are built on activities and progressions developed earlier. Emphasis is placed on learning more standard gymnastics activities.

Whenever possible, all children should be active and performing. Safe formations for teaching and maximizing active learning time are described in detail in this chapter. Spotting and safety techniques must be taught to children.

Go to this website to view a lesson on gymnastics skills development:

 http://www.geocities.com/Colosseum/Stadium/7261/devgym6a.htm

Instructional methodology and styles of teaching gymnastics to children are described in detail in this chapter.

SAFETY CONSIDERATIONS

Safety is a foremost consideration in the gymnastic program. The inherent hazards of an activity and how to avoid them must be included in the instructional procedures.

Spotting

The purpose of spotting is twofold. First and most important is the performer's safety and the prevention of injury. Of secondary importance is guiding the performer through the stunt to help develop proper body awareness. When spotting for safety, the goals are to assist the performer, help support the body weight, and prevent a hazardous fall. A particularly difficult problem is working with obese children in tumbling activities. Students must be carefully taught to spot before being asked to spot. Children should be paired up by similar size and weight.

STUNTS AND TUMBLING ACTIVITIES

The stunts and tumbling activities are organized in order of difficulty for each of the three developmental levels. In this chapter you will find lists of all of the activities in each of the levels and a page reference for rapid access to descriptions of each activity within the textbook. Individual and partner stunts and tumbling activities are described in detail in the chapter.

Developing Gymnastic Routines

The teacher can put together in sequence various stunts and other movements. The teacher can also offer movement challenges/problem-solving tasks for the students or groups of students to develop routines.

Additional information on gymnastics can be found at the following websites:

 http://www.usa-gymnastics.org

 http://www.usa-gymnastics.org/publications/technique/2004/10/recreational.pdf

 http://www.onlinesports.com/pages/I,HK-0-87322-708-5.html

INSTRUCTIONAL FORMATS

A videotape of a lesson demonstrating the teaching of gymnastics, stunts, and tumbling to elementary children should be used as an overview. In addition, the instructor using suggested movement patterns listed in this chapter or in the lesson plan book should lead an activity session. The introduction of the chapter material and activity session may be followed by cooperative learning assignments, which provide critical thinking activities for the student. In the cooperative learning groups, the students will discuss and practice the materials listed on the Cooperative Learning Task Sheet. Each group can become a "content expert" for sections of the Cooperative Learning Task Sheet. Oral summary reports or demonstrations may be presented to the entire class covering all or part of the discussion items.

KEY TERMS

squad formation	U-shaped formation	spotting
semicircular formation	demonstration mat	start-and-expand technique

DISCUSSION TOPICS

1. Discuss the reasons why some people may shy away from teaching gymnastics in the public schools.

2. Discuss a variety of methods for demonstrating stunts and gymnastics skills.

3. If the teacher is unwilling or unable to demonstrate movements described in this chapter, discuss solutions that will allow one to teach well and offer the children the experience of gymnastics.

SAMPLE WRITTEN ASSIGNMENTS

1. Have a videotape of a gymnastics lesson available for students to view. Assign the student a paper to evaluate the lesson viewed for management skills with the focus on active learning time as well as safety.

2. Write a lesson plan covering a variety of three-person stunts.

3. Research and write a brief history of educational gymnastics.

4. Research and write a report on children under 16 who have been in the Olympics in gymnastics events.

5. Write a Task Sheet for practicing previously taught gymnastics/stunts skills.

ACTIVITY SESSION EXPERIENCES

Lead the students through the following activities:

*   Lead the students through methods for teaching the stunts, tumbling, and gymnastics skills presented in the chapter. Videotapes may be used to aid in demonstrations.

*   Teach a model lesson demonstrating the most efficient methods of teaching stunts and tumbling activities while maximizing activity and minimizing waiting. The use of task sheets and stations will aid the management and instruction of these skills.

*   Teach a model lesson for each developmental level using the lessons written in the lesson plan book with gymnastics skills as the lesson focus.

*   Have the students peer teach lessons using gymnastics skills as the lesson focus.

COOPERATIVE LEARNING TASK SHEET

Chapter 20: Gymnastic Skills

Directions: Your cooperative learning group will become the content experts by finding the answers to the items listed below. Discuss the following items with your group and be ready to report on one or all of them at the end of the class period.

1. Identify activities that need to be taught with the use of a spotter. View a videotape on spotting techniques or ask your instructor to demonstrate spotting selected activities. Practice spotting these skills on each other on a safety mat in a gym.

2. Each person in the group should select a different basic gymnastics position or gymnastics dance position described in the chapter. After studying the movement, teach it to your group.

3. Each person in the group should select a different Developmental Level I activity and teach it to your group.

4. Each person in the group should select a different Developmental Level II activity and teach it to your group.

5. Each person in the group should select a different Developmental Level III activity and teach it to your group.

6. Each person in the group should select a different partner/group stunt. Study it and then teach it to your group. Write a gymnastic routine by combining in sequence various gymnastics movements and stunts for each developmental level.

CHAPTER 21

Cooperative Skills

SUMMARY

Cooperative activities teach youngsters to work together for the common good of other players. The activities in this chapter provide students with the opportunity to learn skills associated with cooperation and apply those skills in a rewarding activity. This chapter includes cooperative and parachute activities. Cooperative challenge activities help youngsters work together in an effort to complete the group task.

STUDENT OUTCOMES

Upon completion of the reading of this chapter, the student will:

- Understand the role of cooperative activities in physical education.

- Understand the steps that should be taken when teaching cooperative activities.

- Communicate the importance of questioning and discussion following cooperative activities.

- Describe several group challenges appropriate for elementary school children.

- Present various parachute activities and explain their role as cooperative activities.

MAIN CONCEPTS

For the purpose of this chapter the term "cooperative activities" is used to describe activities that work on team building, cooperative learning, cooperative, and adventured education to teach cooperation.

There are two primary objectives that guide the teaching of cooperative activities:

1. Cooperative activities provide students with the opportunity to apply a variety of fundamental motor skills in a unique setting.

2. Cooperative activities teach children personal and social skills necessary to function in daily life. In these activities students must outwardly cooperate for the good of the group.

Cooperative activities also teach other social skills. Students are often required to work with classmates they may have never worked with before. Working together allows students to learn that all students are important, everyone has similarities and differences, and all students can assume a role that contributes to the group's effort to accomplish the common goal.

TEACHING COOPERATIVE ACTIVITIES

Steps to Teaching Cooperative Activities

1. Set the Stage

During this step it is the teacher's job to sell the activity with the following information:

    a. What is the challenge?

    b. What are the rules?

    c. What are the consequences for breaking the rules?

    d. Are there any safety issues that need to be addressed?

During this step, only the essential information to get the group going is provided.

2. Facilitate

Once the stage has been set, the teacher's role is to step back and let the students work. For many teachers this is a difficult task because they want to tell students how to accomplish the task or at least give them a few hints. During this step, it is best to simply answer questions and monitor the group for safety.

3. Debrief

Debriefing may be the most important component in effectively implementing cooperative activities. Up to this point, little has been said about cooperation. This step of the cooperative activity process allows for students to share their experiences and affords teachers the opportunity to meet their own objectives (e.g., to discuss listening) and to connect what was learned to daily living.

The foundation of debriefing is open-ended questions. The following are examples of open-ended questions:

- What did you have to do in order to accomplish the goal?

- What does "communicate" mean?

- What happened that was positive?

- What happened that could have been better?

- How could you have changed things?

- What does it mean to be patient?

- How can you compromise?

- What would you have done differently? What would you have repeated exactly as you did it today?

GROUP CHALLENGES

Group challenges are designed to place students in an unfamiliar situation that requires some form of cooperation. The activities and rules are created in such a manner that the task cannot be accomplished alone. Students must cooperate in an effort to meet the challenge.

The chapter includes group challenge activity examples that are intended for Developmental Levels II and III. For Developmental Level I, basic cooperative skills such as sharing, listening, and individual or partner decision-making are taught throughout the curriculum and described in this chapter.

Additional material on group challenges, team building activities, and cooperative activities can be read at the following websites:

 http://www.pecentral.org/lessonideas/searchresults.asp?subcategory=cooperative+learning

Specific team building activities can be found at these sites:

 http://www.corporategames.com

 http://www.wilderdom.com/games/InitiativeGames.html

 http://www.teachingideas.co.uk/pe/contents.htm

ACTIVITIES WITH PARACHUTES

Movement concepts and fundamental motor skills can be learned and reinforced through parachute play. Levels of movement, speed, weight transfer, force, direction, balancing, pulling, bending, twisting, and all locomotor movements can be incorporated and taught while using the parachute.

Parachutes provide an interesting and fun way to accomplish physical fitness goals: a good development of strength, agility, coordination, and endurance. Strength development is focused especially on the arms, hands, and shoulder girdle. At times, strength demands are made on the entire body. A variety of movement possibilities, some of which are rhythmic, can be used in parachute play. Locomotor skills can be practiced while manipulating the parachute. Rhythmic beats of the tom-tom or appropriate music can guide locomotor movements. Lastly, parachute play can also be used to teach cooperation. The success and enjoyment gained from many parachute activities are dependent on group and individual cooperation. Without every student working together, the tasks cannot be completed. If one child decides to not sit on his part of the chute to make the dome, the air will escape and the dome will collapse.

Instructional procedures, activities, games, and skills are described in detail in the chapter.

INSTRUCTIONAL FORMATS

An overview of the material in this chapter may be presented using the lecture style and the Power Point slides. A videotape of a lesson demonstrating the teaching of cooperative and parachute activities to elementary children should be shown. In addition, an activity session should be led by the instructor using activities listed in this chapter or in the lesson plan book. The introduction/review of the chapter material and activity session may be followed by cooperative learning assignments that provide active learning and critical thinking activities for the student. In the cooperative learning groups, the students will discuss the materials listed on the Cooperative Learning Task Sheet and/or other topics you may assign. Each group can become a "content expert" for sections of the Cooperative Learning Task Sheet. Each group may be asked to present a relay or personal challenge activity to the entire class for each or a selected developmental level.

KEY TERMS

cooperative activities   parachute activities

DISCUSSION TOPICS

1. Discuss the portions of the lesson and the lesson topics for cooperative activities that are most appropriate.

2. Discuss the portions of the lesson and the lesson topics for parachute activities that are most appropriate.

SAMPLE WRITTEN ASSIGNMENTS

1. Create a new cooperative activity and write down the instructions.

2. Develop a new parachute activity and write down the description of the activity so someone else could teach it.

ACTIVITY SESSION EXPERIENCES

Lead the students through the following activities:

- Several parachute activities for each developmental level.

- Several cooperative activities listed in the textbook for each developmental level.

- Teach a model lesson for each developmental level using the lessons written in the lesson plan book with parachutes.

- Teach a model lesson for each developmental level using the lessons written in the lesson plan book with cooperative activities.

- Have students peer teach lessons including cooperative activities.

- Have students peer teach lessons using parachute activities.

COOPERATIVE LEARNING TASK SHEET

Chapter 21: Cooperative Skills

Directions: Your cooperative learning group will become the content experts by finding the answers to the items listed below. Discuss the following items with your group and be ready to report on one or all of them at the end of the class period.

1. Each person in the group should select a developmental level to study. Be sure all three levels are accounted for. Each person should select a different cooperative activity and present it to the group. Allow all members of the group to present the activity they studied.

2. Each person in the group should select a developmental level to study. Be sure all three levels are accounted for. Each person should select a different parachute activity to study and present to the group. Allow all members of the group to present the activity they studied.

3. Create a new cooperative activity and write instructions for it. Try the activity out on the group to make sure it is fun, challenging, and appropriate for instruction.

4. Create a new parachute activity and write instructions for it. Try the activity out on the group to make sure it is fun, challenging, and capable of being executed.

CHAPTER 22

Game Skills

SUMMARY

Games are excellent activities for developing social skills. Students can be taught to display appropriate interactive skills such as leading, following, and making decisions. Cooperative skills that include following directions, accepting individual differences, and participating in a teamwork situation are necessary for reaching common goals. Game situations offer many scenarios for teaching sportsmanship behavior. Games that involve only a few children, allow some children to dominate, or offer little opportunity for skill development, should not be part of the program. Children should be allowed the opportunity to create and modify games to meet their needs. Safety is a primary concern in the selection and presentation of game activities.

STUDENT OUTCOMES

Upon completion of the reading of this chapter, the student will:

- Explain various ways in which games can be created or modified.

- Understand safety precautions associated with the teaching of games.

- Cite instructional procedures to enhance the teaching of games.

- Identify games that provide maximum participation and afford an opportunity for skill development.

- List games that can be explained and implemented quickly.

- Classify various games according to developmental levels.

MAIN CONCEPTS

Games make a valuable contribution to the growth and development of youngsters.

Through games, children have an opportunity to experience success and accomplishment.

Objectives that can be accomplished through games are: the development of interpersonal skills, understanding rules and limitations, and learning how to behave in a variety of competitive and cooperative situations.

Games are where children apply physical skills in a game-like setting.

Games can contribute to the development of large-muscle groups and enhance: running, dodging, starting, and stopping under control while sharing space with others.

Children learn to apply strategy in games as well as the importance of alertness and the mental aspect of participation.

EVALUATING GAMES

Games need to be scrutinized and evaluated in terms of what they offer children before they are used.

Games can be modified by you or your students to increase the number of participants or practice certain skills previously learned.

Games that involve few children, allow some to dominate the game, or offer little in the way of skill development should be eliminated form the program.

Games should be evaluated by looking at the skills required, the number of active participants, the complexity of the rules, the amount of strategy used, and the length of the game.

Successful participation demands that youngsters have learned requisite skills in a practice setting.

Games require cooperation and learning how to compete against peers in a meaningful way.

Use a progression of games moving from partner activities to small-group games to team games. Children must be taught how to cooperate with teammates and compete against peers.

The number of rules and the amount of strategy required in games increase the difficulty of a game. Developmental Level I games have little emphasis on team play or scoring. Level I children find it difficult to play a game that has many rules.

Most elementary school children are not able to concentrate on performing game skills and strategy simultaneously.

Complex games require team members to play specific roles and may not appeal to many youngsters. Many of the popular games are spontaneous and demand little concentration on strategy.

Chase and tag games in Developmental Level II become more complex and demand more maneuvering.

Assure children receive positive feedback from game experiences. Children become bored and tire of playing long games.

Fatigue is also a factor in the interest level of children.

Games require a combination of skills. Lead-up games are developed for the express purpose of limiting the number of skills needed for successful participation. Evaluate the number of skills required and build a progression of games that gradually increases the use of skill combinations.

CREATING OR MODIFYING GAMES

Games can be modified and new variations created by teachers or students. Suggestions for modification include:

1. Increase or decrease the distance to be run in a game.

2. Change the directions for locomotion such as: hopping, walking, skipping, galloping, running, etc.

3. Play the game with one or more partners.

4. Change the method of tagging in simple tag games.

5. Make goals or restricted areas larger or smaller.

6. Vary the boundaries of the game (larger or smaller).

7. Change the formation in which the game is played.

8. Change the requirements necessary for scoring.

9. Increase the number of players, taggers, runners, number and type of equipment, etc.

10. Change the rules or penalties of the game. (Allow more players, allow more dribbles, etc.)

COOPERATION AND COMPETITION

Games require cooperation before competition can be an outgrowth of the activity.

Cooperation involves two or more children working together to achieve a common goal.

Opponents working against each other as each tries to reach a goal or reward characterize competition.

Since cooperation precedes competition and is more difficult for youngsters to learn, emphasis should be placed on this phase of game activity. Through games, players develop a spirit of working together, a concern for teammates, and an appreciation of the collective skills of the group.

Achieving a balance between offense and defense helps students understand that both phases are important. Teams should be somewhat equal so that all participants have an opportunity to experience success.

Emphasizing cooperation reinforces the need to play with all classmates regardless of ability level.

Rotate students regularly so they have a chance to play with classmates and to play on a winning team. Include youngsters with disabilities in all rotation plans.

SAFETY

Rules and safety must be a primary concern in game situations. The teacher needs to check the area for dangerous objects and damaged equipment, as well as explaining rules carefully and clearly.

Teaching children to stop play immediately when a signal is given conditions youngsters to games with referees and assures safety.

TEACHING GAMES EFFECTIVELY

1. Put youngsters in the formation they are going to use in the game prior to presenting a new game to a class. They can then sit in a formation that will make it easier to understand the instructions.

2. Use a trial period of no scoring during the first stages of learning to avoid the possibility of children feeling resentful about losing a point if they did not understand the activity.

3. Do not use games that isolate one child. An example of this is "Birdie in the Cage." Instead of putting one youngster in the center of the circle to intercept passes made by the circle players, put several in the center.

4. Develop a rotation plan that allows all children to play an equal amount of time.

5. Assure all children have an equal chance to participate in games that require taking turns.

6. Carefully plan before you attempt to teach a new game. Identify safety hazards, anticipate difficult concepts, and adapt the game to the class and the situation. Make physical preparations prior to teaching.

7. When playing low-organized and sport lead-up games, try to avoid using the out-of-bounds rule. Instead, make a rule that whoever gets to the ball first gains possession. Establish a safety zone. Use cones or spots to mark the safety/deceleration zone.

8. Change the makeup of the teams often and play relatively short games. This gives everybody a fresh start and keeps a greater number of students motivated.

9. To identify teams, use pinnies, crepe paper armbands, colored shoulder loops, or team belts worn around the waist.

10. Games are an excellent platform for learning social skills. Encourage players to learn negotiation skills and to resolve differences among themselves rather than having a teacher decide each issue.

11. Help youngsters understand that learning to perform skills correctly is more important than the outcome of the game. Continue instruction throughout the early phases of a game.

12. Use the "rule of three" as a way of simplifying rules. For example, you can only hold the ball for 3 seconds, take 3 steps, or miss three catches, etc. This reduces the number of rules youngsters have to remember and diminishes the disagreements youngsters might have about rules.

SELECTION OF GAMES

Games in this chapter require minimal skill and offer activity for all children.

Analyze the skills children must practice before playing a game. Drills and skill practice become more meaningful when children understand that the skill will be used in a game they will be playing.

The games in the chapter are presented in detail, sorted by difficulty, and placed into three developmental levels.

Sport lead-up games limit the number of skills required for successful participation so children can experience success in a sport setting.

Developmental Level I games do not require competency in sport skills and use basic locomotor skills.

Developmental Levels II and III games require increased competency in specialized sport skills. These games require ball-handling, agility, and movement skills. They offer opportunities for children to practice skills prior to being placed in a competitive situation.

The games in Developmental Levels II and III fall into two categories: sport lead-up games and low-organization games. This chapter includes low-organization games only. The lead-up games in this chapter fall into the low-organization games category. The remainder of the chapter describes sport lead-up games appropriate for each developmental level. Chapters 24-30 offer additional sport-related lead-up games.

INSTRUCTIONAL FORMATS

A videotape of a lesson demonstrating the teaching of games to elementary children should be shown as an example to the students in your class. In addition, an activity session should be led by the instructor using suggested games and skills listed in this chapter or in the lesson plan book. The introduction of the chapter material and activity session may be followed by cooperative learning assignments that provide critical thinking activities for the student. In the cooperative learning groups, the students will discuss the materials listed on the Cooperative Learning Task Sheet. Each group can become a "content expert" for sections of the Cooperative Learning Task Sheet. Each group may be asked to present a game to the entire class for each or a selected developmental level.

KEY TERMS

cooperation   competition   sport lead-up games

DISCUSSION TOPICS

1. Discuss the most appropriate portion of the lesson to include games. Clarify the types of games most appropriate for each portion of the lesson.

2. Discuss reasons for modifying game rules. Cite a game and how it could be modified for a specified reason.

3. Discuss how traditional game rules could be modified to create a new lead-up game.

SAMPLE WRITTEN ASSIGNMENTS

1. Identify a game in this textbook. Write new instructions to modify it for more active participants most of the time.

2. Identify a game found in another textbook or listed on an Internet site. Write new instructions to modify it for more active participants most of the time.

3. Write a lesson plan including a lead-up game.

ACTIVITY SESSION EXPERIENCES

Lead the students through the following activities:

- Lead the students through at least two games in the chapter for each developmental level.

- Teach a model lesson of games for each developmental level using the lessons written in the lesson plan book.

- Teach the students several low-organization games that could be considered lead-up games.

- Have students peer teach games using lessons from the lesson plan book.

COOPERATIVE LEARNING TASK SHEET

Chapter 22: Game Skills

Directions: Your cooperative learning group will become the content experts by finding the answers to the items listed below. Discuss the following items with your group and be ready to report on one or all of them at the end of the class period.

1. Each person in the group should select a developmental level to study. Be sure all three levels are accounted for. Each person should select a different game listed in the chapter to study and present to the group. Allow all members of the group the opportunity to present the game they studied.

2. Create a new game and identify the skills this game will develop or reinforce and write instructions for it. Try the game out on the group to make sure it is appropriate, fun, and challenging.

3. Conduct an Internet search and find a low-organization game. Analyze the virtues of the game. If it is different from those listed in the textbook and your group deems it a worthwhile game, teach it to the class.

CHAPTER 23

Lifetime Activities

SUMMARY

Lifetime activities can be used to maintain an active lifestyle throughout the lifespan. Too often, curriculums are limited in scope and don't offer activities that students can use as they become mature adults. This chapter is designed to introduce students to a number of activities that can be performed alone or in small groups. They can be played in highly competitive situations or enjoyed in recreational settings. Rather than creating outstanding performers, the focus of this chapter will be to turn students on to activities that are not always found in elementary school settings.

Upon completion of the reading of this chapter, the student will:

- Provide an explanation as to why lifetime physical activities should be taught in physical education.

- Identify characteristics of lifetime physical activities.

- Discuss the importance of teaching walking in elementary schools.

- Design an orienteering course for students and list the necessary skills students will need to know before completing the course.

- List a variety of racquet skills and lead-up games involving racquets.

- Discuss a variety of Frisbee activities that can be taught in the elementary schools.

MAIN CONCEPTS

Lifetime physical activities are activities that can be participated in throughout the lifespan. A primary role of physical education is to promote lifetime physical activity for all students. For this reason, it is important that physical education teachers have a firm understanding of what is being promoted. For an activity to be regarded as a lifetime activity it usually meets all or most of the following criteria:

- Offers opportunity for participation at various intensities, including low and vigorous.

- The activity can be noncompetitive; it is an activity that is enjoyable even if competition is not the focus of participation.

- The activity can be done alone or with a partner or teammates.

- The activity can contribute to the overall health of the participant.

For most people, as age increases, the desire and ability to engage in intense physical activity decreases. At the age of 20, football and rugby may be desirable activities; however, football and rugby are not typically an activity of choice beyond the age of 25. In fact, most traditional team sports, because they are usually vigorous in nature, are not thought of as lifetime activities. In addition, team sports, in their purest form, do not meet the criteria of being a lifetime activity. Traditionally, physical education has focused on team sports. However, new data suggests that the types of activities adults participate in are not team sports. The National Sporting Goods Association (2003) reports that of the top 20 activities participated in by adults, two (basketball is #10 and baseball is #19) are team sports As Figure 23.1 in the textbook indicates, not all of the top 20 activities are appropriate for elementary children or the physical education setting. Also, this data does not suggest that these activities are the only activities that should be included in physical education. It merely states that these are the most popular.

The feasibility of including physical activity in a typical day also plays a role in lifetime activity. Most adults work an 8-hour day, care for children, and run errands leaving little time for physical activity. Those people who deem physical activity important must "work" it into their schedules when time permits. Thus, trying to find a group of 6-8 adults who are able to work physical activity into their schedules at the same time and on the same day is difficult. The majority of lifetime physical activities only require one or two people for participation. It makes it much easier to coordinate schedules when the number of participants is limited.

The role of physical education is to promote lifetime physical activity for all students. Because all students have unique needs and desires, it is important to offer a variety of activities. Using the definition of lifetime physical activities presented above, virtually all activities, with a few modifications, can be participated in throughout life. Thus, a variety of activities, including gymnastics, rhythms, traditional sports, and lifetime activities, should be taught via a balanced curriculum.

Examples of lifetime activities described in this chapter include:

- **Walking**

  For more information on this subject, go to the following websites:

  http://walking.about.com/cs/measure/a/webwalkingusa.htm

  http://www.dshs.state.tx.us/diabetes/walktx.shtm

  http://www.walksmartvirginia.com/default_pages/default_home.aspx?s=va

  http://www.walktoschool-usa.org

- **Orienteering**

  For more information on this subject, go to the following websites:

  http://www.us.orienteering.org

  http://www.pelinks4u.org/units.htm

  http://www.eduref.org/cgi-bin/printlessons.cgi/Virtual/Lessons/Physical_Education/Outdoor_Education/OED0001.html

  http://www.orienteering.org

  http://www.4orienteering.com

  http://www.orienteeringunlimited.com

- **Tennis**

  For more information on this subject, go to the following websites:
  http://www.usta.com/home/default.sps

  http://www.tennisone.com

  http://www.tennisserver.com

- **Racquetball**

  For more information on this subject, go to the following websites:
  http://www.usra.org

  http://www.racquetball.org

  http://www.surfermall.com/rball/kids.htm

  http://www.rbdepot.com/racquetball_how_to_play.asp

- **Badminton**

  For more information on this subject, go to the following websites:
  http://www.worldbadminton.com

  http://www.badmintoncentral.com/badminton-central

  http://www.northwestbadminton.org/spokane/play_badminton.htm

  http://www.ehow.com/how_17615_play-badminton.html

  http://www.pier55.com/Sports-Recreation/Play-Badminton.shtml

- **Frisbee activities**

  For more information of this subject, go to the following websites:
  http://www.discgolf.com

  http://www.pdga.com

  http://www.whatisultimate.com

  http://freestyledisc.org/learnToPlay.html

  http://www.frisbee.com/freestyle/index.html

INSTRUCTIONAL FORMATS

An overview of the material in this chapter may be presented using the lecture style and the Power Point slides. An activity session should be led by the instructor using activities listed in this chapter or in the lesson plan book. The introduction/review of the chapter material and activity session may be followed by cooperative learning assignments that provide active learning and critical thinking activities for the student. In the cooperative learning groups, the students will discuss the materials listed on the Cooperative Learning Task Sheet and/or other topics you may assign. Each group can become a "content expert" for sections of the Cooperative Learning Task Sheet.

KEY TERMS

lifetime activities	badminton	orienteering
tennis	racquetball	

SAMPLE WRITTEN ASSIGNMENTS

Have the student write a lesson covering each of the following topics:

- Walking activities

- Orienteering skills

- Frisbee skills

ACTIVITY SESSION EXPERIENCES

Lead the students through the following activities:

- Walking activities

- Orienteering activities

- Badminton

- Tennis

- Racquetball

- Frisbee skills

COOPERATIVE LEARNING TASK SHEET

Chapter 23: Lifetime Activities

Directions: Your cooperative learning group will become the content experts by finding the answers to the items listed below. Discuss the following items with your group and be ready to report on one or all of them at the end of the class period.

1. Describe lifetime activities. Give examples of lifetime activities.

2. Explain the problems associated with teaching only team sports in relation to adult lifestyle activities.

3. Define and describe appropriate walking activities for the elementary school child.

4. Define and describe appropriate orienteering activities for the elementary school child.

5. Define and describe appropriate tennis activities for the elementary school child.

6. Define and describe appropriate racquetball activities for the elementary school child.

7. Define and describe appropriate badminton activities for the elementary school child.

8. Define and describe appropriate Frisbee activities for the elementary school child.

9. Create a lesson focus for one of the suggested activities that are described as lifetime activities.

CHAPTER 24

Basketball

SUMMARY

Skills instruction for basketball is introduced primarily during the intermediate grades after youngsters have mastered the basic prerequisite skills. The teaching of rules and strategies for basketball should be an integral part of the instructional process. Using proper progression is a key to success when teaching fundamental skills and lead-up games associated with basketball. Lead-up games provide an opportunity to emphasize development of selected basketball skills in a setting that is compatible with the ability of participants.

STUDENT OUTCOMES

Upon completion of the reading of this chapter, the student will:

- Structure learning experiences efficiently with respect to appropriate formations, progressions, and coaching techniques.

- Know the basic rules of basketball.

- Develop a unit plan and lesson focus for basketball.

- Identify safety precautions associated with teaching basketball.

- Describe essential elements for a successful lead-up game.

- Cite assessment procedures for evaluating basketball skills.

MAIN CONCEPTS

Basketball instruction in the elementary school focuses on developing skills and competence so students can participate later in life.

Emphasis should be placed in lead-up games that allow all students to experience success and enjoyment.

Intramural programs and recreational leagues can offer opportunities for more skilled students to play the game of basketball.

Smaller balls and lower baskets help develop technically correct shooting patterns and increase the success of the participants.

INSTRUCTIONAL EMPHASIS AND SEQUENCE

Developmental Level II: Little emphasis is placed on regulation basketball at Developmental Level II. Instead, concentration is placed on the fundamental skills of passing, catching, shooting, and dribbling.

Lead-up games allow participants to learn skills in a setting that offers enjoyment and success.

The lay-up shot and the one-hand push shot should be taught at Developmental Level II.

Development Level III: Passing, catching, dribbling, shooting, and defending games can be introduced at Developmental Level III. Drills to enhance skill performance and rules for regulation basketball are presented. Self-officiating should also be taught.

Go to the below listed websites to view other lesson ideas on teaching basketball:

 http://www.usask.ca/education/ideas/tplan/pedlp/basketball.htm

Visit this site to view a lesson on the "set shot:":

 http://www.usask.ca/education/ideas/tplan/pedlp/setshot.htm

At this site you will find information on reference books for basketball:

 http://www.fbbasketball.com/youthbasketball

INSTRUCTIONAL PROCEDURES

1. Many basketball skills can be taught with the use of any type of ball.

2. Many skills can be practiced individually or in pairs with playground balls.

3. Baskets should be lowered to 7, 8, or 9 feet depending on the size of the youngsters.

4. The program should concentrate on skills and include many drills.

BASIC BASKETBALL RULES

The game of basketball at the elementary school level should be modified to assure the opportunity for success and for proper skill development. Putting the ball into play, violations, fouls, scoring, and substitution modification of rules are listed in this section of the chapter. Additionally, appropriate drills are carefully described in this section of the chapter.

INSTRUCTIONAL FORMATS

An overview of the material in this chapter may be presented using the lecture style with the accompanying Power Point slides and/or overhead transparencies that are available with this textbook. A videotape of a lesson demonstrating the teaching of basketball to elementary children should be shown. In addition, the instructor using suggested lead-up games should lead an activity session using basketball skills listed in this chapter or in the lesson plan book. The introduction/review of the chapter material and activity session may be followed by cooperative learning assignments, which provide active learning and critical thinking activities for the student. In the cooperative learning groups, the students will discuss the materials listed on the Cooperative Learning Task Sheet and/or other topics you may assign. Each group can become a "content expert" for sections of the Cooperative Learning Task Sheet. Each group may be asked to present a lesson focus activity for basketball to the entire class for a selected developmental level.

KEY TERMS

jump shot   one-hand push shot   feinting

DISCUSSION TOPICS

1. Discuss the appropriate types of basketball skills to teach at each developmental level.

2. Discuss appropriate lead-up games that can be used in teaching basketball.

SAMPLE WRITTEN ASSIGNMENTS

1. Develop a new game using basketball skills. Write down the instructions.

2. Write a lesson plan using a lead-up game for basketball.

ACTIVITY SESSION EXPERIENCES

Lead the students through the following activities:

- Teach a model lesson for each developmental level using the lessons written in the lesson plan book with basketball as the lesson focus.

- Lead the students through the lead-up games listed in the chapter.

- Show the videotape on teaching sport skills that accompanies this textbook.

- Have students peer teach basketball as the lesson focus using lessons from the lesson plan book.

COOPERATIVE LEARNING TASK SHEET

Chapter 24: Basketball

Directions: Your cooperative learning group will become the content experts by finding the answers to the items listed below. Discuss the following items with your group and be ready to report on one or all of them at the end of the class period.

1. Each person in the group should select a developmental level to study. Be sure all three levels are accounted for. Each person should select a different basketball skill listed in the chapter to study and present to the group. Allow all members of the group the opportunity to present the skill they studied.

2. Each person in the group should select a different developmental level to study than they did in the above assignment. Be sure all three levels are accounted for. Each person should select another skill to study and present to the group. Allow all members of the group to present the basketball skill/game they studied.

3. Each person in the group should select a different lead-up game to study. Be sure all people in the group select a different game. Each person should study this game and present it to the group. Allow all members of the group to present the basketball lead-up game they studied.

4. Create a new lead-up game and identify the skills this game will develop or reinforce and write instructions for it. Try the game out on the group to make sure it is fun, challenging, and doable.

CHAPTER 25

Football

SUMMARY

Skill instruction for football is introduced during the intermediate grades after youngsters have mastered the basic prerequisite skills. The teaching of rules and strategies for football are an integral part of the instructional process. Using proper progression is a key to success when teaching fundamental skills and lead-up games associated with football. Lead-up games provide an opportunity to emphasize development of selected football skills in a setting that is compatible with the ability of participants.

STUDENT OUTCOMES

Upon completion of the reading of this chapter, the student will:

- Structure learning experiences efficiently with respect to appropriate formations, progressions, and coaching techniques.

- Develop a unit plan and lesson focus for football.

- Identify safety precautions associated with teaching football.

- Describe instructional procedures for implementing a successful lead-up game.

- Cite assessment procedures for evaluating football skills.

MAIN CONCEPTS

Specialized skills are needed for throwing and catching a football. The shape of the football makes it more difficult to throw and catch than a round ball.

Flag football is the game derived from regulation football that is taught to physical education elementary students.

INSTRUCTIONAL EMPHASIS AND SEQUENCE

Foam-shaped footballs are recommended to teach basic skills since the pointed football can hurt when caught.

Developmental Level II

Passing, centering, and catching skills should receive the most attention. Lead-up games can be used with these skills.

Developmental Level III

Emphasis shifts to passing skills with moving receivers in football drills. Punting and kicking games are introduced. More specialized skills such as blocking, carrying the ball, exchanging the ball, and football agility skills provide lead-up work for the game of Flag Football.

Go to this website to read a lesson plan on teaching flag football:

http://www.usask.ca/education/ideas/tplan/pedlp/football.htm

FOOTBALL SKILLS

The football skills described in this chapter that are appropriate for elementary school children include: forward passing, lateral passing, catching, handing off the ball, carrying the ball, centering, stance, blocking, and punting.

Instructional Procedures

1. All children need the opportunity to practice all skills, and a system of rotation should be set up to ensure this.

2. Drills should be performed with attention to proper form, and they should approximate game conditions.

3. Junior-sized foam footballs should be used.

4. Roughness and unfair play must be controlled by supervision and strict enforcement of the rules.

5. Appropriate games, drills, and activities for Level II and III students are described in detail in this chapter.

INSTRUCTIONAL FORMATS

An overview of the material in this chapter may be presented using the lecture style and the accompanying Power Point slides and/or overhead transparencies. A videotape of a lesson demonstrating the teaching of football skills to elementary children should be shown. In addition, the instructor using suggested lead-up games should lead an activity session and skills used in football listed in this chapter or in the lesson plan book. The introduction/review of the chapter material and activity session may be followed by cooperative learning assignments that provide active learning and critical thinking activities for the student. In the cooperative learning groups, the students will discuss the materials listed on the Cooperative Learning Task Sheet and/or other topics you may assign. Each group can become a "content expert" for sections of the Cooperative Learning Task Sheet. Each group may be asked to present a lesson focus activity for football to the entire class for a selected developmental level.

KEY TERMS

punting	lateral pass	centering

DISCUSSION TOPICS

1. Discuss when it is appropriate for boys and girls to participate in football together and when it would not be appropriate.

2. Identify several lead-up games appropriate to use for Developmental Level III students.

SAMPLE WRITTEN ASSIGNMENTS

1. Write a lesson focus lesson plan for teaching basic football skills.

2. Write up the instructions for a new lead-up football game.

ACTIVITY SESSION EXPERIENCES

- Teach the students the formations listed in this chapter.

- Teach the students a lesson covering football as the lesson focus listed in the lesson plan book.

- Lead the students through the basic techniques associated with football:

  - Throwing and catching the football.

  - Passing, kicking, punting, and centering a football.

  - Passing skills using moving receivers.

- Assign the students to peer teach football as the lesson focus using lessons from the lesson plan book.

COOPERATIVE LEARNING TASK SHEET

Chapter 25: Football

Directions: Your cooperative learning group will become the content experts by finding the answers to the items listed below. Discuss the following items with your group and be ready to report on one or all of them at the end of the class period.

1. Identify appropriate formations, progressions, and coaching techniques to be used in elementary schools for football skill development.

2. Develop three lesson focus lesson plans for football.

3. Make a chart showing safety precautions associated with teaching football.

4. Describe instructional procedures for implementing a successful lead-up game. Select a lead-up game listed in this chapter and teach it to members of your group. Evaluate the lesson with each other. Allow each member of your group the opportunity to teach a different game.

5. Cite assessment procedures for evaluating football skills. Create an accompanying check-off list that an instructor could easily use.

6. Conduct an Internet search regarding the history of football. Discuss your findings before presenting the information to your classmates.

7. Conduct an Internet search on a famous football player. Present the findings to your group and then to the class.

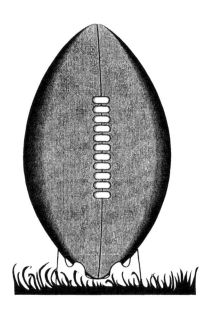

CHAPTER 26

Hockey

SUMMARY

Skill instruction for hockey should be introduced during the intermediate grades after youngsters have mastered basic prerequisite skills. Teaching of rules and strategies for hockey is an integral part of the instructional process. Using proper progression is a key to success when teaching fundamental skills and lead-up games associated with hockey. Lead-up games provide an opportunity to emphasize development of selected hockey skills in a setting that is compatible with the ability of participants.

STUDENT OUTCOMES

Upon completion of the reading of this chapter, the student will:

- Structure learning experiences efficiently using appropriate formations, progressions, and coaching techniques.

- Develop a unit plan and lesson focus for hockey.

- Identify safety precautions associated with teaching hockey.

- Describe instructional procedures used for implementing a successful lead-up game.

- Cite assessment procedures used for evaluating hockey skills.

MAIN CONCEPTS

Hockey is a fast-moving game that is a lead-up to ice hockey and field hockey.

Hockey can be played indoors with a plastic puck.

Boys and girls can play on an equal basis.

Success at hockey in the elementary school demands running and team play.

Teach fundamental skills and position play.

Instructional Emphasis and Sequence

The chapter describes appropriate activities for Developmental Level II and III students.

Level II

Little strategy is taught. Drills are used to develop fundamental skills such as: dribbling and carrying the puck, fielding, and making short passes.

Level III

Skill development continues, with more emphasis on ball control and passing accuracy. Lead-up games using skills involved in regulation hockey are played.

HOCKEY SKILLS

The hockey skills taught at these levels include: gripping and carrying the stick, dribbling and carrying, loose dribble, controlled dribble, passing, forehand passing, driving and shooting, fielding, tackling, jab shot, dodging, face-off, and goalkeeping.

INSTRUCTIONAL PROCEDURES

1. Hockey is a new experience for many elementary school children. Introduce it as such.

2. Teach the basic skills in a sequential manner and to allow ample time in practice sessions for development.

3. Teach the proper methods of stick handling to ensure safety.

4. A stick and a ball/puck should be provided for each child.

5. You can teach with a plastic puck, wiffle ball, or yarn ball depending on the surface where you teach.

6. Hockey is fun when all teammates are given ample playing time. Do not allow ball hogs.

7. Students with restricted movement abilities may enjoy playing goalkeeper.

8. Hockey requires running, agility, and endurance. You may need to include frequent rotation and rest periods in your teaching.

Hockey drills and lead-up games are described in detail in this chapter.

INSTRUCTIONAL FORMATS

An overview of the material in this chapter may be presented using a videotape of a lesson demonstrating the teaching of hockey skills to elementary children. Content can be presented with the use of the accompanying overhead transparencies and Power Point slides. In addition, an activity session should be led by the instructor using suggested skills used in hockey listed in this chapter or in the lesson plan book. The chapter material and activity session may be followed by cooperative learning assignments, which provide active learning and critical thinking activities for the student. In the cooperative learning groups, the students will discuss the materials listed on the Cooperative Learning Task Sheet and/or other topics you may assign. Each group can become a "content expert" for sections of the Cooperative Learning Task Sheet. Each group may be asked to present a lesson focus activity for hockey to the entire class for a selected developmental level.

KEY TERMS

hockey puck   slap shot   face-off

DISCUSSION TOPICS

1. Discuss the difference between teaching skills to Developmental Level II and III.

2. Identify the basic skills needed in hockey.

SAMPLE WRITTEN ASSIGNMENTS

1. Write a series of lesson focus lesson plans concentrating on position play and responsibilities.

2. Develop a lead-up game for hockey skills. Write the lesson up so others could teach the lead-up game.

ACTIVITY SESSION EXPERIENCES

Lead the students through the following activities:

- Lead the students through the drills and skills described in this chapter.

- Lead the students through the lead-up activities described thoroughly in this chapter.

- View a videotape on hockey skills. Discuss the activities that are appropriate for elementary children to develop.

- Have students peer teach hockey as the lesson focus using lessons from the lesson plan book.

COOPERATIVE LEARNING TASK SHEET

Chapter 26: Hockey

Directions: Your cooperative learning group will become the content experts by finding the answers to the items listed below. Discuss the following items with your group and be ready to report on one or all of them at the end of the class period.

1. Identify appropriate formations, progressions, and drills to be used in elementary schools for hockey skill development.

2. Develop three lesson focus lesson plans for indoor and outdoor hockey.

3. Make a chart showing safety precautions associated with teaching hockey.

4. Select a skill listed in this chapter and teach it to members of your group. Evaluate the lesson with each other. Allow each member of your group the opportunity to teach a different skill.

5. Select a lead-up game listed in this chapter and teach it to members of your group. Evaluate the lesson with each other. Allow each member of your group the opportunity to teach a different game.

6. Cite assessment procedures for evaluating hockey skills. Create an accompanying check-off list that an instructor could easily use in class.

7. Conduct an Internet search regarding the history of hockey. Discuss your findings before presenting the information to you classmates.

   Below are three sites you may refer to:

   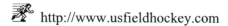 http://www.usfieldhockey.com

   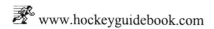 http://www.fieldhockey.com

   🏒 www.hockeyguidebook.com

8. Conduct an Internet search on a famous hockey player. Present the findings to your group and then to the class.

CHAPTER 27

Soccer

SUMMARY

Skill instruction for soccer is introduced during the intermediate grades after youngsters have mastered basic prerequisite skills. Teaching of rules and strategies for soccer is an integral part of the instructional process. Using proper progression is a key to success when teaching fundamental skills and lead-up games associated with soccer. Lead-up games provide an opportunity to emphasize development of selected soccer skills in a setting that is compatible with the ability of participants.

STUDENT OUTCOMES

Upon completion of the reading of this chapter, the student will:

- Structure learning experiences efficiently using appropriate formations, progressions, and coaching techniques.

- Develop a unit plan and lesson focus for soccer.

- Identify safety precautions associated with teaching soccer.

- Describe instructional procedures used for implementing a successful lead-up game.

- Cite assessment procedures used for evaluating soccer skills.

MAIN CONCEPTS

Soccer is the most popular and most active sport in America for youth, with tremendous growth rate among girls.

Below is the official site of the American Youth Soccer Organization (AYSO):

 http://www.soccer.org

Effective soccer stresses position play and team work.

Organized practice that emphasizes handling the ball as often as possible is essential. Offer students frequent opportunities on offense to kick, control, dribble, volley, and shoot as well as frequent opportunities on defense to mark, guard, tackle, and recover the ball.

Success in soccer depends on how well individual skills are coordinated in team play.

This site provides you with lead-up games for soccer:

 http://www.kidsfirstsoccer.com/ldupgame.htm

MODIFICATIONS OF SOCCER FOR CHILDREN

Balls: Junior-sized soccer balls should be used for elementary school children. Foam balls that are covered with a tough plastic skin to simulate the appearance of a soccer ball can negate the fear of being hurt. Beach balls are excellent for teaching beginning skills such as heading.

Decrease the number of players in games to assure that there is more opportunity to practice skills. When learning soccer the 11-person game is not suitable. Mini-Soccer is an excellent game with 6 to 7 players on a side.

Decrease the size of the goal to approximately 18 to 21 feet in width and 6 to 7 feet in height to offer success.

SKILL DEVELOPMENT

This chapter presents appropriate activities, skill development, and drills for Developmental Levels II and III. The skills included are: dribbling, passing, kicking, ball control, heading, volleying, defensive maneuvers, jockeying, throw-ins, shooting, goalkeeping, and punting.

Basic soccer rules for lead-up games are included along with a variety of developmentally appropriate lead-up games.

Instructional Procedures

1. Soccer skills must be practiced if children are to participate successfully in the sport.

2. Many combination drills featuring both offense and defense should be included in lessons. Drills and lead-up activities can be used to make the skills challenging, but all activities should be appropriate to the developmental level of the students.

3. Use small-group games (2 to 5 players) to ensure maximum activity. Increase the number of players as the skill improves.

4. Lead-up games are designed to encourage the use of the skills practiced in drills.

5. The grid system is useful when organizing drills, activities, and small-sized games. Using cones or chalk, mark a grid system of 10-yard squares on the field. One square for every three students is recommended. The squares are used as boundaries for tackling, keeping possession, and passing diagonally or sideways.

6. Balls smaller and lighter than regulation soccer balls should be used. Partially deflated 8-inch rubber playground balls can be used.

7. Since soccer can be a rough game, rules need to be strictly enforced. Rough play such as pushing, shoving, kicking, and tripping must be controlled.

8. Modified scoring can be used to make the activity more enjoyable for more children. Cones and spots can be used to mark goal outlines. Regulation soccer goals are not necessary for the elementary school program.

SOCCER DRILLS

Soccer drills for individual and group activities are described in detail.

1. Individual practice is excellent for developing dribbling techniques. This is one approach to developing soccer skills.

2. Heading skills can be practiced with two children. One tosses a beach ball overhead to a partner and the partner heads the ball.

3. Children can rebound the ball (foot juggling) to themselves to learn ball control.

4. A skill approach to teaching soccer involves both offensive and defensive players and perhaps a target. In drills using the skill approach, the goal is to outmaneuver the opponent.

SOCCER SKILL TESTS

A variety of skill tests are included in the chapter. They include: passing against a wall, figure-eight dribbling, and controlling.

Placekicking, punting, penalty kicking, and short passing for accuracy are also covered.

INSTRUCTIONAL FORMATS

An overview of the material in this chapter may be presented using a videotape of a lesson demonstrating the teaching of soccer skills to elementary children. The Power Point slides and/or overhead transparencies can be used to present the content of the chapter. In addition, an activity session should be led by the instructor using suggested skills used in soccer listed in this chapter or in the lesson plan book. The cooperative learning task sheets will provide critical thinking activities for the student. In the cooperative learning groups, the students will discuss the materials listed on the Cooperative Learning Task Sheet. Each group may be asked to present a lesson focus activity for soccer to the entire class for a selected developmental level.

KEY TERMS

tackling	shooting	passing
heading	dribbling	trapping

DISCUSSION TOPICS

1. Discuss the positions used in the soccer game and what each player is responsible for covering.

2. Discuss the basic skills needed in soccer.

3. Discuss the skills that are best practiced individually or with a partner.

4. Discuss the rules and how they could be modified for each developmental level.

SAMPLE WRITTEN ASSIGNMENTS

1. Write a series of lesson focus lesson plans for soccer appropriate for Developmental Level II.

2. Write the instructions for a new lead-up game.

3. Write a paper on the history of soccer in the United States.

ACTIVITY SESSION EXPERIENCES

Lead the students through the following activities:

- Lead the students through the basic skills included in the game of soccer: kicking, passing, controlling, dribbling, heading, shooting, guarding, marking, and recovering the ball. Use the lesson plan book along with this textbook for model lesson ideas.

- Demonstrate the lead-up games described in this chapter.

- Demonstrate soccer rules and modifications that could be applied to each developmental level to offer success to the children.

- View a videotape on the game of soccer. Discuss the difference between the way soccer should be played at the elementary school level versus high school, college, or professional soccer.

- Have students peer teach soccer as the lesson focus using lessons from the lesson plan book.

COOPERATIVE LEARNING TASK SHEET

Chapter 27: Soccer

Directions: Your cooperative learning group will become the content experts by finding the answers to the items listed below. Discuss the following items with your group and be ready to report on one or all of them at the end of the class period.

1. Identify appropriate formations, progressions, and teaching techniques to be used in elementary schools for soccer skill development.

2. Develop three lesson focus lesson plans for soccer.

3. Make a chart showing safety precautions associated with teaching soccer.

4. Describe instructional procedures for implementing a successful lead-up game. Select a lead-up game listed in this chapter and teach it to members of your group. Evaluate the lesson with each other. Allow each member of your group the opportunity to teach a different game.

5. Cite assessment procedures for evaluating soccer skills. Create an accompanying check-off list that an instructor could easily use.

6. Conduct an Internet search regarding the history of soccer. Discuss your findings before presenting the information to you classmates.

7. Conduct an Internet search on a famous soccer player. Present the findings to your group and then to the class.

8. Discuss the difference between AYSO soccer and "club" soccer in your area. What are the values and virtues of each?

CHAPTER 28

Softball

SUMMARY

The introduction of softball skills occurs during the intermediate grades after youngsters have mastered basic prerequisite skills. Teaching of rules and strategies for softball is an integral part of the instructional process. Using proper progression is a key to success when teaching fundamental skills and lead-up games associated with softball. Lead-up games provide an opportunity to emphasize development of selected softball skills in a setting that is compatible with the ability of participants.

STUDENT OUTCOMES

Upon completion of the reading of this chapter, the student will:

- Structure learning experiences efficiently using appropriate formations, progressions, and coaching techniques.

- Develop a unit plan and lesson focus for softball.

- Identify safety precautions associated with teaching softball.

- Describe instructional procedures used for implementing a successful lead-up game.

- Cite assessment procedures used for evaluating softball skills.

MAIN CONCEPTS

Emphasis in softball should be on instruction and lead-up games. Children have many opportunities after school, at noon, and during recess to play the regulation game.

Instructional Emphasis and Sequence

Youngsters may not be ready to participate in some of the softball activities in this chapter until 8 years old.

Developmental Levels I and II

Students need to be taught the proper form and technique of the fundamental skills of batting, throwing, and catching at this level.

Lead-up games using the basic rules of the game should be taught. As youngsters mature, specific skills for pitching, infield play, base running, and batting make up the instructional material.

Developmental Level III

Developmental Level III youngsters develop the background to play the game of regulation softball.

Tee Ball provides a good opportunity for developing all softball skills except pitching and catching.

SOFTBALL SKILLS

The skills of gripping, throwing, pitching, fielding, positioning, catching, batting, base running, and basic softball rules are covered in this chapter.

Skills Covered

The following skills are included in this chapter in-depth for teaching children: Gripping the Ball, Throwing (Right-handed), Overhand Throw, Sidearm Throw, Underhand Throw, Pitching, Fielding, Fly Balls, Grounders, Sure Stop for Outfield Balls, First-Base Positioning, Catcher's Position, Batting (Right-Handed), Bunting (Right-Handed), and Base Running.

Instructional Procedures

1. Safety is of the utmost importance. The following safety precautions should be observed:

   a. Throwing the bat is a constant danger. Members of the batting team should stand on the side opposite the batter.

   b. Techniques used to teach the batter not to throw the bat:

   i. Have the batter touch the bat to the ground before dropping it.

   ii. Call the batter out if the bat is thrown.

   iii. Have the batter carry the bat to first base.

   iv. Have the batter change ends of the bat before dropping it.

   v. Have the batter place the bat in a 3-foot circle drawn on the ground before running.

   c. Sliding can lead to injury and destruction of clothing. Do not permit sliding.

   d. A catcher who stands close behind the plate while catching must wear a mask. A body protector is also recommended.

   e. Colliding while running for a fly ball can be avoided by teaching players to call for the ball and stay out of another player's area.

   f. When changing field positions at the beginning of an inning, the batting team stays on the first-base side of the infield. The field team goes to bat via the third-base side of the infield.

   g. Soft softballs should be used, particularly in the early stages of development. Fleece balls are excellent for introductory fielding skills.

2. Batting skills must be stressed. Make sure that youngsters know the correct stance and proper mechanics of batting.

3. To avoid a pitcher-batter duel, have a member of the batting team pitch or allow 2 to 3 swings per batter to eliminate the problem.

4. Rotate the positions of the players often.

5. The distance between the bases should be lessened or increased according to the game and the capabilities of the players.

6. Umpires can be appointed, or the team at bat can umpire. Other ideas are presented in this chapter.

7. Encourage players to give approval and support those who are less skillful.

8. Each player should run out a hit, no matter how hopeless it seems.

9. Analyze the purpose of lead-up games and be sure to practice the skills needed before introducing the game.

10. Teach respect for officials and acceptance of the umpire's judgment.

ORGANIZING FOR INSTRUCTION

Station teaching is effective in teaching softball skills. Suggestions for instruction include:

1. Assure children many opportunities to practice different skills. Use small groups and rotate the student's skill practice in each group.

2. You will most likely experience ability differences in your class. Skillful youngsters in your class can be used in various phases of instruction, provided that you give them specific instructions.

3. Carefully plan and explain the activities and procedures to be used at each instructional station. Teach your "helpers" the activities before you present them to the class. Cover softball rules.

4. During a class session, groups/teams may practice at one instructional station for part of the time and then participate in an appropriate lead-up game. You can pick-up the lesson the next day and rotate the children to a new station for skill development/practice.

5. Place signs with clear directions at each instructional station.

6. You can use mimetic drills without equipment to provide skill practice such as batting, pitching, throwing, and fielding.

7. Older students might be able to help you out at each station.

8. A motivational factor can be introduced through comparisons of the rotational system with varsity or major league practices.

9. Activities can be selected from the lead-up games in this chapter.

BASIC SOFTBALL RULES

Modified softball rules are listed in this chapter.

If you go to this website, you can find resources for softball:
http://www.usasoftball.org

Softball Drills and Lead-Up Games

An extensive set of drills and combinations of skills plus lead-up games are presented in this section of the chapter.

Softball Skill Tests

A variety of appropriate skill test items are described in this section of the chapter.

INSTRUCTIONAL FORMATS

An overview of the material in this chapter may be presented using a videotape of a lesson demonstrating the teaching of softball skills to elementary children. In addition, an activity session should be led by the instructor using suggested skills used in softball listed in this chapter or in the lesson plan book. The chapter material and activity session may be followed by cooperative learning assignments, which provide active learning and critical thinking activities for the student. In the cooperative learning groups, the students will discuss the materials listed on the Cooperative Learning Task Sheet and/or other topics you may assign. Each group can become a "content expert" for sections of the Cooperative Learning Task Sheet. Each group may be asked to present a lesson focus activity for softball to the entire class for a selected developmental level.

KEY TERMS

sidearm throw	fielding	batting
pitching		

DISCUSSION TOPICS

1. Discuss the lead-up games for softball that the students find most appropriate. Illustrate the elements of the game that are developed in the game selected.

2. Discuss the pros and cons of coeducational softball.

3. Discuss a variety of methods that can be used to teach softball skills to youngsters.

4. Discuss the challenge of dealing with students in one class with very different softball skill levels.

5. View a videotape on the game of softball. Discuss the difference between the way softball should be played at elementary school versus high school or college.

SAMPLE WRITTEN ASSIGNMENTS

1. Write a series of two lesson focus lesson plans for softball appropriate for developing softball skills progressively at Developmental Level II.

2. Write a paper on the history of softball in the United States.

3. Identify lead-up games that can be used for Developmental Level II students.

ACTIVITY SESSION EXPERIENCES

Lead the students through the following activities:

- Lead the students through the basic skills included in the game of softball: throwing, pitching, fielding, batting, base running, and rules of the game. Use the lesson plan book along with this textbook for model lesson ideas.

- Have students peer teach softball as the lesson focus using lessons from the lesson plan book.

COOPERATIVE LEARNING TASK SHEET

Chapter 28: Softball

Directions: Your cooperative learning group will become the content experts by finding the answers to the items listed below. Discuss the following items with your group and be ready to report on one or all of them at the end of the class period.

1. Identify appropriate formations, progressions, and teaching techniques to be used in elementary schools for softball skill development.

2. Develop five lesson focus lesson plans for teaching softball skills to Developmental Level III students.

3. Each person in the group should select one of the lesson plans developed and teach it to your group. Discuss the effectiveness of the lesson.

4. Teach one of the lessons peer taught in #3 to another group. Discuss the effectiveness of the lesson with the new group.

5. Make a chart showing safety precautions associated with teaching and playing softball.

6. Describe instructional procedures for implementing a successful lead-up game. Select a lead-up game listed in this chapter and teach it to members of your group. Evaluate the lesson with each other. Allow each member of your group the opportunity to teach a different game.

7. Cite assessment procedures for evaluating softball skills. Create an accompanying check-off list that an instructor could easily use.

8. Conduct an Internet search regarding the history of softball. Discuss your findings before presenting the information to your classmates.

9. Conduct an Internet search on a famous softball player. Present the findings to your group and then to the class.

CHAPTER 29

Track, Field, and Cross-Country Running

SUMMARY

Skill instruction for track, field, and cross-country running are introduced during the intermediate grades after youngsters have mastered basic prerequisite skills. Teaching of rules and strategies for track, field, and cross-country running is an integral part of the instructional process. Using proper progression is a key to success when teaching fundamental skills and lead-up games associated with track, field, and cross-country running. Lead-up games provide an opportunity to emphasize development of selected track, field, and cross-country running skills in a setting that is compatible with the ability of participants.

STUDENT OUTCOMES

Upon completion of the reading of this chapter, the student will:

- Structure learning experiences efficiently using appropriate formations, progressions, and coaching techniques.

- Develop a unit plan covering the lesson focus portion for track, field, and cross-country running.

- Identify safety precautions associated with teaching track, field, and cross-country running.

- Describe instructional procedures used for implementing a successful lead-up game.

- Cite assessment procedures used for evaluating track, field, and cross-country running skills.

MAIN CONCEPTS

The elementary program in track and field consists of short sprints (40 to 100 yards), running and standing long jumps, high jumps, hop-step-and jumps, and relays.

Jogging and distance running are encouraged throughout the program.

INSTRUCTIONAL EMPHASIS AND SEQUENCE

The primary emphasis is on practice and personal accomplishment. Modified competition in cross-country running is acceptable. Hurdling can be included when the equipment is available.

Students should be allowed to experience the differences between walking, sprinting, running, striding (for pace), and jogging.

Sprinting techniques are particularly important, with instruction centering on correct form for starting, accelerating, and sprinting.

Developmental Levels I and II

At Developmental Level I running for short distances and long jumping skills should be taught. At Developmental Levels I and II distance and cross-country running can be introduced. Children also enjoy relay activities.

Development Level III

At Developmental Level III, more serious efforts should be used to achieve proper form. The scissors style of high jumping can be introduced. Students should be taught how to check marks with the running long jump. Running for distance and cross-country activities are emphasized. Hurdling using modified hurdles is an exciting event.

Connecting to this site gives you excellent references to the sport of track and field:
 http://www.trackandfieldnews.com

TRACK AND FIELD SKILLS

The following skills are described in detail as they are appropriate for the elementary school program: Starts, Sprinting, Distance Running, Relays, Baton Passing, Horizontal Jumping, Standing Long Jump, Long jump, Hop-Step and Jump, and High Jumping.

In the high jump, the critical points of the Scissors Jump, the Straddle Roll, and the Western Roll should be taught. These skills are described in this chapter.

Connect to this site to read the history of high jumping:
 http://www.trackandfieldnews.com/results/newsletter/200006/quande.html

Hurdling skills are also discussed in this chapter.

Developing pace in distance running without strong elements of competition is taught.

Connecting to this site gives you tips and motivational reasons to run:
 http://www.runnersworld.com

The hop-step-and-jump extends the range of jumping activities in which children can participate.

Relays and baton passing are given increased coverage at level III.

Hurdling Skills

For safety, use hurdles that are designed specifically for elementary schools. Hurdles should tip over easily when struck by runners.

Techniques for hurdling: The runner should adjust his stepping pattern so the takeoff foot is planted 3 to 5 feet from the hurdle. The lead foot is extended straight forward over the hurdle; the rear leg is bent, with the knee to the side. The lead foot reaches for the ground, quickly followed by the trailing leg. A hurdler may lead with the same foot over consecutive hurdles or may alternate the leading foot.

INSTRUCTIONAL PROCEDURES

1. Spiked running shoes are not permitted.

2. Form should be stressed, but it should be appropriate to the individual. Youngsters should be encouraged to develop good technique within their own style.

3. The program should offer something for all boys and girls regardless of their skill level. Children with physical problems need to be included in the activities. Activities can be modified for those students.

4. The amount of activity, particularly distance work, should be increased progressively.

5. Warm-up activity should precede track and field work and should include jogging as well as bending and stretching exercises.

6. Pits for the long jump and high jump must be maintained properly and checked regularly for compliance.

7. For high jumping, commercial impact landing pads are necessary. If they are not available, high jumping should be restricted to the scissors style with tumbling mats used for the landing area. Crossbars can be varied for use in a class; the chapter provides detailed suggestions.

8. For track meets, the use of a track starter signal is recommended. The clapboard track starter can be used instead of a starter's gun.

9. The goal of the program should be to allow students to develop at their own rate. Instructional sessions should be strenuous enough to ensure some overload, but not so strenuous that students become discouraged or physically ill.

ORGANIZING FOR INSTRUCTION

Track, field, and cross-country running differ from other areas of the elementary school program in that considerable preparation must be made before the classes begin.

1. A track or cross-country course must be identified and marked.

2. A hurdling area should be marked.

3. Pits are needed for running long jump, high jump, and hop-step-and-jump.

4. High jump equipment should be checked.

5. Takeoff boards for the long jump and the hop-step-and-jump should be set up.

6. Accessory materials should be gathered including batons, starter clapboards, watches, hurdles, and yarn for the finish line.

Meet organization is also important.

TRACK AND FIELD DRILLS AND ACTIVITIES

The chapter gives great detail to drills and activities appropriate to children in this section of the textbook.

CONDUCTING TRACK AND FIELD DAYS

Planning, organization, and meet director duties are clearly outlined in this section of the chapter.

More information is available at this site:
http://www.usatf.org

Cross-Country Running and Meets

In this section of the chapter cross-country events and meets are described.

INSTRUCTIONAL FORMATS

An overview of the material in this chapter may be presented using Power Point slides, the overhead transparencies, and/or a videotape of a lesson demonstrating the teaching of track and field skills to elementary children. In addition, an activity session should be led by the instructor using suggested skills listed in this chapter or in the lesson plan book. The chapter material and activity session may be followed by cooperative learning assignments that provide active learning and critical thinking activities for the student. In the cooperative learning groups, the students will discuss the materials listed on the Cooperative Learning Task Sheet and/or other topics you may assign. Each group can become a "content expert" for sections of the Cooperative Learning Task Sheet. Each group may be asked to present a lesson focus activity for track and field to the entire class for a selected developmental level.

KEY TERMS

hop-step-and-jump	Norwegian start	baton passing
Western Roll	shuttle relays	scissors jump

DISCUSSION TOPICS

1. Discuss appropriate organizational procedures for working with Developmental Level III students on a track and field unit.

2. Discuss rules of track and field in your state.

3. Discuss the modifications of each track and field event that can be used with the different developmental level classes.

4. Discuss cross-country running skills and teaching techniques.

SAMPLE WRITTEN ASSIGNMENTS

1. Write a series of four lesson focus lesson plans for track and field appropriate for developing track and field skills progressively at Developmental Level II.

2. Identify races that can be used for Developmental Level II students.

3. Create task cards that can be used at stations for teaching track and field.

4. Draw a feasible cross-country running area that could be used for an elementary school in your area.

ACTIVITY SESSION EXPERIENCES

• Lead the students through the basic skills included in track and field events: starts for sprinting, long distance running relays, baton passing, hurdling, long jump, high jump, discus throwing, and shot put. Use the lesson plan book along with this textbook for model lesson ideas.

• Teach several model lessons with each of the track and field skills described in this chapter as the lesson focus for each lesson taught.

• Set up a station-teaching lesson for your class to experience using several skills in track and field.

• Lead the students around the cross-country running track at your university. Point out the different challenges within the course.

COOPERATIVE LEARNING TASK SHEET

Chapter 29: Track, Field, and Cross-Country Running

Directions: Your cooperative learning group will become the content experts by finding the answers to the items listed below. Discuss the following items with your group and be ready to report on one or all of them at the end of the class period.

1. Identify appropriate formations, progressions, and teaching techniques to be used in elementary schools for track and field and cross-country skill development.

2. Develop five lesson focus lesson plans for teaching track and field skills to Developmental Level III students.

3. Each person in the group should select one of the lesson plans developed and teach it to your group. Discuss the effectiveness of the lesson.

4. Teach one of the lessons peer taught in the assignment listed above to another group. Discuss the effectiveness of the lesson with the new group.

5. Create task cards that can be used at stations for teaching track and field.

6. Develop a chart for teaching track and field safely using a variety of stations in one lesson.

7. Make a chart showing safety precautions associated with teaching track and field.

8. Describe instructional procedures for implementing a successful relay race activity including baton passing. Teach a relay event to members of your group. Evaluate the lesson with each other. Allow each member of your group the opportunity to teach a different event or relay race.

9. Cite assessment procedures for evaluating track and field skills. Create an accompanying check-off list that an instructor could easily use.

10. Conduct an Internet search regarding the history of track and field or cross-country running. Discuss your findings before presenting the information to your classmates.

11. Conduct an Internet search on a famous runner. Present the findings to your group and then to the class.

CHAPTER 30

Volleyball

SUMMARY

Skills instructions for volleyball are introduced during the intermediate grades after youngsters have mastered basic prerequisite skills. Teaching of rules and strategies for volleyball is an integral part of the instructional process. Using proper progression is a key to success when teaching fundamental skills and lead-up games associated with volleyball. Lead-up games provide an opportunity to emphasize development of selected volleyball skills in a setting that is compatible with the ability of participants.

STUDENT OUTCOMES

Upon completion of the reading of this chapter, the student will:

- Structure learning experiences efficiently using appropriate formations, progressions, and coaching techniques.

- Develop a unit plan and lesson focus for volleyball.

- Identify safety precautions associated with teaching volleyball.

- Describe instructional procedures used for implementing a successful lead-up game.

- Cite assessment procedures used for evaluating volleyball skills.

MAIN CONCEPTS

To play volleyball successfully on the elementary level, a foundation of basic volleyball skills needs to be developed during the elementary school years.

> This is a thorough reference site for the sport of volleyball:
> 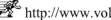 http://www.volleyball.org/general/index.html

Children need to be taught serving, passing, and effective ball control skills. This requires sufficient practice of the sills and the development of hand-eye body coordination for effective ball control. Attention to proper technique is essential.

> To read more about tips on teaching volleyball, connect to this site:
> http://volleyball.about.com/sports/volleyball/msubmenu3.htm

> To read more about skills, go to:
> http://volleyball.about.com/od/skillshowtosinfo/

Informal practice begins with activities that mimic volleyball skills: passing, serving, rebounding, and blocking. Setting and spiking are skills that will challenge the most skilled youngsters. Little time should be spent on these skills with the majority of the students.

INSTRUCTIONAL EMPHASIS AND SEQUENCE

Nets should be lowered to 6 feet or less to ensure success.

An adequate number of balls are necessary for individual skill practice and skill development.

Beach balls and foam balls can be used to enhance the early learning of basic skills and to supplement the equipment for the class.

In elementary school physical education classes the emphasis of volleyball should be on keeping the ball in play, thereby increasing activity, skill development, and enjoyment. The overhand serve, setup, and spike are skills that are usually introduced when a competitive situation exists, such as intramurals or in an interschool program.

Students should learn about the setup, spike, and blocking techniques, but attention should not be focused on these skills.

Rebounding and ball control is an excellent related experience. Beach balls and balloons can be used for these skills, particularly for younger children. These preliminary experiences in visual tracking are advantageous for volleyball skills learned in the upper grades.

In the primary grades, children should practice ball-handling activities related to volleyball skills.

Developmental Level II

At Developmental Level II, Beach Ball Volleyball is a good culminating game. The larger ball allows for greater success.

Developmental Level III

At Developmental Level III the majority of instruction focuses on the underhand serve and the overhand and forearm passes. Strategy can also be introduced.

VOLLEYBALL SKILLS

The following skills are described in detail as appropriate to the elementary school teaching environment: Serving, passing, setting, digging, spiking, and blocking.

INSTRUCTIONAL PROCEDURES

1. Most volleyball-type games begin with a serve, so be sure children can serve.

2. Players should roll the ball back to the server.

3. Beach balls are excellent for beginning players.

4. Initial instruction should be individual or with partners. Each child should have a ball for individual practice.

5. 8-inch foam balls or a "volleyball trainer" ball should be used in early stages of learning, following the beach ball instructional period.

6. Rule out hitting with fists.

7. Rotation should happen often in lead-up games.

ORGANIZING FOR INSTRUCTION

Organizational methods are described for the individual player, partners, and small groups.

Rules

Basic volleyball rules and rule adaptations are described in this chapter.

Additionally, this chapter describes numerous lead-up games and activities.

INSTRUCTIONAL FORMATS

An overview of the material in this chapter may be presented using the Power Point slides and a videotape of a lesson demonstrating the teaching of volleyball skills. In addition, activity sessions should be led by the instructor using volleyball skills listed in this chapter or in the lesson plan book. The chapter material and activity session may be followed by cooperative learning assignments that provide active learning and critical thinking activities for the student. In the cooperative learning groups, the students will discuss the materials listed on the Cooperative Learning Task Sheet and/or other topics you may assign. Each group can become a "content expert" for sections of the Cooperative Learning Task Sheet. Each group may be asked to present a lesson focus activity for volleyball to the entire class for a selected developmental level.

KEY TERMS

forearm pass	setup	spike

DISCUSSION TOPICS

1. Identify local elementary schools and/or middle schools that have intramural volleyball programs. Plan a field trip to observe the program(s).

2. Discuss the proper volleyball skills to teach for each developmental level.

SAMPLE WRITTEN ASSIGNMENTS

1. Write a series of four lesson focus lesson plans for volleyball appropriate for developing volleyball skills progressively at Developmental Level II.

2. Identify lead-up games that can be used for Developmental Level II students.

3. Identify skills that can be used for Developmental Level III students.

4. Identify lead-up games that can be used for Developmental Level III students.

ACTIVITY SESSION EXPERIENCES

Lead the students through the basic skills included in the game of volleyball: underhand and overhand serving, overhand pass, underhand/forearm pass, dig pass, and rules of the game. Use the lesson plan book along with this textbook for model lesson ideas.

Teach model lessons from the lesson plan book for each developmental level using volleyball as the lesson focus.

Have students peer teach volleyball using lessons from the lesson plan book.

COOPERATIVE LEARNING TASK SHEET

Chapter 30: Volleyball

Directions: Your cooperative learning group will become the content experts by finding the answers to the items listed below. Discuss the following items with your group and be ready to report on one or all of them at the end of the class period.

1. Identify appropriate formations, progressions, and teaching techniques to be used in elementary schools for volleyball skill development.

2. Develop five lesson focus lesson plans for teaching volleyball skills to Developmental Level III students.

3. Each person in the group should select one of the lesson plans developed and teach it to your group. Discuss the effectiveness of the lesson.

4. Teach one of the lessons peer taught in #3 to another group. Discuss the effectiveness of the lesson with the new group.

5. Make a chart showing safety precautions associated with teaching and playing volleyball.

6. Describe instructional procedures for implementing a successful lead-up game. Select a lead-up game listed in this chapter and teach it to members of your group. Evaluate the lesson with each other. Allow each member of your group the opportunity to teach a different game.

7. Cite assessment procedures for evaluating volleyball skills. Create an accompanying check-off list that an instructor could easily use.

8. Conduct an Internet search regarding the history of volleyball. Discuss your findings before presenting the information to your classmates.

9. Conduct an Internet search on a famous volleyball player. Present the findings to your group and then to the class.